Fashion Drawing FOR DUMMIES®

by Lisa Smith Arnold and Marianne Egan

John Wiley & Sons, Inc.

Fashion Drawing For Dummies®

Published by
John Wiley & Sons, Inc.
111 River St.
Hoboken, NJ 07030-5774
www.wiley.com

Library of Congress Control Number: 2012935366

ISBN 978-0-470-60160-0 (pbk); ISBN 978-0-470-88762-2 (ebk); ISBN 978-0-470-88763-9 (ebk); ISBN 978-0-470-88764-6 (ebk)

Manufactured in the United States of America

10 9 8 7 6 5 4 3 2 1

4863   3142   06/12

WILEY

About the Authors

Lisa Smith Arnold: Lisa Smith Arnold is an illustrator and painter who graduated from Syracuse University with a bachelor of fine arts degree and headed straight to New York City. She has worked for Conde Nast Publications and other fashion-oriented companies. As a result, most of her paintings still have that exaggerated fashion influence. She now lives in Westport, Connecticut, with her husband and three kids.

Marianne Egan: Marianne grew up outside of Chicago and earned her bachelor of arts degree in fashion design from the International Academy of Design & Technology in Chicago. She also earned a master of science degree in apparel design from Oregon State University, where she focused on *couture* construction and illustration.

Marianne has worked as a designer and freelance illustrator, and she currently teaches fashion illustration, computer design, and corset and strapless dressmaking full time at Oregon State University. Marianne also runs a small custom bridal business; you can visit her website at www.marianneegan.com.

When she is not chasing after her son, you can find Marianne tribal belly dancing, running, drawing, or glued to her sewing machine.

Dedications

From Lisa: I dedicate this book to my mom, Charlotte Smith. Thanks for being the first to encourage me and introduce me to the world of fashion.

From Marianne: This book is dedicated to my son, George. Be nice and do the right thing, my sweet boy.

This book is also dedicated to my amazing friends Lydia and Ashley. Lydia, your ability to love is matched by no other, and I could not be who I am without you. Ashley, you radiate strength and grace, and you know just when to bring a girl ice cream and wine when she can't get up from the kitchen floor. I am so blessed to have you both in my life.

Authors' Acknowledgments

From Lisa: Thanks to all at Wiley who were involved in this project.

From Marianne: I would like to thank the amazing staff at Wiley: Thanks go to developmental editor Sharon Perkins for making me laugh and putting up with me — you rock! I'd also like to thank senior project editor Vicki Adang for laughing at my sense of humor (and not requiring me to explain how to draw the meat dress) and senior copy editor Danielle Voirol (who has the steps down for the meat dress!). More thanks go to copy editor Jessica Smith for all her hard work and to technical editor Barbara Rhodes for all her time and edits over edits. To acquisitions editor Michael Lewis, thanks for not giving up on me and for convincing me to work with such amazing people! And thanks to everyone else who's been a part of bringing this book to life.

I would also like to thank my incomparably supportive loved ones, Juliette, Todd, Trevor, and Noel — without your support, this book would never have happened! Thank you, Ashley (thanks to you, there's one less truck on the road) and Travis, for just being you. Thanks to Lydia (cheers!), Eva, Ethan, and little Isaiah for all your sweet dancing moves! Thanks to my supermom running sistas, Kara, Tonya, and Kellie. To Jaimie, Morgan, and Tonja, thank you for all those late and middle-of-the-night phone calls. To my Wild Iris dancing sisters, Shellece, Erika, Carol, and Eva, thank you for keeping me moving. Thanks also to my supermom girlfriends who keep me going: Anne, Heidi, Wendy, Amy, Adrienne, Aylssa, Betsy, Claire, and anyone else I forgot.

Thanks so much to all my colleagues at Oregon State, especially Dr. Kathy Mullet and Dr. Leslie Davis Burns, who push me every day and refuse nothing but everything I can give. Thank you, Nate, for late night tacos!

Finally, I have to thank my family: Dad and Diana; Mom (kitchen gnome) and Steve (Team Steve!); my loving brother Matthew (Da Bears) and his brave wife, Jenny (for marrying into our crazy family and giving us little Alice, Bears fan in training); my dreamer sister Mollie (what a year!); my awesome brother Ryan; and my I-don't-mess-around sister Breanna. I love you all.

Publisher's Acknowledgments

We're proud of this book; please send us your comments at http://dummies.custhelp.com. For other comments, please contact our Customer Care Department within the U.S. at 877-762-2974, outside the U.S. at 317-572-3993, or fax 317-572-4002.

Some of the people who helped bring this book to market include the following:

Acquisitions, Editorial, and Vertical Websites

Developmental Editor: Sharon Perkins

Senior Project Editor: Victoria M. Adang

Acquisitions Editor: Michael Lewis

Senior Copy Editor: Danielle Voirol

Copy Editor: Jessica Smith

Assistant Editor: David Lutton

Editorial Program Coordinator: Joe Niesen

Technical Editor: Barbara Rhodes

Editorial Manager: Michelle Hacker

Editorial Assistants: Rachelle Amick, Alexa Koschier

Cover Illustrations: Marianne Egan

Cartoons: Rich Tennant
(www.the5thwave.com)

Composition Services

Project Coordinator: Sheree Montgomery

Layout and Graphics: Claudia Bell, Timothy C. Detrick, Cheryl Grubbs, Joyce Haughey, Sennett Vaughan Johnson, Corrie Niehaus

Proofreaders: Rebecca Denoncour, Betty Kish

Indexer: Ty Koontz

Special Help
Alissa Schwipps, Clint Lahnen

Publishing and Editorial for Consumer Dummies

Kathleen Nebenhaus, Vice President and Executive Publisher

Kristin Ferguson-Wagstaffe, Product Development Director

Ensley Eikenburg, Associate Publisher, Travel

Kelly Regan, Editorial Director, Travel

Publishing for Technology Dummies

Andy Cummings, Vice President and Publisher

Composition Services

Debbie Stailey, Director of Composition Services

Contents at a Glance

Table of Contents

Introduction

If you like fashion and you like to doodle figures, then you've come to the right place. *Fashion Drawing For Dummies* is a great way to ease into the world of fashion drawing. Don't panic if you have no experience; we give you all sorts of practice exercises that will have you sketching out stylish, long-limbed figures in no time. If you do have experience, this book can help you brush up on techniques and point you in the right direction to pick up more fashion advice and drawing tips.

Fashion is a playful world where almost anything goes, but you have to have the foundation to back up your ideas. Take a look at the work of some of your favorite fashion illustrators and designers. Chances are they've broken some rules to get noticed, but they also have pretty decent fashion drawing foundations under their belts.

Whether you're interested in being a fashion designer, a fashion or trend forecaster, a buyer, or a fashion art director, you have to know how to draw a basic fashion figure. And if you want to be a fashion illustrator? Jump on the train! If you're nervous, don't be — if we could learn how to draw fashion illustrations, anyone can! Keep that positive attitude, practice drawing all the time, and enjoy yourself along the way.

About This Book

Fashion drawing is not like figure drawing; fashion drawing is an art where the figure is exaggerated in an elegant way and clothes are drawn with texture and precision. We've worked in the fashion industry for many years, and in this book, we give you a taste of what this special world is about. At the same time, we show you what you need to develop, grow, and go beyond mere competence to create your own signature look.

Many fashion books are filled with glorious illustrations that you may adore looking at, but when you're just starting out, you may not know where to begin. *Fashion Drawing For Dummies* is a complete how-to book for people who like fashion and want to know how to draw the unique and quirky fashion figure. We take you on a step-by-step drawing journey from fashion head to fashion feet and everything in between. Plenty of sketching exercises help you develop your drawing skills so you can create a fashion figure and dress her right down to the finishing touch of a pair of sparkling earrings. This book helps you over the trouble spots (like hands and feet!) and gives you practical and logical steps, tips, and techniques.

The purpose of this book is to introduce you to fashion drawing basics. We start with a basic review of figure drawing that you may find helpful, whether you've done a lot of drawing or not. We then go over the fashion drawing rules (there are some!) that will help you get launched and discover your own fashion drawing style. With our tips and fashion techniques, you'll become comfortable drawing the fashion figure and all types of clothing.

Conventions Used in This Book

We used a few conventions to help you navigate this book more easily:

- Numbered steps and keywords in bulleted lists appear in **boldface.**

- When we introduce new terms, we *italicize* and define them.

- Web and e-mail addresses appear in monofont to make them easier to see.

What You're Not to Read

As an artist, you may or may not like to read. If you don't, you're in luck, because you can skip over some parts of this book. The copyright page is one part, and text in sidebars (short boxed sections printed on gray backgrounds) is another. Knowing what you can *not* read may give you more time to practice your drawing!

Foolish Assumptions

When we wrote this book, we made some assumptions about you and your interests. If we had to guess, we'd assume that you fit into one or more of the following categories:

- You love clothes and are interested in designing your own.

- You're a fashion design student who may have a bit of drawing experience but no fashion drawing experience.

- You love to draw, and fashion illustration looks like fun, but you don't know where to start.

- You're a beginning fashion illustrator looking to improve your art.

How This Book Is Organized

This book is divided into five parts, allowing you to zoom in and focus on what's most important to you. You can then flip from part to part or chapter to chapter for easy access to related fashion information. Here's an outline of what you'll find where.

Part 1: Fashion Drawing 101

This section is all about the basics of drawing, including a quick refresher on figure drawing. We also talk about the fun of purchasing the necessary art supplies for fashion illustration and how to set up your own studio. If you've ever wondered where to start in drawing a fashion figure, this part gives you everything you need to know.

Part 11: Building a Fabulous Fashion Figure

In this part, we tell you the golden rules of fashion drawing. (Later, we tell you how to break them!) Special proportions are important in fashion illustration, and we explain all about those fabulous lengthy legs and arms that give your drawings star quality. Exaggeration is key when you're creating a powerful fashion drawing from head to toe.

Part 111: Dressing Your Fashion Figure

After you master basic female, male, and child fashion figures, you're ready to put some clothes on them. In this part, we explain how to draw hats, shoes, and everything in between for men, women, and kids.

Part 1V: Taking Your Fashion Drawing to the Next Level

In this part, we stretch your fashion drawing skills even more and encourage you to try new techniques to make your drawings really stand out. One way to distinguish your art is by adding great textures and patterns that viewers will long to touch. You also want to convey action and attitude in fashion. You have so many ways to show your fashion model's stuff when you know how to show her striking a pose, walking down a runway, or tossing her hair. As you get more comfortable with fashion drawing, you'll want to develop your style; this means knowing when to break the rules, so we give you some pointers on how to do just that. And after you've created a masterpiece or a dozen, you'll want to show off your work — perhaps to a prospective client or boss — so we end this part by offering you tips on putting together a portfolio.

Part V: The Part of Tens

The Part of Tens includes short lists that contain valuable information on discovering more about fashion and promoting your work. Now that you can draw the fashion figure and more, you can work on keeping up and staying in touch with the ever-changing fashion world. This part serves as a fashion launch pad with advice about the Internet, fashion publications, and more.

Icons Used in This Book

Fashion Drawing For Dummies features some cute little icons in the left margins. Each icon is meant to grab your attention for something particularly important, so check them out.

This icon gives you a friendly heads-up about useful information to keep in mind.

The text next to the Tip icon offers hints to make your fashion drawing journey easier.

When you heed the Warning icon, you benefit from the mistakes we've learned from. Don't go there; making the same mistakes will only complicate your fashion illustration and create confusion.

This icon is where the pencil hits the paper. When you see this icon, pull out your drawing supplies and try your hand at the concept or technique we're explaining. After you've completed the exercise once, try it again, but change it up a bit. For example, if the practice exercise is about long, bouncy curls, modify it so you draw short, bouncy curls instead.

Where to Go from Here

Even though we wrote this book and would love for you to read it from cover to cover, we urge you not to read *Fashion Drawing For Dummies* in one sitting, unless you're the kind of person who just has to know how a book ends! Take time to digest and practice what we show you in each chapter. If you're already familiar with the basics, feel free to jump around from chapter to chapter to pick out the fashion drawing tidbits that interest you the most. You can go back and read through everything more thoroughly later on.

Part I
Fashion Drawing 101

The 5th Wave   By Rich Tennant

"I'll be doing my fashion drawings on these, so
I was wondering if this sketch pad comes in
navy blue velveteen with scalloped edging."

In this part . . .

In this part, you get the lowdown on getting started with fashion illustration. We begin at the beginning and explore basic drawing techniques, including how to draw a figure (for those of you who have drawing experience, this is a great refresher). We also cover art supplies and how to create a workspace just for you.

Chapter 1

Finding Your Footing in Fashion Drawing

If you picked up this book to figure out how to draw fashion illustrations, you likely want to be a fashion illustrator or to work in the fashion industry. Although they're two very different types of jobs and industries, fashion illustration connects them. In this chapter, we talk about how to get started in drawing fashion and the ways in which fashion drawing differs from figure drawing. We also cover where to find work and how to get started in your career.

Getting Started with Fashion Drawing

Maybe you've been copying figures from magazines or dressing paper dolls with your own creations since you were a kid. If so, you already know how much your art improves when you work at it. If you've been drawing since you were young, you may also have picked up a number of bad drawing habits or have skipped drawing certain types of clothing or body parts because they're more complicated. And if you haven't been sketching everything in sight up to this point in your life, now is the time to start.

Fashion drawing tends to be much more stylized than figure drawing, so you may have to change your techniques. In the following sections, we offer some ideas about how to get started in fashion drawing.

Filling your sketchbook

Getting good at any kind of drawing is like getting to Carnegie Hall — you need to practice, practice, practice! To practice drawing no matter where you are, you need a sketchbook, better known in the industry as a *design process notebook*. Anything that fires up your brain and helps you create goes into the sketchbook. Your design process notebook may be full of fabric swatches, magazine clippings, drawings, words, or anything and everything you use to inspire yourself when designing. It's like a glimpse into your brain working out all the details of a design.

Saving every scrap

When sketches pile up in your work space, resist the urge to dump your older sketches, and never throw out your old work! You never know when a throwaway sketch will jog your imagination and turn into a saleable idea.

Marianne knew musicians who talked about getting great ideas from pressing the record button even when they were just messing around. She learned from them that you never know when something you're just fooling around with can become a great idea. The same holds true with your design ideas. You may just be doodling around with a sketch and end up with a fantastic design idea that sells itself someday! That's what happened with the notebook sketch of an evening dress shown here.

So what do you sketch when you're out and about, watching television on the couch, or paging through the latest fashion magazine? Whatever catches your eye! You can also use your notebook to practice the sketches we outline later in this chapter and throughout the book — they're even marked with a Sketchbook icon!

Studying the masters

Great fashion illustrations are not generally hanging on the walls of famous museums. Instead, you find these works of art in fashion magazines, on billboards, in the newspaper, and on the Internet. Spend time looking at fashion illustrations and pay attention to the poses they use, along with the amount of lines and details. Check out the work of artists such as John Galliano, Karl Lagerfeld (for Chanel), and Betsey Johnson.

Certain illustrations will just wow you, although you may not understand exactly why. Try to figure out what you like about certain illustrations.

Keep a file of art that appeals to you by saving pictures of the types of work you'd like to do yourself. After a while, you'll see a pattern emerging. Collecting images of what you like helps you learn visually and develop your own style. (For more about developing your own style, see the later section "Making Your Art Your Own.")

Use the images you collect for inspiration, not for copying in your own work! You don't want to violate any copyright laws. A work is protected by copyright as soon as the artist creates it.

Grasping the Basics of Fashion Drawing

If you're a born artist, doing fashion illustration will certainly come easily to you. But if you want to draw but hate the way your figures come out, don't throw in the towel. Anyone can learn how to draw. We can't stress this enough.

A desire to draw is a huge motivator. If you have a picture in your head, you can figure out how to translate it to paper step by step. Drawing starts with a single line — and anyone can draw a line! In this book, we show you how to use shapes to draw the human body and the clothing people wear. All drawings start with circles, triangles, ovals, squares, rectangles, trapezoids, and cylinders, shapes you've been drawing since you were a child.

Learning how to draw is really all about learning how to see, paying attention to what you see, and understanding what you see. Many of the most amazing artists were formally trained, proving artistic skill isn't all about being born with the talent to draw — although it certainly does help! In the end, illustration is all about mastering the basics of fashion drawing, creating your own style, and practicing, practicing, practicing.

Separating fashion from figure drawing

Although related, fashion and figure drawing are two different approaches to the same craft. Yes, they both draw the human form, but that's where the similarities end. You can find the differences in the details.

The most noticeable difference between the two styles is the fact that fashion drawing depends on exaggeration, and figure drawing features a more realistic drawing style. A woman drawn by a figure artist looks pretty true to life. Her body is in a natural pose, her features may be plain, and her arms and legs are in scale with her physical dimensions.

Ask a fashion artist to draw the same woman, and you're not likely to recognize her on paper. She'll be as thin as a rail, her arms and legs will be extremely long and lean, and she may have limited facial features — or even none at all! The goal of fashion drawing is to express style and create a specific effect, and you use exaggeration, movement, and attitude to get it!

Choosing a good pose

Watch how the fashion models move on the runway, and you'll instantly realize that fashion models don't move or stand like normal people — they pose. Fashion models are trained to stand in certain ways in order to show off the styles of the time.

Not all poses you see on real-life models translate well onto paper, but it's helpful to recognize different poses and understand what types of poses work well with different types of clothing. A fashion model in an evening dress doesn't strike the same poses as a teen dude in an urban outfit. The fashion model stands tall and straight to show off the gown's bodice and skirt; the teen dude is likely to assume a slouched pose to demonstrate how the clothing moves with ease over his body.

In fashion illustration, you utilize four different views of poses for most of your artwork (see Chapter 4 for details):

✔ The back view (Figure 1-1a)

✔ The front view (Figure 1-1b)

✔ The three-quarter view (Figure 1-1c)

✔ The side view (Figure 1-1d)

Figure 1-1:
Four views
of fashion
poses.

To draw a basic fashion figure, you must first understand what a "good" pose is. When drawing fashion poses, follow these informal rules:

✔ Make sure your model isn't leaning on anything. She should be standing on her own two feet.

✔ Keep your model from falling over on the page like the model in Figure 1-2. You create balance by keeping the head, shoulders, hips, knees, and feet in a straight line from head to toe (more on this in Chapter 5).

✔ Angle the shoulders in one direction and the hips in the opposite direction, as in Figure 1-3. Doing so gives the impression of movement and attitude — two must-haves in fashion drawing. We talk more about angles in Chapter 4.

Drawing a basic fashion figure

When drawing fashion illustrations, you first create a rough sketch of the body, also referred to as a *croquis.* Then you draw the clothes that go on top.

Figure 1-2:
Fashion fig-
ures should
never look
like they're
falling over.

Figure 1-3:
Angling is
an important
part of the
fashion look.

Are you ready for your first dip into fashion drawing? Grab your pencil, a black pen, some tracing paper, sketch paper, and a fashion magazine if you have one handy. Here's how to begin drawing a front view *croquis:*

1. **Lay tracing paper over a full-body picture of a model from a magazine (or use our outline in Figure 1-4a) and trace around the perimeter of her body using a pencil.**

2. **Draw lines to show the angles of the shoulders and hips. Trace a center line down the front of her body and draw an oval for the head, as in Figure 1-4b.**

   We give you more details about the center front line and angled lines in Chapter 5.

3. **Break your figure down into basic shapes, using trapezoids for the torso and cylinders for the arms and legs. Include circles for the elbows and knees, as in Figure 1-4c.**

Breaking the body down into basic shapes simplifies the drawing process. To find out more about using shapes in your drawings, flip to Chapters 3 and 4.

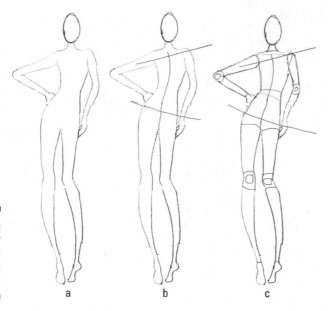

Figure 1-4: Tracing over an outline of a posed figure.

a   b   c

4. **Remove the tracing paper from your model.**

5. **On a piece of sketch paper, redraw your fashion model freehand, but lengthen the torso, arms, and legs, as in Figure 1-5a.**

   The new figure is taller and narrower and has a smaller head in comparison to the rest of her body. Fashion figures almost always have long, slim torsos and long, slender limbs, which make the clothes look better. Find out more about drawing the torso in Chapter 5 and drawing arms and legs in Chapter 6.

6. **Use a black pen to draw over the areas of the body that you want to show. Erase the pencil lines.**

   See the final croquis in Figure 1-5b.

After you've drawn a few croquis, you can move on to adding the clothes on top. After all, your goal is to illustrate the fashions!

Figure 1-5:
Freehanding
a fashion
drawing
with basic
lines and
shapes.

a   b

For this exercise, you need a croquis drawn in pencil because you'll erase the form of the body as you add clothes to it. Follow these steps to draw a dress and knee-high boots on your croquis:

1. **To create the neckline, begin with two *V* shapes on the neck, as in Figure 1-6a.**

   Make sure the ends of the *V* shape curve to show that they're going around the neck. You want the clothing to look dimensional and wrap around the body.

2. **Add a sleeve, as in Figure 1-6b.**

   To form the top of the sleeve, trace over the shoulder of the bent arm and go down to the midpoint of the upper arm. For the hem of the sleeve, draw a long line that starts at the end of the sleeve and angles in toward the body; curve the line to wrap around behind the arm. Draw a line from the sleeve's hem to the line of the croquis' torso to form the bottom of the sleeve. The sleeve is loose and needs to fall with gravity.

3. **Draw the other sleeve, as in Figure 1-6c.**

   For the top of the sleeve, draw a line curving over the shoulder and down the arm, ending slightly above the elbow. Draw a hem across the arm, ending at the torso.

   Add in a line for the armhole seam of each sleeve by connecting the line at the shoulder to the bottom of the sleeve.

4. **Follow the sides of your model's torso and hips and draw lines for both side seams of the fitted dress, as in Figure 1-6d.**

   End the side seams below the crotch and draw a slightly curved line for the hem. Curved hemlines keep the clothing from looking flat.

5. **Add in details such as topstitching, ribbing, and curved lines on the sides of the waist, as in Figure 1-6e.**

   Topstitching, which you represent with dashed lines, is stitching visible from the outside of the garment. Draw topstitching on the sleeve hems, on the hem of the dress, and on the seams of the curved shapes at the sides of the waist. Draw short, parallel lines to add ribbing to the neckline. For more on details such as topstitching, head to Chapter 9.

6. **Draw slightly curved lines above the knee for the thigh-high socks and two slightly curved lines below the knee for the tops of the knee-high boots, as in Figure 1-6f.**

7. **Trace along the calf lines and around the feet to draw the boots, as in Figure 1-6g.**

   Don't forget to add a wedge heel to the boots. To get the skinny on drawing ultra hip boots, check out Chapter 13.

8. **Finish the drawing with a fun face, hair, and arms, as in Figure 1-6h.**

   Turn to Chapters 7 and 8 for pointers on drawing a fashion face and hair.

Don't worry if your fashion figure doesn't turn out exactly how you want her to look. Perfecting your drawing skills takes time and practice. In Parts II and III of this book, we give you lots of Sketchbook exercises that allow you to practice drawing individual parts of the body and various pieces of clothing. After you've worked through those exercises, come back to this exercise and redraw it. You'll be amazed at how far your skills have come.

This book shows you how to draw a basic fashion figure and a variety of clothing. However, it's impossible to show every variation of every piece of clothing out there. When you feel you've mastered the exercises we include in this book, look for other garments you like and try your hand at drawing those. This is where your sketchbook comes in handy.

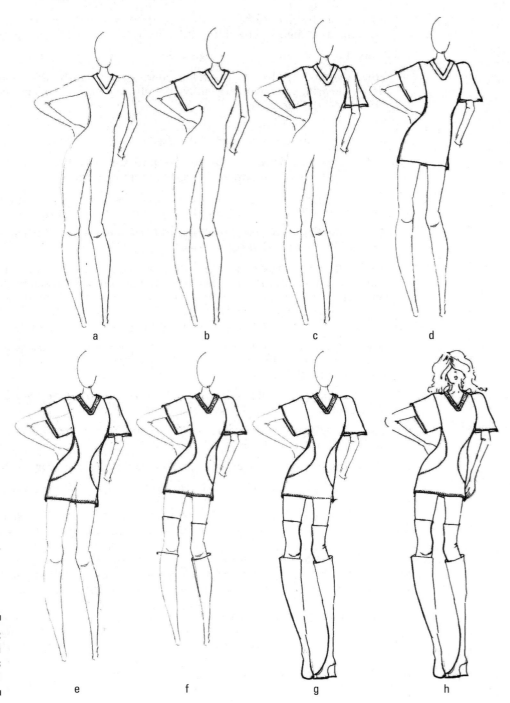

Figure 1-6:
Rocking a
cute dress
and boots!

Making Your Art Your Own

As you expand your drawing experiences, you'll want to include more of yourself in your art. No, we don't mean that you should sketch your own face on your models! As you get more comfortable with pencil and paper, work on incorporating a technique or two that tells the viewer that this drawing was done by *you,* not one of the hundreds of other artists out there. The following sections give you some tips on putting your own stamp on your art.

Developing a signature style

The Great Masters of art have recognizable styles, and you need to have a distinctive style as well. You see the world with your own lenses and put your own spin on it — that uniqueness needs to come through in your artwork!

Look at other artists and take from them the things you love, but never try to imitate someone else's style. Here's why:

- ✔ You won't do it as well as they do.
- ✔ You won't have as much fun as you would creating your own style.
- ✔ Imitating someone else is harder than following your instincts.

So what exactly makes a style, especially in the fashion world? Generally, fashion illustration styles fall into one of two types: loose rendering and tight rendering:

- ✔ Loose leaves out lots of details and draws as few lines as possible; the viewer has to use her imagination and fill in the missing details.
- ✔ Tight is very detailed; the viewer has a better idea of what the illustrator or designer intended.

Figure 1-7 shows two versions of the same drawing with different levels of detail.

Along with the loose versus tight rendering styles, illustrators find other ways to add their own signatures to their drawings. Some illustrators are very realistic with human details, and others let their imaginations run wild with poses and body parts that don't really exist! See Figure 1-8 for a rather wild style. When you're ready to develop your own style, turn to Chapter 16, where we offer some ideas about other ways to render fashion illustrations.

Figure 1-7:
Loose or tight, make your style your own.

a   b

Keeping your work fresh and refining techniques

After you find ways to make your drawings your own, continue to practice and work on your skills. Be open to taking classes or experimenting with different styles. Even after you develop a drawing style, you can continue to improve or change up your work. Remember, improving doesn't mean your drawings aren't good the way they are — there's always room to develop your technique.

Never stay satisfied with the status quo in your art, or your drawings will get stagnant as you draw things the same way every time. It's one thing to develop a signature look and quite another to draw *predictable* work.

Figure 1-8:
Some
illustrators
add a lot of
whimsy.

Marianne loves to explore other artists and build off their influence — she's constantly changing her inspirations while staying true to her techniques. This allows her to get out of her box and to experiment with new ideas. We think it's a great way to constantly stay fresh, and it keeps you drawing all the time!

Other ideas for branching out include getting inspiration from anything and everything you see, from still life to real life and everything in between! Look at the physical part of illustrating, too — experiment with other mediums, such as paint and digital design using a mouse or drafting tablet. Your techniques will always be your own, but they'll evolve when you expose yourself to new ideas.

Exploring the Field of Fashion Illustration

Back in the days before the Internet and great cameras, fashion illustrators were essential for showing a designer's creations. Today, you find fewer true fashion illustrators who make their living through drawing fashion.

But the art of fashion drawing itself will never die, no matter how advanced technology gets. Illustrating is and always will be important because it gets the idea out of your head and makes it real on paper. That's why illustration is an important skill for a designer to have. Can you imagine how hard it would be to just use words to describe a design and expect someone to be able to make it? Drawing transcends language and is the perfect visual representation of your design.

To see why drawing will never go out of style, look at a designer's process notebooks and watch an idea grow from a rough sketch to a finished product. Doodling on a computer doesn't allow you to work through a sketch like a series of hand drawings does — at least not yet!

Considering careers in fashion illustration

Making a career out of drawing today in any field is tricky, not just in fashion drawing. A lot of art has gone digital, and some illustrations are done solely on the computer using a mouse or drafting tablet. But don't throw away your drawing paper just yet — even artists who work on computers need the ability to draw.

The truth is that the need for hand design will never disappear completely. Magazines may no longer *need* illustrations of the latest trends because the camera captures it all, but readers still like to see drawings and organic art. Illustrations can exaggerate and introduce elements of fantasy in ways that are difficult or impossible for cameras.

Can you make a living in fashion illustration? Perhaps. A lot of fashion illustration overlaps with fashion design. Most people who want to draw fashion also want to design their model's clothes. Most of the time, when you show your skills in illustrating, you're also showing your designing skills.

Consider some of the following potential career choices beyond designing and marketing your own line of clothing:

- Work for a designer who has great ideas but has trouble transferring them to paper!
- Teaching others to draw is a thriving career choice. You have to complete some schooling to teach others, but inspiring new artists to develop their talent is a great way to spend your professional life.

✔ Be open to illustrating jobs that aren't directly related to fashion. Children's books especially depend on illustrators to capture the story and bring it to life, and the human characters in the story have to wear clothes! Try your hand at drawing some cute kids and let them play dress-up — we include some kid-specific tips throughout the book.

✔ Check out a career creating *line sheets,* which are drawings of garments that the manufacturer plans on producing. Merchandising garments and designs are cheaper when the garment simply has to be illustrated, not made. Line sheets help buyers see products so they know whether they want to order them.

Looking at careers in fashion design

The textile industry is the largest industry in the world — one walk through the mall can clearly illustrate the power of clothing in the retail world. Everyone wears clothes! Because clothing styles change frequently and because clothes don't last forever, fashion is a constantly changing market. Careers in fashion design are abundant! From *sourcing* (which is finding all the notions and fabrics to create the garment along with finding a factory to construct the garment) to product development, fashion employs millions around the world.

If you want to get into the design industry as an illustrator, learning the trade and creating a portfolio is the way to go (check out Chapter 17 when you're ready to put together your portfolio). Schools offer two- to four-year programs about pattern drafting, grading, fashion design, textiles, and fabric design, giving people the skills to go out into the fashion design world and create living, breathing designs.

Breaking into the fashion world

To be an artist is to be a salesperson, if you ever want anyone else to see your work. No one will come knocking down your door to see your work unless you put it out there. Working in a creative field today requires not only some knowledge of social media but also a working knowledge of the Internet.

Marketing online is not only easy but also less painful for artists who don't have the killer instincts that make great salespeople great. Rejection is always easier online than in person! Although getting noticed is easier than ever, there's tremendous competition, because everyone else is using the same channels to show their work.

You can do it, though, with talent, luck, and persistence (and the advice we provide in Chapter 19). Marianne now teaches fashion illustration, and she never went to school to teach. She was persistent about recording her work, loved to network at all times, and found a way to incorporate her passion into her work.

Chapter 2

Gathering Supplies and Setting Up Your Work Space

In This Chapter

▶ Stocking up on drawing supplies

▶ Setting up a terrific studio

▶ Discovering how to store your art

*W*e love art supplies — maybe even more than clothes! Simply using the proper tools can make your fashion illustrations go from good to great, and using the wrong stuff can ruin a drawing. Trust us — we know.

Art supplies can be pricey, and it's tempting to go overboard when you see all that's offered. Co-author Lisa remembers the first list of art supplies she was told to buy in art school; it was pages long! Of course she bought them all, and then she realized later that she had some things she never even touched.

 Take your time and be deliberate when choosing your supplies. This ain't no shopping spree! Buy what you know you can use now, and pick up additional supplies as you need them.

In this chapter, we show you how to start with the necessities and build up your supplies cabinet as you go along. We also walk you through setting up a work space to call your own. If you have a spot that has proper lighting, a well-organized workstation, and a "no trespassing" sign, you're good to go! Finally, we provide you with some information on how to store your artwork.

Stopping at the Art Supply Store

Although we love the sights and smells of any art supply store, we've narrowed down the list of where we shop for supplies. As you become more familiar with supplies and art supply stores, you'll figure out who offers the best deals and most choice and who has the most helpful staff.

After you settle on your favorite store, you'll return to it again and again. But when you're starting out, roaming down aisle after aisle filled with pads of paper can be pretty scary. Rows upon rows of pencils can make you start chewing your nails, and seeing so many different types of erasers can make you want to scream. Don't be afraid to ask for help; many people who work in art supply stores are artists themselves.

Because the world of online shopping is literally at your fingertips, you don't have to leave home to buy anything these days if you don't want to. However, co-author Lisa shops online only if an artist friend gives her a good site recommendation, because she prefers to actually see and touch her future supplies. In fact, she doesn't advise buying your supplies online unless you have no access to an art store. If you do venture online for supplies, know exactly what you need and the names of particular brands that you've tried out.

In the following sections, we give you the rundown on the must-have supplies as you start creating your own fashion drawings. Make a list of supplies you want to try, or take this book with you to the art supply store. Browse the aisles, feel and try out the different papers, handle the drawing instruments, and ask the staff for advice if you have questions. If an item we haven't mentioned catches your eye, pick it up and try it out. Who knows — it may become your favorite tool of all time!

Picking out papers

Welcome to the wonderful world of paper, where you find shelves and shelves of individual sheets and pads. You can really rack up a hefty bill in this department, so be careful. Less is more! You don't need to start out with a ton of paper, so read our descriptions and choose according to your needs.

You may be torn between buying a pad of paper or individual sheets. When you're starting out, buy pads of drawing paper because you get more bang for your buck. When you have a full pad of paper at your disposal, you're more likely to flip the page and keep experimenting with figures and colors, which helps you improve your skills. Buy individual sheets only if you want something really special. Individual sheets are more expensive, usually quite large in size (watch out on a windy day!), and harder to store.

If you find a spiral notebook with sketch paper, even better! The sketch book doesn't need to be expensive with fancy perforated paper; just get one with a simple lightweight sketch paper for doodling.

Here are some choices you need to make when buying paper:

- ✔ **Size:** A sketch pad that's too small or too big can cause problems. We suggest an 11- x 14-inch sketch pad for starters. Anything smaller can tighten up your style, and anything larger can overwhelm you with the amount of space you think you need to fill with your drawing. Plus the larger the sketch pad gets, the harder it is to carry and store. With an average-sized pad, you can draw one large figure per page or several smaller figures. Wait until you're comfortable with your drawing style before you move to a bigger or smaller size.

- ✔ **Paper weight:** Weight, which is related to paper thickness, can make a tremendous difference in your drawings. The weight of paper can run from 20 pounds up to 140 pounds; the higher the weight, the better the quality of the paper. That said, you don't have to run out and buy the heaviest paper for everything you draw. Use lighter paper for practice and preliminary sketches, and use heavier paper, which is pricier, for final drawings and pieces that you plan to put in your portfolio.

Looking at the textures you find in paper

The texture of the paper you choose can make all the difference in your drawing style and the look of your drawing. Paper can run from smooth to rough — *medium* tooth falls somewhere in the middle:

- ✔ **Smooth paper:** You can create a great detailed drawing on smooth paper. It lends itself to the shading of pencil and fine line strokes, and it provides better control of detail. If you want to illustrate a fashion figure with an outrageous dress that's poufed with tulle, this type of smooth (and often glossy) paper is for you. Markers also work well on smooth paper because the colors blend well and sit on the surface, allowing you to do some really cool things, such as blending and layering colors.

- ✔ **Rough paper:** Paper with texture is super for softer pencil lead, charcoal pencils and sticks, and black and gray pastels. The textured paper helps absorb your medium of choice. Try using a stick of charcoal on a scrap of smooth paper and then on a scrap on textured paper. What a difference! Students are always surprised at the way their softer drawing materials turn to dust on smooth papers but settle in nicely on paper with a tooth. Markers also look super cool on textured paper. The paper tends to absorb the color, creating vibrant illustrations.

Marianne suggests starting by purchasing a pad of smooth paper and a pad of textured paper.

Choosing types of paper for your toolbox

You can explore many, many fantastic types of paper, but you should start off with the basics and work your way up to the specialty papers. This list shows you the practical and affordable basics you can safely begin with:

- ✔ **Bristol board:** Bristol board is a smooth, sturdy, and reliable paper favored by many artists. Weighing in at about 90–100 pounds, Bristol board is great for detailed fashion illustrations.

- ✔ **Sketch or drawing paper:** Sketch or drawing paper is exactly what it says it is: a basic paper to sketch and doodle on.

- ✔ **Newsprint:** Excellent for super-rough sketches, newsprint is the cheapest of all papers. It is flimsy, crumples easily, and is absolutely the least frightening of the lot. Don't expect to create a keeper on this paper, however. You simply doodle and sketch on this flimsy stuff.

- ✔ **Tracing paper:** Tracing paper is the best stuff ever! We don't know what we'd do without it. It's light (20–25 pounds) and transparent, and you can make adjustments and test drawing techniques without touching your original drawing. Just lay it over your drawing and test away.

The types of papers are endless, and there are no exact rules as to the type you must use for a particular type of drawing. However, you can get suggestions on which papers will work or enhance the type of media you're using.

For example, pencils, charcoal, and other dry media work well on drawing paper, and marker works well on marker paper, which is smooth and doesn't bleed. Most pads of paper describe their suggested uses right on the cover sheet. If you're not sure, ask a salesperson or other artists.

When you see a paper you're interested in, touch it and see whether you like the texture of the surface, and hold it to see whether you like the weight of a single page. In art supply stores, you often find test paper that's available for a scribble or two, so take advantage of these scraps before you spend a lot of money on paper. The store may have a supply of test pencils near the papers, but it's a good idea to carry a few pencils of your own, too, especially your favorites.

You can be as creative or experimental as you want with paper types. Don't be afraid to try papers not typically used for sketching, such as the following:

- **Vellum:** A smooth translucent paper similar to tracing paper, but it has more body
- **Plike:** A soft velvet-like paper
- **Brown recycled paper:** Just like a brown paper bag

Purchasing pencils

Why are some pencils so popular? Because folks have used them since kindergarten! They're the comfort food of art supplies. You use pencils to begin your sketch, put the finishing touches on it, and add all sorts of details in between.

Many beginning artists don't realize how many varieties of pencils they can choose from. Using different kinds of pencils for your drawings makes a tremendous difference, so check out the following sections to discover the various pencil properties.

Lining up the different leads: Hard or soft, light or dark

The *lead* (which is actually made of ground-up graphite and a filler) is the center of the pencil. Graphite pencils come in a few grades, based on the hardness and darkness of the lead:

- **H:** H stands for *hard* pencils. They're commonly designated as 2H, 4H, 6H, or 8H, although different brands use different labeling. Some brands also include a 9H. What is consistent is that a higher number means a harder lead, which creates a lighter pencil line. You use an H pencil when you're not planning on erasing the lines after you're finished drawing or when you want your lines to be very light.

- **B:** B stands for *black* pencils. They're commonly designated as 2B, 4B, 6B, and 8B, with some brands including a 9B. For B pencils, higher numbers mean darker lines. B pencils come in handy when you want to add dark features, texture, or thick lines or when you're using a darker paper and you need to be able to see your lines better.

✔ **HB:** At the center point of the lead range is an HB pencil. This is the kind of pencil most artists use, because it's not too dark and not too light. It's great for beginners who are just discovering pencil types, as it's great for everyday sketching when you're not concerned about a drawing being light or dark.

Look at Figure 2-1 to get a better idea of the range of pencil leads. An 8H pencil, for example, draws a line that's very light. At the other end of the pencil spectrum is the 8B pencil, which is the cousin of a charcoal pencil and is very dark. Note that the scale isn't standardized, so two brands with the same grade may not be equally dark.

Here's a little fashion secret: Try to avoid 4H, 6H, and 8H pencils of any brand. The lines they make are often too light, and erasing can be tough because these pencils leave indentations in the paper.

Figure 2-1:
The range
of pencil
hardness.

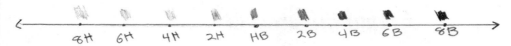

Pointing out our favorite pencils

There are no good or bad pencils; there are just pencils that do what you want them to do! The pencils you prefer may differ from someone else's, even if you draw similar types of art. Here's a list of our preferred pencils:

✔ **Faber-Castell graphite pencils:** We love these smooth and even pencils, which range from 6H to 8B.

✔ **Prismacolor Turquoise drawing pencils:** We suggest the Turquoise line of graphite pencils for many of our students. It has a nice feel to it, doesn't break easily, and ranges from 9H to 9B.

✔ **Raffiné Art Sketch 7000 Creative Mark pencils:** Ranging from 6H to 8B, this brand is popular in art schools.

✔ **Prismacolor (formerly Sanford Design) Ebony pencils:** If you're looking for a powerful and bold line, this pencil is for you. The dark, wide lines and instant smoothness of this "jet black" graphite pencil are great for fashion attitude.

✔ **Mechanical pencils:** A lot of artists that we know love mechanical pencils on both smooth and textured papers. Mechanical pencils don't come in a range of graphite types.

✔ **General's charcoal pencils (extra soft):** We reach for these pencils (make sure you sharpen them well) when we want to make a line that goes from thick to thin with just a slight smudge. We *never* use charcoal sticks; this is the only kind of charcoal pencil that works for us when it comes to fashion illustration.

Test different pencils to find your favorite ones. Try them on various types of paper as well. Hold the pencils in your hand and write a few words, and then draw some circles and straight lines. Notice how smooth the line is, along with how light or dark it is. Hold the pencil on its side to see how easy or difficult it is to color in a shape. Turning a pencil on its side can help you determine whether the pencil is good for shading.

Keeping your pencil in tiptop shape

Both electric and manual pencil sharpeners have their merits. Electric ones are so easy and fast, and Marianne loves the good old-fashioned on-the-wall ones for how long and sharp they make her pencils.

Pencils have *spines,* which are made of the line of graphite inside. Try not to drop your pencils or treat them casually; otherwise, the spines inside can break. Breaks inside the spines, even though you can't see them, make the pencils more difficult to sharpen.

Examining erasers

Drawing pencils typically don't come with erasers on them, so you need to purchase a separate eraser. Marianne likes to use two main types:

- **Art gum erasers:** These are cheap, light brown, rectangular, and about an inch or so long. They're great for erasing a large area.
- **Kneaded erasers:** Kneaded erasers are great for pressing on your paper to remove smudges or just to lighten up the pencil lines. They're also great to knead and shape into a sharp point if you need to erase a small area.

Markers: Making a permanent addition to your drawing arsenal

You can use markers for a variety of purposes. Some artists love to add marker lines over a pencil sketch to get that sharp, clean look (ultra-fine black Sharpies are great for this). You can also use markers to add color to your fashion drawings.

We always have our students begin their marker supplies with a few key colors in high-quality markers and the rest of the colors in cheaper versions (100-color sets). The high-quality markers we suggest you buy include the following:

- A few skins tones (light to dark)
- Warm and cool grays
- A light yellow
- A bright red

Stay away from the rainbow sets — you'll find that you rarely use most of those colors. As you develop your fashion illustration skills, you'll determine the colors you use the most and invest in higher-quality markers as you see fit.

Quality markers are quite an expensive investment, but they're well worth it! These markers dry fast, have more than one point (they're double ended), allow you options in blending colors, and are true to the color on the outside of the marker. They also last a long time before they dry out or run out of ink.

Don't buy water-soluble markers. They take longer to dry and have a tendency to smear — usually when you're just about to complete your drawing. Permanent markers are a must!

Here's a list of brand-name markers you may want to try:

- **Ultra-fine black Sharpies:** We couldn't live without these staples. Seriously. This marker can produce an ultra-thin line every time. It's terrific for finalizing pencil outlines and for adding details, linear shading, and textures. And when you feel really confident, you can use this marker to turn out some amazing runway-like sketches with just a few lines.

- **Prismacolor markers:** This line of markers has a long life span, as long as you take care of them. Prismacolor offers a wide selection of color markers, though we suggest you stick with the gray shades for now. Their double-ended markers have a broad, flat edge on one end and a fine point on the other. They also won't give you the dreaded marker headache because they don't smell.

- **Pantone Universe Twin markers:** Pantone offers a decent line of markers with both a brush-shaped end and a fine-point end in one marker. Test out their cool and warm grays — they're wonderful for a bold shading style. When you feel confident, a quick stroke of a marker is the way to go in fashion illustration.

- **Copic markers:** These markers are pricey but well worth it. They're one of the best quality markers on the market! They all come double-ended — each end has a different tip. Co-author Marianne loves to use the ones with the brush tip. Most Copic markers can be refilled (which saves money and waste), and the range of colors available is endless.

- **Tombow Dual Brush Pens:** These brush tip markers (also known as *stamping markers*) are so much fun! They're less expensive than the other markers, and they work like paint brushes, laying down bold colors with a softer tip. After being introduced to these markers, some students inevitably get hooked!

Here are a few tips on using your markers:

1. **Sketch in pencil and get your fashion illustration in good shape.**

   Permanent markers are called "permanent" for a reason.

2. **Try to pick up some graphite from your pencil lines using your kneaded eraser.**

3. **Run your marker over the pencil lines.**

   Try not to rub the marker into a paper hard enough to pill the paper and ruin the tip of the marker.

4. **Put those caps on tightly after using your markers.**

   Otherwise, you'll dry them out faster than you can say "waste of money."

   Dried-out markers can be annoying because markers are pricey, but don't throw them out — they can be great for depicting sheer and textured fabrics because they leave less pigment on your paper, which creates white spots that are almost impossible to purposely create.

5. **Let your marker lines sit a bit and then erase your pencil lines.**

   You'll marvel at the crispness produced.

Sealing with fixative

Drawing mediums such as graphite pencils and charcoal lay down loose pieces that can smear long after you've finished a drawing. Layering an illustration with marker on top of the pencil does a good job of sealing the graphite, but it's not ideal. Besides, you won't use markers on all drawings.

Fixatives fill the bill for sealing your illustrations. *Fixatives* are liquid varnishes you usually spray from a can. Most fixatives specify the media they work best for; they're labeled as a spray fixative for charcoal or pastels, for example. Read the cans carefully to purchase the best type for your media. Make sure to read the instructions about how to use them; they can be highly toxic!

Buying a toolbox for art supplies

After you've purchased your supplies, you need somewhere to stash them. Ideally, your toolbox should be portable so you can take it to class, use it on location at a fashion show, or easily store it in your studio. You can consider using a cigar box, a tackle box, baggies, canvas shopping bags, and more. No hard and fast rule exists for what makes a good toolbox, but make sure it's something that allows you to get to your supplies easily. You don't want to have to burrow for your supplies when you need them.

We prefer a nice-size tackle box for storing and organizing art supplies. The small compartments are perfect for erasers and sharpeners, and the larger part is great for pencils and markers. And the entire box opens up so you can see all your supplies at once. Don't forget to keep the size reasonable, however; the larger the box, the more stuff you collect and the heavier and harder it becomes to carry around!

Creating a Studio Space

A space of your own where you can focus on your work without being disturbed — doesn't that sound amazing? The thought conjures up visions of floor-to-ceiling windows and a sun-drenched room, but sadly, that isn't most people's reality. Although attractive surroundings are wonderful, you can be creative anywhere. If you could see some of the places where we've worked, you would be shocked! But we've always managed to personalize those spaces, which is critical.

In the following sections, we help you determine which type of space works for you and your personality (and family dynamic). We also show you how to choose the right equipment, including lighting, a drawing table, and a side table, to create a studio that you'll love. Finally, we provide suggestions on how to keep your space spic and span (or at least comfortably uncluttered).

Quiet, bustling, at home, or in town: Claiming a space that suits you

You have to know yourself pretty well to establish your own studio space, and you have to be almost territorial in claiming it. Before considering furniture and other equipment, first consider your personality and your family and roommates. Ask yourself these questions:

- Do you like to work with other people, or do you need to be alone to produce your best work?
- Is absolute silence the rule, or will too much silence put you on edge?
- Can you afford to rent space away from home? If not, can you stake out your own space where you live?
- If you do draw at home, can you establish no-entry zones? In other words, will your family or roommates actually stay out of your work space?

For example, co-author Lisa needs quiet to work, but she gets really weird if she's alone too long. So she works at home and people come and go, but she knows their patterns of activity and when she can get good quiet time. She also has a simple rule about her supplies and work area: No one can even think about going near anything! If you're firm from the start, you shouldn't have too much trouble.

Marianne, on the other hand, can draw anywhere, anytime! She just needs room to lay out herself and her stuff.

Lighting that works

Lighting is one of the most important investments you can make in a studio space. Every artist should be obsessed with her eyesight. After all, good eyes are crucial to your livelihood. And trying to draw in too dim a light can cause eyestrain or worse. Spending a little extra money on lighting is money well spent.

We prefer drawing in the sunshine, but for when that isn't an option, you can invest in some adjustable studio lamps. Lisa has two studio lamps, one planted on each side of her desk. Both have flexible arms, allowing her to adjust them as needed. If you can't find a decent studio lamp at a store, go online and hunt down exactly what you're looking for.

For light bulbs, consider using compact fluorescent light bulbs at 100 watts. Or for true colors when you're coloring in your drawings, you can use full-spectrum bulbs.

Hammering out your drawing surface

A good working surface is important for drawing. Without a sturdy surface, you won't be able to produce your best work. You have several options for choosing a surface that's perfect for you and your space:

- ✔ **A slanted drafting or drawing table:** These tables are large rectangles mounted on a system that allows them to tilt. This lets you sit up straight. You can adjust some to your own height by cranking them up and down.

  Here's one negative about working on a slanted drafting table: One false move, and your pencils, rulers, erasers, and more can start an avalanche! Some furniture stores have little ledges you can mount at the bottom of the rectangle to catch the pencils. Or you can do what Marianne does and drill in a stick of wood by the bottom — that catches the pencils, too!

  A new drafting or drawing table will set you back between $50 and $200. However, check out office supply store sales, art store sales, and even tag sales and rummage sales as well as online resale sites — you may just get lucky and find a good deal!

- ✔ **A sturdy, flat table:** Although a slanted drafting or drawing table is ideal, plenty of artists do great work without a drafting table. In fact, many artists prefer to lean over work that rests on a flat surface. Kitchen tables and desks are perfect for many people. A world of tables awaits you, so just be creative!

  Be cautious with a flat table that causes you to lean over your work. Leaning over for long periods of time can take a toll on your back. An ergonomic chair can alleviate stiffness and pain. (We discuss some chair options later in the chapter.)

- ✔ **A drawing board or slant board:** A slant or drawing board is a smaller, portable version of the drafting table. Slant boards are about 18 inches x 24 inches, and they work for many different sizes of paper. They're made out of masonite, and they have a clip attached to keep your papers from flying around. Their portability is a huge plus.

Packing up a studio to go

Sometimes you may be a fashionista drawing on the go. For example, co-author Lisa got her first job doing fashion sketches at a runway show, and her second job had her traveling to a studio to sketch a designer's line. Lisa was in a total panic about how she could carry all her supplies without looking like a total pack mule. It's a valid concern, but never fear. You can learn to pack light and travel with only the must-haves, including the following packed away in a *très chic* canvas bag:

- ✔ Your sketchbook
- ✔ Pencils of choice
- ✔ Erasers
- ✔ An ultra-fine Sharpie marker

You don't want to be setting up camp at a fashion show or in a designer's studio, so plan ahead to pack just the essentials — but also make sure you have everything you really need.

Before you invest in a slant board or slanted drawing table, find out whether you enjoy working on a slant. Grab something with a smooth flat surface (a piece of wood or the back of a large drawing pad) and then prop it up against something stationary. Lay your paper on it and see whether you feel more comfortable working on a slant.

Wherever you decide to work, make sure you get up and stretch periodically during your drawing time. It's amazing how bad your posture can get when you slump and curl like Quasimodo.

Taking a seat

You're going to spend countless hours seated at your drawing table, so look for a top-notch chair. Even if you prefer to stand while you work, you're going to want to take a load off every so often.

If you don't buy a chair with cushioning, you're cooked! You need that extra bit of comfort to offset the amount of time you're going to spend in your chair. Look for a chair that has good back support and armrests.

If you tend to go back and forth between your drawing surface and your computer, you may want to find a chair with wheels. Make sure your chair height is adjustable — you need to be in a comfortable position. Also check that your chair is a good fit with your drawing table; you don't want your knees hitting the table every time you roll up to it.

Your best bet is to purchase your chair in a store so you can test its fit and comfort level for you. If you order a chair online, you risk ending up with a chair you don't like — and no one wants the hassle of trying to return a chair in the mail.

Organizing your side table

You don't have to get fancy with side tables, but they can be helpful. You can simply use an extra table from your home to set next to your drawing table. It can be any height, but choosing one that's about level with your table is more convenient than having to bend over to reach things.

It's amazing how quickly you can accumulate supplies (and forget that you have them as well), so keep everything as organized as possible. Consider, for example, keeping all overflow supplies in containers and bins so stuff doesn't get jumbled together. Knowing where everything is saves you time and money. A side table's main advantage is offering easy access to your supplies, especially if you have a deadline.

Place your side table on the same side as your dominant hand. Because Lisa's a leftie, she parks her table on the left side of her drawing table. This placement keeps everything within easy reach.

Cleaning up!

Becoming a slob in your own studio is very easy. After all, it's tempting to walk away from your mess when you're tired or in a rush. However, consider the ways you pay for letting it all hang out:

- If you don't put those pencils and markers in their proper storage bins, they run away from you.
- When you leave the caps off of your markers, they dry out.
- If you toss your latest work on the floor, your sneaker print is going to ruin your drawing.
- Dirty hands can smudge up the very piece you're working on. Take a break and wash up every now and then.
- Don't eat or drink anything near your drawings. Ever. You *know* what's going to happen!
- Dropping a kneaded eraser, which is similar to gum, guarantees you'll step on it and have to spend time picking it out of your shoe treads or out of your carpet.

Here are some golden rules for keeping your space clean:

- Keep a roll of paper towels in the studio to clean up messes quickly.
- Empty your wastebasket every day. Sitting next to a garbage mountain is just too depressing.
- Get rid of all those shavings from pencil sharpeners, including those in electric sharpeners.

Co-author Lisa's studio is small and loaded with stuff hanging on the walls, but her work area is tidy, and she knows where every single item is. Find a method to your madness. Consider what another artist said: People like to complain about crummy places as an excuse for creating crummy work.

Storing Your Work

The sooner you get into the practice of storing your work, the better you and your artwork will fare. You've worked hard on those fashion illustrations, so treat them with respect and store them properly, thus avoiding tearing or crumpling, fading from sunlight, damage from curious children, or spills. Too many beautiful pieces of work get shoved randomly into sketchbooks, where they quickly get tattered from wear and tear.

Seeing artists treat their art without respect shows that they don't really value their own work.

In the following sections, we detail several ways you can store your creations: on computer or in a portfolio.

Saving work on the computer

These days, artists store more and more of their work as JPEG files on their computers. When you store art on your computer, you create an art file, allowing you to keep things on record and send samples of your work by e-mail. You need to take a few steps before your artwork appears on screen, however. Here's how to save your work electronically:

- ✔ **Scan the image.** Scan at a high resolution, such as 300 DPI (dots per inch). This will retain much of the detail and allow you to scale the image.

- ✔ **If the original piece doesn't fit in your scanner, photograph your work with a digital camera in good lighting.** You can then download the images onto your computer.

After you have your work on the computer, you can easily share it with people around the corner or around the world. Consider your options:

- ✔ **Send images by e-mail.** If your files are small enough, you can attach them to an e-mail and then send them to 1 or 100 people at once.

- ✔ **Create a CD-ROM.** You can save dozens of images on a CD and send that CD to clients anywhere in the world. CDs are an excellent way to go global with your work.

  CDs are also an excellent way to store your images or create backup files.

- ✔ **Upload your images to an online portfolio.** You can choose from many free websites that allow you to create a portfolio to store your work online, or you can look into creating your own website. A digital portfolio can be so valuable: You can send your web address all over the world, or people researching on the Internet may just stumble upon your site! Plus, an online portfolio provides instant gratification. A CD has to be mailed and can easily get lost.

We discuss digital portfolios in more detail in Chapter 17.

Investing in portfolios

Not everyone has easy computer access, and even if you do, you need to store original drawings somewhere. Even when you send a CD, you're still expected to show the original work as well.

Usually the best place to store your original artwork is in a *portfolio,* which is a large, flat, rectangular briefcase with a handle and zipper closure. A portfolio holds clear plastic sheets that contain your projects. You should invest in a portfolio or two if you really care about your artwork. You don't have to spend a fortune on those top-of-the-line cases, but it's worth paying a little more to store your pieces.

Consider these points when picking out a portfolio:

- ✔ Consider a decent vinyl case with handles. A fancy leather one looks great, but it's not a necessity for budding artists.

- ✔ Buy a portfolio with removable sheets so you can add and remove work easily and don't have a bunch of empty pages hanging out.

- ✔ Make sure your portfolio is roomy enough for your work, but also make sure that you're physically comfortable carrying it around. The two best sizes carry removable sheets that are 11 inches x 14 inches or 14 inches x 17 inches. Going smaller leaves too little space to show your drawings, and larger portfolios are difficult to travel with.

Evaluate and purge your work over the years. Yes, certain illustrations are fabulous, and, yes, some are sentimental, but at some point, you have to get tough with the rest. You don't want to be a hoarder unless you have endless storage space and an organized system for storing sketches. Only pieces done within the last three years stay in co-author Lisa's studio; the rest go up to the attic and are stored in large portfolios away from the sun. (For more details on fashion portfolios, including tips on which drawings to include, flip to Chapter 17.)

Chapter 3

Beginning with Figure Drawing Basics

You can't really start to develop fantastic fashion illustrations until you master basic drawing techniques. Although figure drawing and fashion drawing are quite different, familiarity with the basics of figure drawing gives you a solid foundation to build on when you turn your hand to fashion. Knowing normal body proportions and appearances gives you a starting point when you're ready to exaggerate the fashion figure in creative ways.

In this chapter, we guide you through the figure drawing basics of creating different parts of the body. Even if you've been doing figure drawing for years, the tips in this chapter can help you apply figure-drawing concepts as you switch over to fashion drawing. We also review some simple techniques that can add depth and dimension to your drawings, whether you're working on figure drawing or fashion illustration.

If this is your first time picking up a pencil and you want more information on figure drawing, *Figure Drawing For Dummies,* by Kensuke Okabayashi (Wiley), can get you started.

A Little Warm-Up: Starting with Lines, Curves, and Shapes

All fashion drawings consist of lines, curves, and geometric shapes. Figuring out how to draw smooth, flowing lines and shapes that vary from dark to light, thick to thin, and bold to subtle isn't always easy. Fortunately, practice really does make perfect, so the more you draw, the better you get and the more comfortable you become with varying your technique.

If you're a lefty, put a piece of paper towel under your hand as you draw. Lefties tend to drag their hands across the paper when they draw, making it more likely that they'll smudge their work.

Playing around with basic shapes

You can reduce almost everything you draw into a collection of circles, ovals, squares, rectangles, trapezoids, triangles, and heart shapes. After you master the basic shapes, putting them together into a figure drawing becomes much easier.

Ovals, squares, and circles are essential for outlining the shape of the head. The oval shape also helps you establish the fashion head count, which helps you figure out body proportions (more on proportions in the later section "Laying out body lines," as well as in Chapter 4). As for triangles and the rest? You use them for patterns, for facial shapes, to exaggerate parts of the body, and for so much more.

Try experimenting with shapes like this:

- ✔ Draw basic shapes — circles, ovals, squares, rectangles, trapezoids, heart shapes — until you're comfortable with them. Figure 3-1a shows a collection of circles and squares in various sizes.

- ✔ Experiment with the space between the shapes by connecting and stacking shapes in different ways, as in Figure 3-1b.

- ✔ Overlap your shapes. Figure 3-1c shows shows several circles, all about the same size and evenly spaced. Squares of different sizes overlap the field of circles, making the design more interesting.

Figure 3-1:
Try stacking,
connecting,
and overlap-
ping the
shapes.

a   b   c

To play around with shapes, have lots of cheap paper handy and don't worry too much about the finished results. The important point is to relax and practice, practice, practice.

Taking lines from long to short, thick to thin

What's the big deal about drawing a long, straight line? A lot! First of all, a steady hand is required (no rulers allowed), and that takes practice. Drawing a good freehand line comes in handy when you're drawing plaids, adding great-looking hair, and penciling in lines of symmetry, which we describe in the upcoming section "Creating the line of symmetry." Lines of different widths and lengths are a must for creating texture in clothes, hair, and more.

By experimenting with dark lines (great for shadowing) and light lines (super for detail), you can achieve fashion textures that are pleasing to the eye. Practice with your pencil by doing the following:

- Draw long, straight lines, as in Figure 3-2a.

- Draw some straight lines that go from thick to thin, as in Figure 3-2b. Start by using the side of your pencil and then gradually turn it so the point creates a thin, wispy finish.

- With a bit of pressure from your hand, go really dark. Then ease the pressure on the pencil to lighten the line. See Figure 3-2c.

- Draw quick, short lines, as in Figure 3-2d.

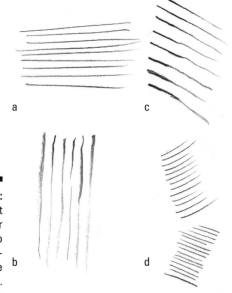

Figure 3-2: Experiment with your pencil to create different line styles.

You can achieve different looks by using different pencils and varying the pressure you apply with your hand. We discuss pencils and the darkness of their lines in Chapter 2.

Drawing cool curves

Curved lines definitely work in fashion illustration! You use curved lines when drawing hair, ruffles, an arched eyebrow, or a high-heeled pump, not to mention a million other things. Practice drawing curves in long loops bunched closed together as well as in arcs, and you see how useful curves can be in creating fashion clothes and hair. For example, you often use parallel curves when drawing necklines, waistbands, and cuffs.

Try your hand at different types of curves, from arcs to complete loops:

✔ Practice drawing curves of different lengths and curvatures, as in Figure 3-3a.

✔ Draw curves in long loops, as in Figure 3-3b.

✔ Draw curves in tight bunches, as in Figure 3-3c.

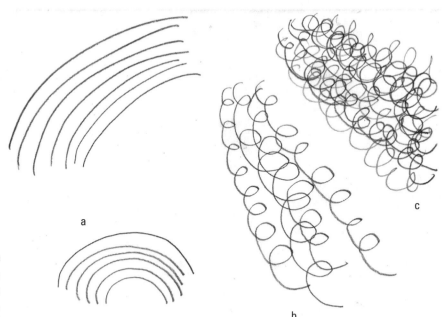

Figure 3-3:
Curves go everywhere.

Starting with a Stick Figure

Drawing a stick figure, or line figure, is a perfect way for beginners to get comfortable with basic figures, and it serves as a refresher for people who've done figure drawing before. Starting with simple stick figures serves several purposes:

✔ It helps you get something on paper, because *beginning* to draw a figure can be a bit daunting.

✔ By starting with a stick figure, you can lay out lines of proportion, which are critical to making a figure drawing work. You can later add geometric shapes to bulk up your stick figure.

✔ Building on fluid stick figures helps you lay out fashion illustrations. You can figure out poses and placement before getting too far into a drawing.

In the following sections, we help you draw an artist's stick figure.

Creating the line of symmetry

The *line of symmetry,* or *balance line,* runs down right through the center of the stick figure's head and continues to the bottom of the stick feet. The line of symmetry serves a number of functions in both figure and fashion drawing:

✔ It marks the center of the body.

✔ It aids you in comparing one side of the body to the other.

✔ It helps you keep both sides of the body balanced as you draw.

✔ It keeps the figure grounded, not falling over, as you start to draw poses.

✔ It helps you set proportions.

To establish a line of symmetry, draw a simple stick figure, as in Figure 3-4a. Then draw a dashed line straight through the middle of your figure, as in Figure 3-4b.

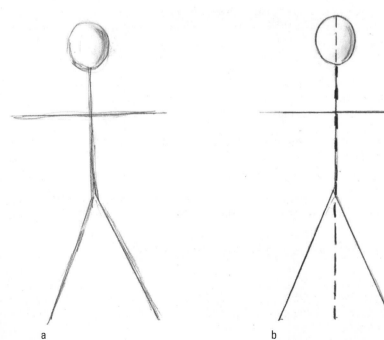

Figure 3-4: Draw a line of symmetry on your stick figure.

a

b

TIP

Grand gestures: Capturing a figure with a few fast lines

Stick figures give you straight, simple lines to use for placement and proportion. But we also suggest practicing a drawing technique that's a little more flexible: *gesture drawing*, which consists of drawing using a few quick and key lines to help you master the figure. In a nutshell, you just keep the pencil moving on the paper and try not to think too much! Gesture drawing has to do with curved lines, not lifting the pencil, and being fluid. You use as few lines as possible to get the basics of the figure down.

Gesture drawing allows the hand and brain to relax and conveys movement and action, two fashion illustration must-haves! When you relax your hand and brain, you draw lines organically. Don't worry about imperfections — they add character and personality to the drawing.

Laying out body lines

Proportion keeps your figure from looking like the body's too long for the head or the head's too big for the body. Fashion drawing plays with normal proportions, making the proportions not exactly representative of real people (kinda like models aren't representative of "real" people!). However, figure drawings do represent real people.

The *head count* is a term that describes a quick and easy rule for proportioning that uses the head as a measuring tool (see Chapter 4 for more about the importance of head counts). After you draw an oval to represent the head, the height of the head you've drawn becomes a unit of measurement, like an inch or centimeter. You can then talk about the number of *heads* that fit into various parts of the body — legs that are 4 heads long, a waist that's 3 heads down from the top of the figure, and so on.

In figure drawing, the head fits into the adult body seven to eight times total, so the figure is 7 to 8 heads tall. When we talk about a head count, it always includes the head along with the rest of the body.

Your stick figure will be 8 heads long; the actual head counts as 1 head, and the body is as long as another 7 heads stacked on top of each other. Here's how to start a figure drawing:

1. **Draw an oval to represent the figure's head and then draw a dashed line of symmetry, as in Figure 3-5a.**

2. **Draw in seven more ovals stacked along the line of symmetry. Draw a horizontal line 4 heads down to represent the hips or crotch. (See Figure 3-5b.)**

3. **A third of the way through the second head, draw a horizontal line for the shoulders as wide as two of the ovals on their sides, as in Figure 3-5c.**

4. **For arm placement on each side of the body, draw a straight vertical line that goes from the shoulder line to the bottom of the 5th head, as in Figure 3-6a.**

5. **From the line at the hips, draw two angled lines for legs that are 4 heads long, as in Figure 3-6b.**

6. **At the ends of the two leg lines, draw two small triangles for feet, as in Figure 3-6c.**

After you become proficient at drawing using heads to determine proportion, just create a series of hash marks to mark off lengths equal to the height of the head — you don't need to draw full ovals. This shortcut helps save time and decreases the amount of erasing you need to do.

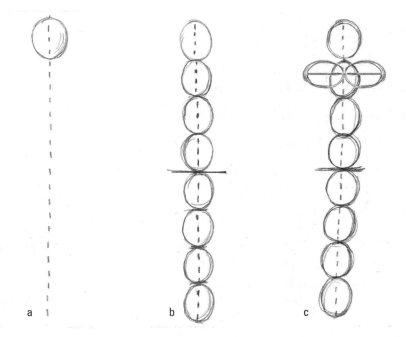

Figure 3-5: Proportioning your figures.

a   b   c

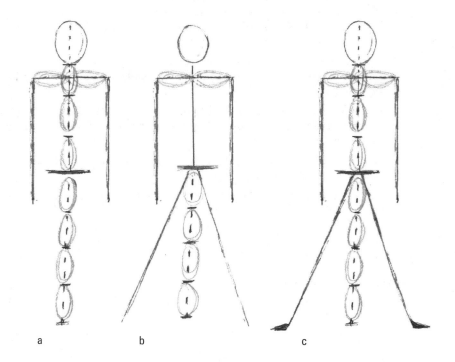

Figure 3-6:
Adding arms
and legs.

a b c

Choosing sides: Drawing a stick figure from another angle

When drawing a stick figure from the side, start again with the 8-head count. A stick figure drawn from the side looks a bit more relaxed because you show a bit of a curve in the spine by the waist. The head shape is slightly angled, but the proportion lines remain the same.

Try these steps to draw a figure facing right:

1. **Draw a head shape in a three-quarter view, as in Figure 3-7a.**

   The curved line going down the head marks the center of the face.

2. **Draw a straight line by counting down 7 heads. For the foot, end with a small triangle that starts about ½ head from the bottom. (See Figure 3-7b.)**

3. **At 4 heads from the top, draw a horizontal line for the hips. Add a slight curve to the back above the hips. (See Figure 3-7c.)**

4. **Start the arm line below the stick figure's actual head and have the arm hang straight down. Start the hand slightly below the top of the 5th head and extend the hand and fingers almost to the bottom of that head. (See Figure 3-7d.)**

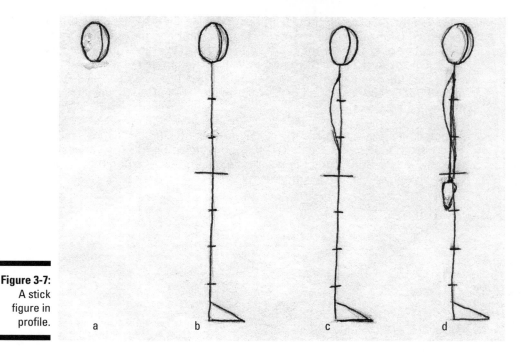

Figure 3-7:
A stick figure in profile.

Creating a Figure Drawing

Breaking figure drawings down into basic geometric shapes and using lines of proportion solves half of your problems in creating figure drawings. You use your lines of proportion to guide you. In the following sections, we explain how to draw the main body parts to scale.

Having a real-life model helps tremendously when you're doing figure drawings. Go to a figure drawing class and work from a model if you can. If you can't get to a class, grab a friend who's willing to sit still. The advantage of drawing from real life is being able to see all the real body parts and proportions. If you can't rope anyone into posing, buy a wooden mannequin at an art supply store to help you with form and shape.

Getting a head start

Start with a basic oval when drawing a head. Take a look at your head in a mirror. Ignore your facial features and hair, and see that your head is longer than it is wide — the definition of an oval. You can also think of the head as a large egg shape.

Next, draw a face grid on your oval. Face grids have nothing to do with sports. A *face grid* is is a fancy term for a simple drawing tool that helps you establish the placement of the features of the face — you just draw horizontal and vertical guide lines that cross at the center of your oval. The vertical line is a line of symmetry that marks the center of the face (down the nose), and the horizontal line is the figure's eye level. Mapping out a face grid gives you a starting point when you're looking at an empty oval that needs to be turned into a face. You don't use measuring tools to place the facial features; just eyeball everything.

Some people prefer to curve the guide lines slightly, following the oval's natural curve, as in Figure 3-8. A slight curve to your face grid adds dimension so that the facial features don't appear to be rigid or flat. We find that a slight curve gives facial features a more active feeling.

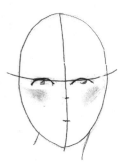

Figure 3-8: Sketch the oval and add a face grid with slightly curved lines.

The eyeline is halfway down the head, so keep the horizontal face grid line in the center of the oval, or you'll end up with eyeballs on the forehead! When you're ready to fill in the facial features, flip to Chapter 7, where we tell you all about drawing eyes, noses, and mouths for fashion figures.

Moving on to the neck and shoulders

After you have your fashion head down, you need to attach a beautiful upper body! Start with the neck and add in shoulders to see your fashion figure start to come alive. Keep in mind that not all drawings include the entire body; you can end your figure at the waist, especially if you're focusing on upper body clothing.

Get the trunk of the body started by drawing the neck and shoulders:

1. **Draw an oval head shape, as in Figure 3-9a.**

2. **Draw the neck by starting on both sides of the chin area and creating a short cylinder-like shape about ⅓ head high, as in Figure 3-9b.**

3. **The shoulders, which are bigger for men than women, ease out of the neckline. They extend slightly beyond the head or about the length of 2 heads turned sideways, and they form the top of the arms. (See Figure 3-9c.)**

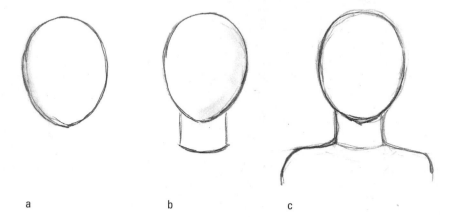

Figure 3-9:
Drawing
the head,
neck, and
shoulders.

a   b   c

Taking up arms

You have to draw the arms in proportion to the rest of the body, or your drawing will look very off-balance. A common beginner's mistake is to make the arms too short, so use the correct head count. Arms should be 2½ heads long, not including the wrists and hands.

The elbows should line up with the waistline, about 3 heads from the top. Use your stick figure proportions as a guide to find the correct arm lengths.

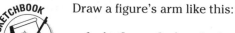

Draw a figure's arm like this:

1. **At the end of each shoulder line, lightly pencil in two cylinders for the upper and lower arms, as in Figure 3-10a. A circle between the two represents the elbow.**

   The length of the upper arm is about 1½ heads, and the forearm is about 1 head long. End the first cylinder at the elbow, which is across from the waistline. The waistline is 3 heads down. (See Figure 3-5b.)

   The second cylinder ends arounds the top of the thigh (or 4 heads down) and tapers down to where the wrist and hand begin.

2. **Turn the sides of the cylinders into gentle curves to represent the muscles, as in Figure 3-10c.**

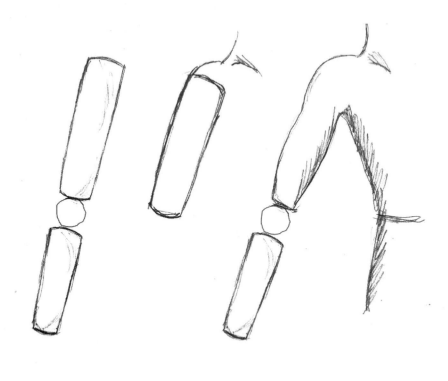

Figure 3-10:
Drawing
an arm.

a   b   c

Keeping your hands out

Many new artists hide the hands by sticking them behind the figure's back or by drawing shapes that looks like paws. But hands don't have to be so hard if you use basic shapes and curves.

Follow these steps to create a flat hand with the fingers extended:

1. **Draw an oval for the palm, as in Figure 3-11a.**

    This oval should be a little less than ½ the length of your figure's head.

2. **Draw a parallel curve above the oval to show where the fingers end. (See Figure 3-11b.)**

    The distance between the curve and the top of the oval is approximately the same as the palm length. The total length of the hand is about ¾ of the length of the head.

3. **Lightly sketch in the fingers, using the top of the oval as the place where the fingers join the palm and the top curve for the fingertips, as in Figure 3-11c.**

   The middle finger is the longest finger, with the pointer finger as the next longest. The ring finger is slightly shorter than the pointer finger (or the same length as the pointer), and the pinky finger, of course, is the shortest.

4. **Add a cylinder-like shape for the thumb and shade for dimension. (See Figure 3-11d.)**

After you understand how to draw the basic hand, try your own hand at drawing a typical fashion model's hand pose. One of the most common hand poses is a side view of the hand with a little fashionable bend to the fingers.

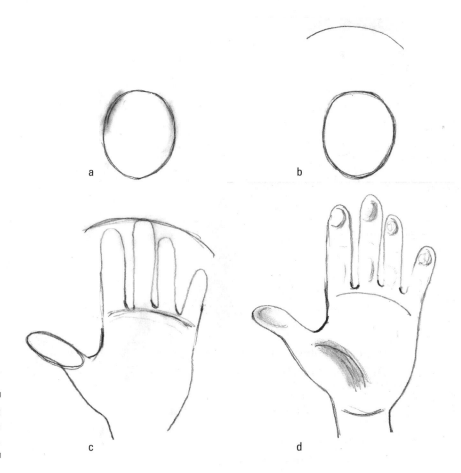

Figure 3-11: Hands take shape.

Here's how to draw the hand from the side:

1. **Start with a circle for the elbow. For the forearm, draw a tapered cylinder that ends with a smaller circle at the end for the wrist, as in Figure 3-12a.**

2. **At the end of the wrist, draw a triangle shape with one point of the triangle touching the circle of the wrist, as in Figure 3-12b.**

   This triangle represents the hand, minus the fingers. The forearm is 1 head long, and the hand is about ½ head long.

3. **From the wide point of the triangle, add in a tube-type shape for the thumb. On the sharp point of the triangle, add two tube shapes bending from the end for the fingers, as in Figure 3-12c.**

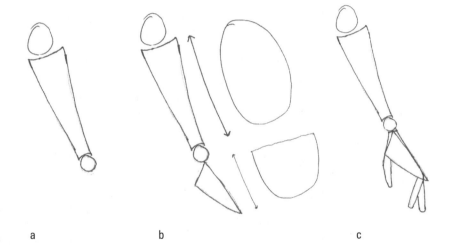

Figure 3-12:
The side view of a hand.

a   b   c

Watching the waistlines

To draw a waistline, revisit the stick figure, check the lines of proportion, and use the head count to properly place the waist. Waistlines come in all shapes and sizes, but the basics remain: a woman's waist is curvy, and a guy's is relatively straight.

To create the waistline:

1. **Draw a figure and count down 3 heads.**

2. **Draw a horizontal line for the waist.**

3. **To shape the man's waist, draw a line that starts in the armpit and angles down and in at the waist. For the woman, start the line at the armpit and create a line that curves in around the middle of the 3rd head and then flares out, creating an hourglass shape.**

Curve the line at the waist for a woman (see Figure 3-13a) and keep the line straight but tapered in for a man (see Figure 3-13b).

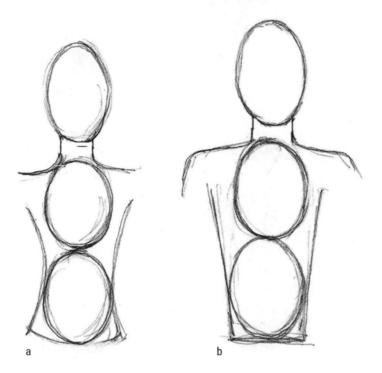

Figure 3-13: Draw the waistline.

a   b

Fitting in the hips

Hips are wider and curvier on women and straighter and thinner for men. By *hips,* we mean the widest part of your lower half. Using the head count, the pelvic area and hips fall within the 4th head down in your figure drawing. Hips serve a very important purpose, aside from the rocking and wiggling action they convey: the pelvic region is part of the body's core.

To mark out the hips and pelvic region on a woman, follow these guidelines:

1. **Starting at the bottom of the 4th head, draw a horizontal line for the crotch; place the *V* of the crotch on that line, as in Figure 3-14a.**

2. **At the top of the 4th head, draw a curved line for the waist. Starting from the sides of the waistline, draw the sides of the lower torso: Use a line down each side, ending at the horizontal line for the crotch, as in Figure 3-14b. Draw a couple of downward arcs to represent the tops of the legs.**

In women, the hips are often just a little wider than shoulder width.

A man's hips tend to be narrower than his shoulders. The entire hip and waist area is boxier on a guy — his waist is just slightly narrower than his hips, as in Figure 3-14c.

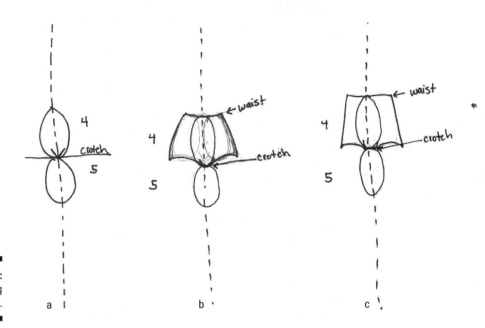

Figure 3-14:
Drawing
the hips.

Setting down sturdy legs

Your head count also works when dividing up the length of the legs. The entire length of legs in a figure drawing runs about 4 heads. The knee joints start within the 6th head.

Men's legs are thicker than women's. Keep a woman's leg long and curvy while making a man's wide and straight with muscular calves.

Start your figure drawing leg this way:

1. **Mark off 4 heads (ovals) to show the length of the leg, as in Figure 3-15a.**

   The knee falls in approximately the bottom ⅓ of the second oval from the top.

2. **Draw in two cylinder-like shapes over the 4-head length, making the top cylinder slightly shorter than the bottom cylinder. Connect the two cylinders with a circle for the knee. (See Figure 3-15b.)**

   The knee circle should be about ½ head tall. End the bottom part of the leg at the bottom of the 8th head.

3. **Erase the head markings from Step 1, leaving the cyclinders and circle to create the leg shape, as in Figure 3-15c.**

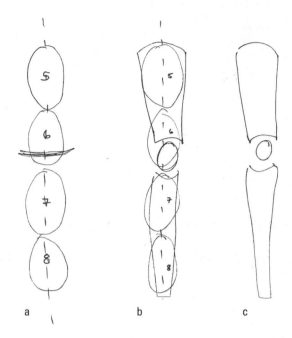

Figure 3-15: Now you've got a leg to stand on.

These feet are made for walking

Feet hold the body up, so don't draw them too small on your figure drawing — the length of your foot is about the length of your forearm, from the crease of your elbow to the start of your wrist. You can draw feet from many angles, but concentrate on the front and side views for now.

Start your feet by drawing a hoof (as in animal) shape — don't laugh, it works!

1. **Lightly draw the outline of a hoof shape, as in Figure 3-16a.**

2. **Inside the hoof shape, lightly draw a curve that follows the line of the front of the foot, as in Figure 3-16b.**

   This line marks where the toes join the foot and determines how long the toes are.

3. **Divide the space between the two lines into five toes, starting with the big toe, and sketch in the anklebones, as in Figure 3-16c.**

   The anklebones are just slight triangle pieces coming out from each side — the anklebone on the inside of the leg is a little higher than the one on the outside. These bones work the same way on the both the right and left foot.

4. **Draw in the toenails using curved lines and add shading by the arch of the foot and below the toes, as in Figure 3-16d.**

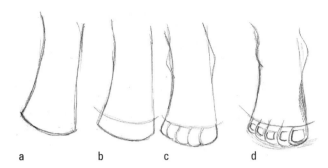

Figure 3-16:
Draw the
foot from
the front.

a   b   c   d

For a side view of the foot, follow these directions:

1. **Draw a right triangle (about the length of a head) and round out the points, as in Figure 3-17a.**

2. **Curve the right angle of the triangle to form a heel. Continue along the bottom of the triangle with a curved line for the bottom of the foot. (See Figure 3-17b.)**

   Curve the line up at about the midpoint of the triangle to form the arch of the foot. Then make a smaller indentation toward the front of the triangle to show where the big toe begins.

3. **To complete the top of the foot, draw a curved line along the front of the triangle from the ankle to the toe, as in Figure 3-17c.**

4. **Finish the foot by penciling in a toenail, the anklebone, and a little shading, as in Figure 3-17c.**

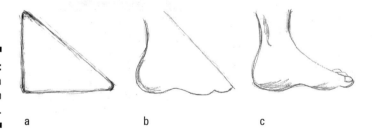

Figure 3-17:
Drawing a
foot from
the side.

a   b   c

Adding Depth with Shading

Shading techniques are used in both figure and fashion drawing but in somewhat different ways. In fashion illustration, you often use shading to create a fabric texture (which we cover in Chapter 14) or to accent a curve in the body. Some fashion illustrators prefer to work without using any shading at all. But for figure drawing artists, shading is essential, because shading molds the body with lights and darks to create dimension. In the following sections, we show you how to use some basic shading techniques.

Shading in all the right places

Shading takes your drawing from a flat, paper-doll look to one with a three-dimensional feeling.

To give a drawing form, shading can't be random or haphazard. We frequently see students who are a bit too eager to add depth to their fashion illustrations and shade everywhere. Casting a shadow across an object requires a light source, whether you're drawing realistic figures or fashion illustrations.

Here's an exercise for you: Take a piece of fruit and put it on a counter on a sunny day. Notice where the sunlight is falling on it and observe the shadow cast over the rest of the fruit. Notice the shadow on the counter where the piece of fruit is resting as well. Now hold the fruit up to a light source. Again, you see the part farthest away from the light source fall into shadow.

After you observe how shadows fall around an object, you can try to capture the shading on paper. Try giving volume to an egg shape:

1. **Draw an oval, as in Figure 3-18a, to represent the basic egg shape.**

   For reference, put a real egg on your counter, shine a light on the side of it, and observe the highlights and shadows.

2. **Use the side of your pencil to add shading to make the oval appear 3-D. Follow the curve of the shape you're shading, and don't forget to draw the shadow it casts on the counter!**

   The light source in Figure 3-18b comes from the left side of the egg, so the right side falls into shadow.

Figure 3-18:
Draw a 3-D oval shape in partial shadow.

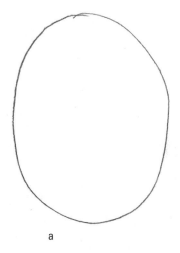

a   b

Use a soft lead pencil to create shadows and then blend in your pencil marks with your finger. Blending with your finger is a wonderful technique to make your shadows smoother looking. Your fingers are valuable tools when comes to smudging and blending your shadow. Don't be afraid of dirty hands!

Creating shine-on shades

In *shine-on shading,* you have a white area in the middle of dark or shaded areas. This technique is for more than shiny hair; you can use it to put the sheen in patent leather shoes and bags as well as on jewelry. Even eyes shine when you're drawing close-ups of the face!

You can create shine-on shading in two ways:

- ✔ **Erase dark areas.** The eraser on the tip of your pencil (or any other eraser you have handy) works perfectly when you want to create the impression of shine. Map out a dark area with the side of your pencil. After you've blended in that dark area, simply drag your eraser through it to get a super highlight.

  If you're using your eraser to get that glow, don't go too dark when drawing the shaded area. The darker the shaded area is, the harder it is to erase.

- ✔ **Leave an area white.** The other way to achieve that special gleam on a darker shade that you've created with your pencil is to simply leave a white area within the darkened space. Pencil in a dark area, stop where you want a shine, and then continue with your dark blending after you've left a white space. You can work with vertical blends or blend along a curve. This technique works with markers, too!

Try creating shine for yourself:

1. **Darken an area using the side of your pencil and blend in that area, as in Figure 3-19a.**

2. **Drag an eraser through the shaded area to create shine, as in Figure 3-19b.**

The best way to figure out which areas should be white is to think about where the light is coming from. It's from above, find the highest surface of your object. Look at Figure 3-19c and notice the areas of white in her hair. The curve near the crown of her head creates a relatively flat, high surface for light reflection.

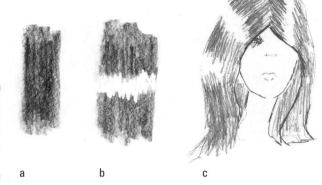

Figure 3-19:
In shine-on
shading, you
put a light in
the dark.

a   b   c

Stippling starters

Stippling involves tiny little dots — lots of them! Stippling is a wonderful way of shading without using pencil strokes or blending with your fingers. And stippling is easy, too. All you have to do is take your pencil and make a cluster of tiny dots using your pencil tip only, keeping them close together to get a dense look.

Use stippling to add texture on clothes as they fall into shadow, not to shade in faces.

Try these step-by-step stippling instructions:

1. **Practice drawing a series of little dots in clusters, as in Figure 3-20a.**

   Work slowly, because if you dot too quickly, your dots may end up looking like tiny little lines or small check marks. You want dots and dots only.

2. **Draw a skirt shape, as in Figure 3-20b.**

3. **Use your stippling technique to create shadow on the side of a skirt, as in Figure 3-20c.**

   Think about where your light source is coming from when you're deciding where to put the dots (see the earlier section "Shading in all the right places" for details). In this example, the light is coming from the left.

Figure 3-20:
Practice
stippling on
a skirt.

a   b   c

Part II

Building a Fabulous Fashion Figure

In this part . . .

If you're ready to roll up your sleeves and start drawing knockout fashion figures, this is the part for you. Here's where you find out how to draw a fashion figure of awesome proportions. To get that long and lean look, you employ the fabulous fashion head count and the *S* curve. After you've mastered those techniques, you can draw slanting shoulders and hips to give your drawing an attitude that stands out. Finally, you top it all off with long limbs and a face and hair that turns heads.

Chapter 4

Working with the Basic Fashion Drawing Rules

To make a fashion drawing look terrific, you have to understand the golden rules of fashion illustration, which are an important set of principles that can make or break your fashion designs. Fashion drawings can look playful, sexy, tough, or whimsical but only if you, the artist, are knowledgeable about proportion, symmetry, body language, and body motion. Without this information, your figure will look stilted and lifeless — and fashion illustration is not about showing off stiff figures. Fashion drawing is about showing off relaxed bodies with attitude!

In this chapter, we introduce you to the golden rules of fashion illustration, and we get you started on mastering some of the basic design elements crucial to fashion drawing. We explain the four views, the basics of drawing fashion figures, and proportion. We wrap up this chapter with some advice on how to handle the inevitable mistakes you'll make as you practice different drawing techniques.

Presenting the Golden Rules of Fashion Illustration

Fashion illustration figures look stilted and lifeless unless you follow these three golden rules of fashion drawing:

✔ Remember that fashion drawing isn't the same as figure drawing.

✔ Use exaggeration and style — they're the foundation of fashion drawing.

✔ Keep your fashion heads small.

You won't find these rules written in stone, but follow them as if they were. Refer to them until you can effortlessly incorporate them into all your fashion drawings. We discuss the three rules in the following sections.

Noting the different goals of fashion drawing and figure drawing

Fashion illustration is not like figure drawing because they have different aims. The goal of figure drawing is to accurately draw the human form. However, realism isn't a goal of fashion illustration; instead, the goal is to present a design or specific look on a body. Commit this first golden rule to memory early in your fashion journey.

Figure 4-1a represents a figure drawing, and Figure 4-1b shows the fashion figure (Marianne is proud to say that Figure 4-1b was drawn by one of her students, Allison Reaves). Notice the exaggeration in the fashion figure; with its curves and simple features, it looks quite different from the figure drawing.

In fashion illustration, a three-dimensional look is lovely, but don't overdo it! Your fashion figure will end up looking like you were in a life-drawing class, which uses shading techniques to create realism.

This book shows you how to draw a fashion figure from a fashion foundation in order to create that fashionable look. Of course, this goal does require knowledge about basic body structure (which originates from figure drawing), but using your imagination, exaggerating the body, and adding a sense of flair is what sets fashion drawing apart.

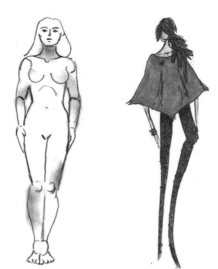

Figure 4-1:
An example of a figure drawing and a fashion drawing.

a   b

Focusing on exaggeration and style

Unlike figure drawing, fashion illustration begs you to exaggerate every element of your design and to add your own style. In fact, exaggeration is the second golden rule! You want to show off your figures by exaggerating facial features and drawing outrageous hair, slim bodies, and long legs. Stamping your own exaggerated style elements on your models helps your art stand out from everyone else's.

The poses you choose, the body parts you exaggerate, the details you add or leave out, and even the boldness and shape of your lines come together to create a specific mood or attitude. Whether your figures look flashy or elegant, friendly or fierce, or relaxed or energetic, your style stirs up emotions that viewers will associate with the clothes.

You can exaggerate features in a fashion illustration by doing the following:

- ✔ Draw a fashion face with big eyes, diamond-shaped lips, and no nose — see Figure 4-2 for an example.

- ✔ Give your creation over-the-top, hip-looking hair.

- ✔ Pose your model in a nearly impossible position with ridiculously long, thin legs.

- ✔ Create long, thin, elegant necks.

You're limited only by your imagination when using exaggeration in your fashion designs. If your drawing resembles actual people in plausible poses, don't be afraid to loosen it up! (For more ideas about exaggerating poses, see Chapter 15.)

Figure 4-2:
A fashion face with extra large eyes, full lips, and no nose.

Keeping your fashion heads small

The final golden rule is simple: Make sure you draw your heads small. A small head gives a figure a more graceful look; check out Figure 4-3 to see what we mean. Fashion models do, for the most part, have smaller heads (as you may have noticed in editorial photo shoots or on the runway when watching television), so drawing them this way won't be a far cry from reality. For details on how to draw the perfect fashion head, check out Chapter 7.

The traditional fashion model is known for her snug head shape, long neck, and broad shoulders. These models are often referred to as *hangers,* which, believe it or not, is a compliment in the fashion industry! This term means that all clothes look great on their slim bodies.

Figure 4-3:
A small head adds a graceful look to fashion illustrations.

The Four Fashion Views

Imagine yourself trying on an outfit and looking in the mirror. What views do you try to get to determine whether a look is for you? They're probably similar to the four views that fashion illustrators use when drawing a model. Here are the four views you see as you turn slowly from front to back:

- ✔ Front view (Figure 4-4a)
- ✔ Three-quarter view (Figure 4-4b)
- ✔ Side view (Figure 4-4c)
- ✔ Back view (Figure 4-4d)

Chapter 5 tells you everything you need to know about drawing the torso from different views, but the following sections provide a preview of how these four views can affect your fashion designs.

Figure 4-4:
The four fashion views.

a   b   c   d

Facing forward: The front view

Artists — and that's you! — often consider the *front view* the easiest to draw. Imagine looking straight on at a person or at yourself in the mirror — that's a front view. The front view allows you to see a complete view of both sides of the body, keeping the imaginary center front line exactly down the middle (see Figure 4-4a to see the center line on the torso).

The front view is great for fashion illustration because seeing all the details is easy; clothes hang well and look fun! Add the angled shoulders and hips that convey attitude in fashion drawing, and you have a great start on fashion illustrations.

Teasing the viewer with the three-quarter view

Think about the stars on the red carpet posing for pictures. As they pose, they tend to turn their bodies slightly for a slimming effect and bring one foot forward. This pose is referred to as the *three-quarter view*. The three-quarter view allows you to see the front of the body, but one side is shown more than the other.

In Figure 4-4b, you can see a sexy yet demure three-quarter view that shows more of the figure's left arm than her right. Compare this to the front view (Figure 4-4a), in which you can see both arms equally well.

With the three-quarter view, the head can face any direction; play with various directions for different looks and feelings. Drawing the three-quarter view is a bit advanced, but that makes it all the more fun to explore, so don't let it scare you!

Turning to the side view

You may not see or use the *side view* as much as the other views, but it's great for showing the side details of a dress or the way a coat nips in at the back waist. The side view, which you see in Figure 4-4c, is also a high fashion and creative way to show a wedding dress or evening gown.

Capturing the side view can be tricky, but with a little practice, your side views will have just as much attitude as your rockin' front views.

Spinning around to see the back view

The *back view* (see Figure 4-4d) is really only needed to show — yep, you guessed it — the back of a garment. Think about all the types of clothing where straining to see your back end is important. Jeans, jeans, and more jeans, without a doubt! And strapless dresses or other types of revealing clothing often have you trying for a good view of the back as well.

Fashion artists often use back views in fashion illustration as companions to the front views of a design. Many times, a design includes both the front and back views to give a detailed look at the garment.

The best part about drawing the back view is that it's almost exactly the same as drawing the front view. With a few minor changes, drawing a figure from the back view comes as naturally as drawing one from the front.

Building a Basic Fashion Figure

Are you itching to draw a fashionista extraordinaire? Well, it's time to get to it. In the following sections, we introduce the *S* curve and show you how to use it to sketch different shapes that don't look like much on their own — but when you put them together, they have the makings of a model who can strut the catwalk with the best of them. So get out your pencils, flip open your sketchbook, and get ready to draw a basic fashion figure.

Starting with the S curve

Nearly all wonderful fashion drawings start with the *S curve*. No, the *S* curve isn't some special code that fashionistas use. It's a drawing tool based on the letter *S* (or some form of it), and it's critical when you're drawing a model's body.

You can draw the *S* curve first or use it when looking at your illustration's torso shapes to make sure you have a good pose. Using the *S* curve forces you to slant the shoulders one direction and the hips in the opposite direction to create great fashion poses. It keeps you from drawing a rigid fashion figure and adds style and flow.

A little observation shows you why the *S* curve is critical in drawing fashions. Have you ever noticed how models often slouch in delightfully languid ways, making long *S*'s with their bodies? And don't those drawings of elegant profiles with tapering heads and snaking ultra-long necks just kill you? Finally, think about those drawings of fashion figures where the shoulders slant one way and the waistline sways in the other direction, curving the body much like an *S*.

Not quite seeing the *S* curve? Stand up straight, bend one leg forward (putting your hands on your hips to grab that attitude), and look in the mirror. Can you see how one hip is higher than the other? Slant your shoulders one way and your hips the other. If you trace down the center front of your upper and lower torso, you notice a curve. If you keep tracing that line down the side of the leg with your weight on it, you create another curve. Put the curves together, and the shape resembles an *S*. If you bring your raised shoulder or hip higher, the *S* curves even more.

Now look at Figure 4-5, where the upper arrow in the figure points to the angled shoulders and the lower arrow points to the angled hips — the black line follows the center of the body and creates the *S* shape. To see how the *S* curve looks in other poses, look at Figure 4-4 earlier in the chapter. Notice how you can follow the curve of each model's body to trace forward and backward *S* shapes.

Read on to see how use the *S* curve to create basic fashion figures.

Curving the spine with the letter S

Fashion figures often twist and move into extreme positions. They raise and lower shoulders and hips while twisting their spines to show various angles of their bodies. Take a look at a women's lingerie catalog for great examples of this. The *S* curve helps you achieve a graceful line of the spine in one swoop.

Figure 4-5:
Trace the
S curve
through
the center
to find the
fashion
attitude.

To master the *S* curve, practice drawing capital *S*'s. Draw large and small *S*'s, exaggerating or elongating the curves. Practice backward *S*'s as well.

After you've mastered capital *S*'s, use the following steps to start making your *S*'s look like a model:

1. **Draw a long, stretched out *S* with a sharper curve in the top half. At the top of the *S*, draw an angled line for the shoulders. Follow the slant of the *S* down and draw an oppositely angled line where the *S* curves back in, directly under the point of the top of the S. (See Figure 4-6a.)**

2. **Draw a trapezoid for the upper half of the torso with the top of the trapezoid following the top angled line. For the lower half of the torso, draw a trapezoid following the bottom angled line. (See Figure 4-6b.)**

3. **Add a cylinder for a neck and connect it to an oval for the head. Add bent lines for arms on either side. (See Figure 4-6c.)**

   The bottom half of the *S* gives you a general idea of the line her legs will follow to keep her balanced.

The *S* curve provides a great base for drawing a fashion figure. You can take your *S* shape — and your model — in any direction you want simply by adjusting the curvature of the *S*. Eventually, you'll be able to visualize the *S* curve without putting it down on paper so you can create sketches more quickly. The next sections show you how.

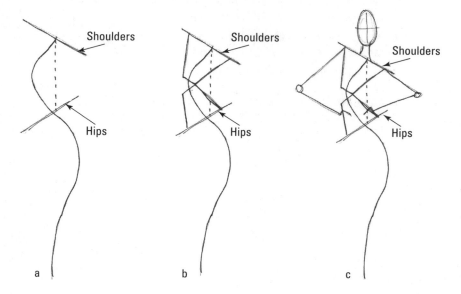

Figure 4-6:
Making your
S look more
like a mod-
el's body.

a   b   c

Taking S-shortcuts: Slanting shoulders and hips

The drama and interplay between the line of the shoulders and the line of the hips really bring fashion illustration to life. You can create a terrific torso by following a simple fashion formula that includes the *S* curve. Or you can make the basic shape even more simple by just sketching the opposite hip and shoulder angles.

Look back at Figure 4-6 and notice the angled lines coming off the *S* curve — one is for the shoulders, and one is for the hips. Sketching these kinds of angles gives you the beginning of a pose that moves. You never want a fashion figure to stand stiffly at attention like a soldier; Figure 4-7 shows the look you want!

To create a dynamic fashion figure without first drawing the *S,* follow these steps:

1. **Draw a balance line to represent your model's full body, and then add a slanting line for the shoulders and a slanting line for the hips. Place the hip line at the halfway point of your balance line, as in Figure 4-7a.**

   The shoulder and hip lines slant in opposite directions, creating a sense of movement just like the *S* curve does.

2. **Starting with the top of the torso, draw a trapezoid shape that follows the angle of the slanted shoulder line. (See Figure 4-7b.)**

   The more you slant the angled line, the more extreme the pose becomes.

3. **Move to the bottom half of the torso and draw a trapezoid following the slant of the hip line. (See Figure 4-7c.)**

4. **Add in shapes such as cylinders for the neck and lines for the arms and legs, as in Figure 4-7d. Don't forget the head, hands, and feet!**

Marianne likes to draw in a lightly dashed line to follow the center front of the body. Drawing this line is a great habit to get into, because almost all clothing patterns are drafted from the center front (or center back) of the body. Therefore, it's an easy reference point for adding clothing later.

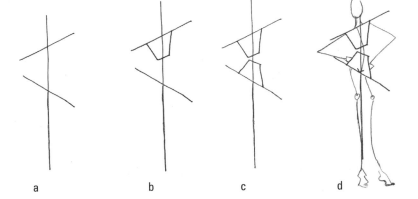

Figure 4-7:
A woman with slanted shoulders and hips.

a   b   c   d

Jutting out the hips

If attitude is what you want in a front view pose (and believe us, you want it), thrust that hip out in your fashion drawing. To get a jaunty hip, simply focus on the bottom half of the torso.

Follow these steps to rock a front pose with just hip action:

1. **Start with the balance line, an angled hip line at the halfway point, and a straight horizontal shoulder line near the top, as in Figure 4-8a.**

   You can angle the hip line in either direction.

2. **Draw the lower half of the torso with a trapezoid that follows the angle of the hip line, as in Figure 4-8b.**

3. **Draw the upper half of the torso with a trapezoid that follows the line of the shoulders, which are not angled. (See Figure 4-8c.)**

4. **Finish with a neck, head, arms, and legs, and you have a front pose with just the rocking hip for attitude! (See Figure 4-8d.)**

TIP

Checking the tilt of the shoulders and hips

Have a friend stand in front of you, and then check out the slant of her shoulders and the angle of her hips. Hold your pencil vertically so it appears directly in front of her. If she's standing at attention, her shoulder line and waistline will be parallel to one another.

Have your friend hold a number of different poses, leaning and tilting in different directions.

By assessing her movement against the straight line of your pencil, you see how the shoulder lines begin to slant and the waistline moves in the same direction or in the *opposite* direction. You can do the same assessment with photos from a magazine if you can't find a friend willing to endlessly pose for you!

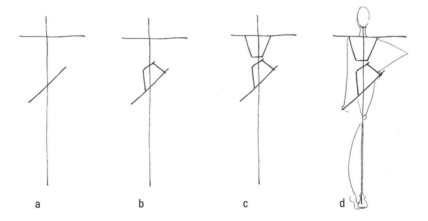

Figure 4-8:
A woman
with hip
attitude.

a   b   c   d

Slanting the shoulders

Follow these steps to rock a pose with attitude all in the shoulders:

1. **Start by drawing the balance line for your fashion figure. Add a horizontal hip line at the halfway point. Draw an angled shoulder line near the top of the balance line, as in Figure 4-9a.**

   You can angle the shoulder line in either direction; just make sure the hip line is straight.

2. **Draw your trapezoid shapes for the upper and lower torso, following the angles of the shoulder and hip lines, as in Figure 4-9b.**

3. **Sketch in the neck, head, arms, and legs, as in Figure 4-9c.**

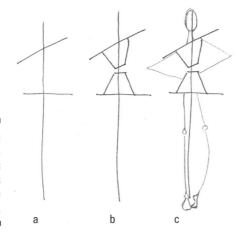

Figure 4-9:
All the atti-
tude in this
pose comes
from the
shoulders.

a   b   c

Exploring New Relationships: Fashionable Proportions

Long and lean is the overall motto of fashion design for women! Legs, arms, and torsos on female bodies are drawn at unrealistic lengths and widths. Male and children's bodies are drawn a little more realistically, but they also have their own fashion proportion rules. In the following sections, we give you some basic guidelines for drawing fashionable proportions.

Using your head to keep fashion figures in proportion

Life-drawing class instructors often pound into students' brains that the head fits into the average adult body seven to eight times (see Chapter 3 for details). In other words, if you were to stack seven or eight heads on top of one another, you'd have the figure's full height. Using the head as a unit of measurement helps you establish the proper proportions between the different parts of a figure.

In most fashion illustrations, the head fits into the adult body 11 times (see Figure 4-10). This rule, often called the *head count,* illustrates one of the biggest differences between figure drawing and fashion drawing, and it's the one most responsible for the elegant look of fashion illustration. The head count keeps the figure's head small in relation to the body and helps you lengthen the arms and legs in a graceful way.

Use the height of a fashion figure's head to see how tall your fashion figure should be. This is where tracing paper can be really handy. You can use the height of your figure's head to determine how tall the illustration should be in several ways; start by drawing a fashion head. Then use one of these methods:

✔ Using your finger and thumb as a measuring tool, count down 10 heads below the shape you just sketched and draw a line. This line shows you roughly how tall your fashion figure needs to be.

✔ Trace your fashion head and move it down along the page (below the one you just drew) ten times for easy visualizing.

Figure 4-10: Use a fashion figure's head to determine her height.

Keep in mind that the rule of 11 heads is a great place to start in fashion drawing, but it's not the be all, end all rule. As you establish your own style, you can decide when and where you want to follow that rule and when and where you want to break it. But whatever head count you use, be sure to go tall! Models are taller today than ever; some are practically skyscrapers, standing over 6 feet. Because fashion is all about keeping up with the times and even projecting looks for the future, your drawings must reflect that as well.

Checking out differences between female and male proportions

In the real world, although men are generally taller and broader than their female counterparts, men's and women's proportions are about the same. But in the fashion illustration world, things get a little more complicated. Both men and women are 11 heads tall, but you must distribute the height differently: Women have longer legs, whereas men have longer torsos.

Table 4-1 breaks down how many heads fit into each body region for men and women. Check out Figure 4-11 for a visual demonstration of these same details.

Table 4-1	Head Counts for Female and Male Fashion Figures	
Body Part	*Women*	*Men*
The head	1	1
The upper torso and neck	2	3
The lower torso	1	1
The upper legs (above the knee)	3	2
The lower legs and feet	4	4

Children's proportions: So cute, so different!

You can't forget the littlest of models. Though children may be mirror images of their parents as far as facial features go, kids are extremely different from their parents in terms of proportions, a fact that's reflected in fashion drawing.

In fashion drawing, a child's head fits into his or her body about 5 times, compared to 11 times for an adult. Obviously, adults are much taller than children, but their other proportions, including head size and neck length, are also completely different. Every little kid has a big head, relatively speaking. Kids also don't have long, elegant necks, even for fashion illustration. Children 10 years old and older start to shoot up in height and grow into more-adult proportions.

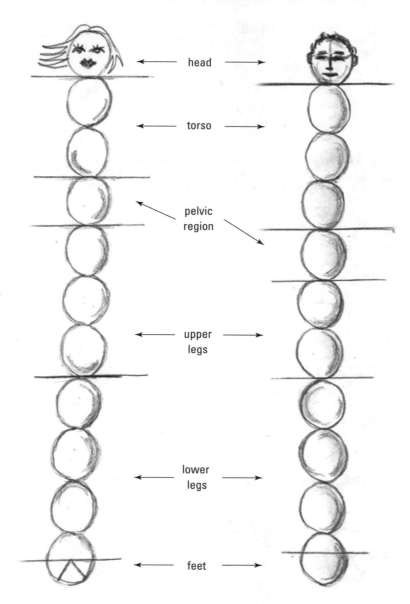

head

torso

pelvic region

upper legs

lower legs

feet

Figure 4-11: Eleven heads broken down into female and male fashion figure proportions.

Here's the most important proportion-related rule to keep in mind when drawing kids: Fashion kids don't have long, lean body lines. Although kids can look really hip instead of prim, you still don't want to exaggerate the body as you would do with an adult in fashion illustration. A long, willowy neck on a 9-year-old would be pretty odd looking! Stay away from long, lean, and mean lines for now, and keep kids looking like kids for as long as you can.

When proportioning a child, remember these rules, which we illustrate in Figure 4-12:

- ✔ The head fits into the figure's full height only five times.
- ✔ One head is enough for the upper torso and neck, and 1 head is fine for the lower torso region.
- ✔ Two heads work from the hips to the feet.

Table 4-2	Head Counts for Child Fashion Figures
Body Part	*Child*
The head	1
The upper torso and neck	1
The lower torso	1
The upper legs (above the knee)	1
The lower legs and feet	1

Figure 4-12: A head count for a child fashion figure.

Fixing, Finishing, or Discarding Your Work

Part of becoming a good fashion illustrator is recognizing when your art works and when it doesn't. Knowing when to hold 'em and when to fold 'em up and put them away — or deposit them in the nearest trash receptacle — is an art in itself. In the following sections, we talk about how to deal with the mistakes that every artist makes. If you aren't making mistakes, you aren't drawing enough!

Deciding whether a drawing can be saved

Yes, friends, it happens: Artists make many, many mistakes when they draw. Loads of them! The thing is not to panic; we've seen so many students crumple up a drawing and start over a little too quickly for their own good. Evaluate what can be saved in your drawing and save paper at the same time!

Before you totally freak out and dissolve into a pool of self-pity, take a deep breath and really look at your illustration. Did you make a humongous mistake, or can you take your drawing in a new direction? You may have a vision in your head about your illustration, but be open to new ideas as well. Sometimes a mistake can be the best thing that happened — ask any fashion illustrator.

Don't let your eraser become a weapon of mass destruction when you've made a mistake. First, assess the damage and use your eraser gently. To keep your paper from crumpling or tearing, hold your paper down with your other hand while you erase. You can use various types of erasers and smudging cloths, ranging from a paper towel to a piece of felt.

If you're wedded to your original idea, start over, but set aside the drawing with the mistake in it. When you look at the "mistake" later, you may find a way to make it work. Then you'll have two distinct drawings from one idea. Another tip someone once taught Marianne is that if you need to redraw a line, try to draw the new line before you erase the old one. That way, you don't draw the same wrong line again. It really does work!

Knowing when to consider a drawing done

"Less can be more" is one of the principles of fashion illustration when you're sketching, drawing, shading, and rendering textures. If you're on a roll and feeling really great about the way your fashion illustration has turned out, leave it alone — it's done! We can't begin to count the number of times we've gotten *so* into a fashion drawing that we ruined it because we just couldn't stop.

If your fashion illustration looks finished, stop drawing. A fashion drawing screams of being amateurish when you don't listen to your instincts and end up with a drawing that's overworked and has too many different styles going on. Knowing when to stop comes from experience, and you'll just have to experience creating your share of muddy shading, too many lines, and weird-looking figures. It's all part of the fashion drill; be patient and keep on drawing. With time, you'll figure out how to create a polished look.

Knowing when to toss it out

Okay, you've goofed and you really can't save your illustration. Be honest with yourself. Can you really find a new direction? If not, give it up and move on. You've given the drawing your best shot, but now it's time to say goodbye. Such is life as an artist!

Knowing when to quit is a sense you gain only by putting in your drawing time. If you draw a lot, you learn to identify this feeling sooner. We all fall in love with our drawings from time to time, and admitting defeat can be hard, but you have to know when to bag it. It's one of the hardest lessons to learn, but it can lead to fashion illustration growth and a more sophisticated style.

Consider not just the drawing itself but the condition of the paper it's on. If the coffee splatters accumulate, the edges tear, or areas wear through from erasing and drawing over an area time and time again, let the drawing go. You can always redraw it.

Don't get discouraged. There are always a million new ideas in that brain of yours. Falling in love with just one drawing isn't allowed. Now see whether you can toss your drawing in the wastebasket in one shot — and get back to work!

Chapter 5

Tackling the Torso

....

....

Work that body, concentrate on the core, get good abs, land the flattest tummy in town: Just like in real life, these goals are preferred in fashion drawing. In fashion illustration, flab and bulging muscle-man biceps are out of the picture! Sleek and sophisticated is the latest fashion look for the torso.

The torso plays an important part in projecting a fashion image. Whether you're going for a sleek, lean fashion male or a toned-and-tough one or you're deliberating between curvy and waif-thin for your fashion female, the torso helps define the attitude of your fashion illustration, which you create by changing the angles of the torso. Kids' torsos are easier — they can just be, because kids normally stand in natural poses and posture less. This chapter shows you how to create a fashion torso that turns heads no matter who you're drawing or which direction you take.

Creating a Terrific Torso

When you're ready for your first attempt at a fabulous torso, trapezoids lead the way. They're the basis for a great torso. After you have your basic shape, you mark the figure's center front and apex, and then you refine the torso and add attitude. In the following sections, we give you the how-to's for creating a torso that sells fashion.

Basic shapes: Setting your traps

The basic torso is simply two trapezoids drawn one above the other. The upper trapezoid is upside-down, and the lower one is right side up. Both male and female torsos have these shapes, but each has a slightly different twist to represent the different dimensions of each gender.

Men are much boxier than women. If you were to measure a man's chest, waist, and hips, the three measurements would vary by 6 to 8 inches. A woman's measurements at her bust, hips, and waist would vary by about 10 inches (34, 24, 34 are the average measurements for a model, according to the British

Association of Model Agents). The more drastic variation in a woman's bust, hips, and waist give a woman her curves.

When drawing the trapezoids for a woman, the sides are more angled than for a man's; in the end, these angles lead to the curvature of the body. Remember these guidelines for the female torso:

- ✔ **Keep the shoulders (Line B) on the upper trapezoid narrower than the hips (Line A) on the lower trapezoid.** Figure 5-1 shows how these lines should look.

- ✔ **Keep the waist narrower than the shoulders and hips, and keep the trapezoids the same height.** You can see that in Figure 5-1, Line C is the same length as Line D. The waist falls where the two trapezoids come together.

Although women normally have a narrower waist and larger hips than men, hips are relatively narrow in fashion illustration, and proportions may be more boy-like.

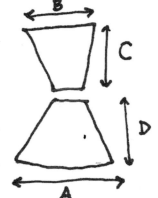

Figure 5-1:
Make a
female torso
by using two
trapezoids.

When drawing the trapezoids for a guy, remember these guidelines:

- ✔ **Keep the upper trapezoid slightly taller than the lower trapezoid.** Check out Figure 5-2, noting that Line A is longer than Line B.

- ✔ **Keep the waist fairly wide and the shoulders wider than the hips.** Take a look at Line C (the shoulders), which is wider than Line D (the hips) in Figure 5-2. The waist falls where the two trapezoids meet.

A child's torso is different from an adult's torso. Kids haven't developed the angles and curves that grown men and women have. Draw the child's torso similar to a man's torso, with shorter trapezoids; stay away from definition at the waist.

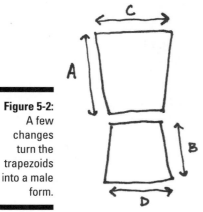

Figure 5-2: A few changes turn the trapezoids into a male form.

Marking the center front and the apex

Like any field, drawing comes with a whole list of shorthand phrases and abbreviations that make it incomprehensible to those who don't work in the field. Two terms, *center front* and *apex,* are crucial to fashion drawing:

✔ **Center front (CF):** As the name implies, this line goes down the middle of the front of the figure's torso, dividing it in half. It's the starting point for all the clothes that your model wears. The center front line comes from pattern-drafting, or drawing patterns for the body; the center front location is the starting point for creating clothing patterns.

✔ **Apex:** The *apex* is the line that passes horizontally through the center of the breast or below the underarms. The apex lines up with the bottom of the armhole. Because many design lines flow directly from the apex line, paying attention to its location can help you design and draw clothing that falls properly on the body.

To sketch out these two important areas of the torso, follow these steps (see Figure 5-3):

1. **Draw two sets of trapezoids — one male and one female.**

2. **Draw a vertical dashed line down the center of each set of trapezoids to create the center front line for a front view.**

   If the figure were to turn, the center front would appear closer to one side of the drawing than the other.

3. **For each set of trapezoids, draw a horizontal dashed line across the center of the upper torso to create the apex line.**

Lightly sketch the apex and center front lines each time you design clothing. Sketching in these lines helps you place seam lines in the correct locations.

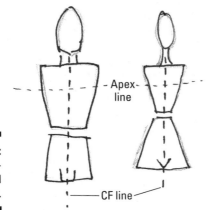

Figure 5-3:
Placing center front and apex lines.

Apex line

CF line

Refining the torso

To refine the fashion figure's torso, you need to add and erase some lines. A couple of trapezoids on top of each other give you the basic idea of the torso's shape, but you need armholes, leg holes, crotches, breasts, and pecs to turn a shape into a person.

Eyeball the proper widths and lengths to get the torso right. And remember that fashion illustration is all about exaggeration, so don't be afraid to lengthen your torso.

Here are the steps for drawing a female torso:

1. **Start by drawing two trapezoids that represent the female figure and then mark the center line and apex line.**

   See Figure 5-4a to see what your illustration looks like. For more info on the center front and apex lines, see the preceding section.

2. **Draw a small _V_ shape for the crotch at the bottom of the lower trapezoid. Add arcs to represent the breasts in the upper trapezoid.**

   The apex line falls halfway through the breast. You can see this step in Figure 5-4b.

3. **Cut into the top of the upper trapezoid's corners for armholes, making sure they end around the apex line, as in Figure 5-4c.**

4. **Cut into the bottom corners of the lower trapezoid with downward arcs to make the leg holes, as in Figure 5-4c.**

5. **Join the two trapezoids where they meet near the middle of the torso to form the waist. Finish with a long, narrow neck and an oval head.**

   Check out Figure 5-4d to see what the female torso looks like.

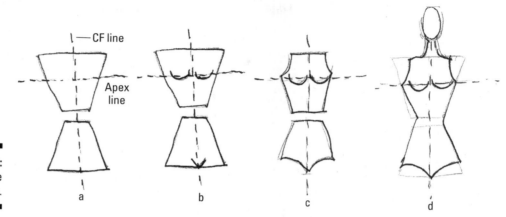

Figure 5-4:
A female torso.

a   b   c   d

To create a great guy torso, follow these steps:

1. **Start by drawing your two trapezoids and then mark the center front line and apex line.**

   The upper trapezoid is taller than the lower, and the shoulders are wider than the hips. The waist is not that much smaller than the hips. See Figure 5-5a to see what your illustration looks like at this point. For more info on the center front and apex lines, see the earlier section "Marking the center front and the apex."

2. **For the crotch, draw two sides and the bottom of a small square in the lower trapezoid. Using the apex line as a guide, add some squared off pecs to the upper trapezoid.**

   The apex line falls about a third of the way though the pecs. Check Figure 5-5b to see the progress.

3. **Cut curved lines into the top of the upper trapezoid's corners for armholes, as in Figure 5-5c.**

   The armhole line should end around the apex line.

4. **Cut into the bottom corners of the lower trapezoid with downward curved arcs to make the leg holes, as in Figure 5-5c.**

5. **Connect the two trapezoids where they meet to shape the waist. Sketch in a wide neck and a head with a square jaw to clearly indicate that you've drawn a guy.**

   Look at Figure 5-5d to see the final torso and head.

For a child's torso, follow the steps for drawing a man's torso but skip drawing in the pecs and crotch. Children's torsos are very boxy with little definition at the waist.

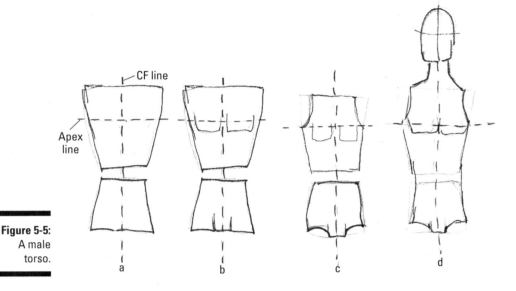

CF line

Apex line

Figure 5-5:
A male torso.

a   b   c   d

A bend at the waist: Adding attitude

The way the lines of the shoulders play off the angle of the hips can make your fashion drawing really fierce! The angles you choose for the shoulders, hips, and waist can convey totally different attitudes.

For a more dramatic look, use a steeper angle between the trapezoids that represent the upper and lower body. Accentuating the angles gives your drawing a haughty and hip look. Women really own these extreme poses. Note that guys don't use shoulder and hip action as much as women do on the runway — guys merely pause at the end of the runway with a slight slant to their shoulders.

To create some extreme attitude for a female fashion figure, try these steps:

1. **Start by drawing a vertical balance line. Add shoulder angle and hip angle lines that slant toward each other, as in Figure 5-6a.**

   The sharper the angles, the more extreme the pose.

2. **Start your upper trapezoid at the shoulder angle line; end your lower trapezoid at the hip angle line, as in Figure 5-6b. Add your center front and apex lines as dashed lines.**

   The bottom line of the upper trapezoid is parallel to the shoulder line, and the top line of the lower trapezoid is parallel to the hip line.

   The center front line should still run through the center of the trapezoids, so curve the line a bit. The apex line remains parallel to the shoulder line.

3. **Sketch in arm and leg holes and add breast arcs. Add a slender neck and oval head to the top of the torso. See Figure 5-6c for the finished product.**

   Keeping the neck and head straight up and down can keep the model from looking like she's falling over.

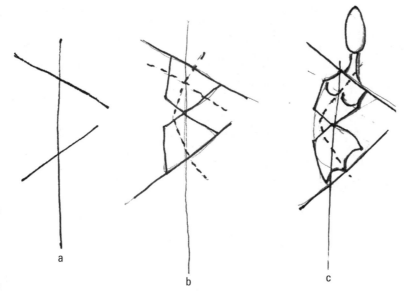

Figure 5-6:
Slanting
lines look so
fine!

Drawing the Torso from Different Views

Drawing figures from the same perspective all the time is *way* boring, so master the different views from the beginning. You don't want to get in a front-view rut. Drawing from a side view, a three-quarter view, or a back view lets you vary your looks (you can see and read more about these views in Chapter 4). Certain types of clothes show best from certain angles. Check out the sketches in Figure 5-7 for the different looks of different views in fashion illustration torsos.

Sidling up for a side view

The look of the torso from the side really counts in fashion illustration: A woman can show off her bod, and a guy can look pretty ripped in a simple T-shirt. Use the *S* curve to show side attitude (see Chapter 4 for more on the *S* curve); women get a more extreme curve than dudes, who get just a slight curve. We show you how to create both female and male side torsos in this section.

Figure 5-7:
Using differ-
ent views
for different
looks.

To create a side look for a female, try these steps:

1. **Draw two rectangles at nearly a 90-degree angle to each other. Draw an *S* curve that passes through the center of both rectangles, as in Figure 5-8a.**

   From the side view, a fashion figure doesn't taper much at the waist, so you can replace the trapezoids with rectangles when drawing the torso.

2. **Sketch in a neck and head facing sideways, as in Figure 5-8b.**

3. **Add an oval for the armhole in the top left corner of the upper rectangle. On the lower rectangle, curve the back of the butt for a round derrière and then add the downward arc for the right leg. (See Figure 5-8b.)**

4. **Connect the upper and lower rectangles at the tummy, using a gradual curve to keep the belly flat. Also connect the rectangles at the back to form the figure's lower back, as in Figure 5-8c.**

5. **Add a perky breast at approximately the same level as the armhole. (See Figure 5-8c.)**

You can add the outline of an arm and leg to make a more complete figure if you'd like. See Chapter 6 for info on drawing these limbs.

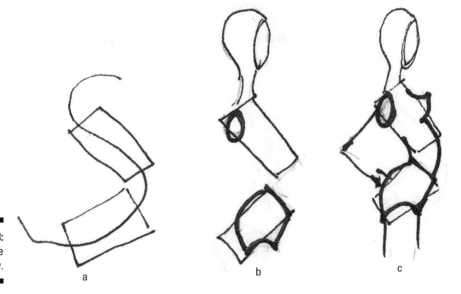

Figure 5-8:
A slinky side
view.

a   b   c

The shape of a guy's torso is getting a lot of media play these days. Shirts are
left unbuttoned, are worn tight to the torso with no room to spare, and are
often sleeveless. All this exposure requires a lot of torso upkeep! When drawing a guy's torso, use a slightly less extreme *S* curve for his back and a slight
and gradual curving line for the front of his torso.

Follow these simple steps to draw the side view of a guy:

1. **Draw two rectangles that are at a slight angle to one another, as in
   Figure 5-9a.**

2. **Sketch in a neck and head facing sideways.**

   Figure 5-9b shows a torso with a head and neck drawn in.

3. **Add an oval for the armhole in the top left corner of the upper rectangle. Slightly curve the left side of the lower rectangle to create a
   rounded buttock — but don't make it too round! Add the downward
   arc for the right leg. (See Figure 5-9b.)**

4. **Finish with a flat chest, a line that connects the rectangles at the
   stomach, and a small curve to connect the two rectangles at the lower
   back. (See Figure 5-9b.)**

Intensifying intrigue with three-quarter views

Three-quarter views of the torso show mood and subtle action. The partial
side view brings your figure to life because you avoid that straight-on stiff
soldier look. Plus, this view is a typical red carpet view that adds lots of
movement to your fashion pose. Even better, this view works like a charm to

make thin appear even thinner. With female figures, you see a slight side view of one of the breasts. In both males and females, the center front line is still in the center front of the figure's torso, but the angle from which you see the line changes.

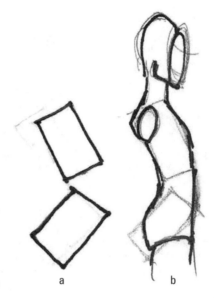

Figure 5-9:
The side view of a guy's torso.

a   b

Here's how to draw a three-quarter view of your female figure:

1. **Draw two stacked trapezoids. Draw the center front line off center, about a third of the way across the torso instead of halfway. Add the apex line in its normal location on the upper torso.**

   See Figure 5-10a to see how your figure may look. For details on the center front and apex lines, see the earlier section "Marking the center front and the apex."

2. **To show the slight side turn to the side, add a breast to the upper torso in slight profile; the breast extends slightly outward from the torso. Draw the other breast so that it extends almost but not quite to the center front line, as in Figure 5-10b.**

   The upper half of the breasts goes above the apex line, and the other half goes below the apex line.

3. **On the upper trapezoid, add an oval for the armhole on your figure's left side. Add a *V* shape for the crotch at the center front line on the lower trapezoid. (See Figure 5-10b.)**

4. **Add downward arcs on the lower trapezoid for the legs, as in Figure 5-10c.**

   The arc on the left leg is wider than the one on the right because you see more of that leg. Finish your figure with a neck and head if you like.

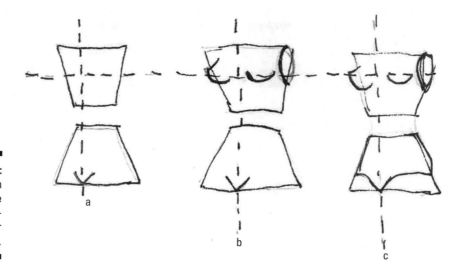

Figure 5-10:
A woman from the three-quarter view.

To add even more fashion attitude, try placing your trapezoids at different angles. Notice in Figure 5-11 that the center front line curves with the body, which helps define your placement of body parts such as the crotch and breasts. When you sketch arms and legs from the three-quarter view, you can draw them at extreme angles to further accentuate the attitude.

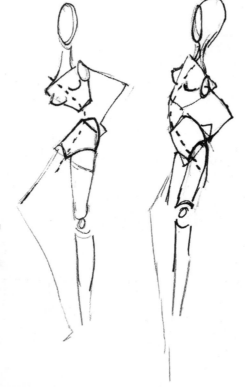

Figure 5-11:
Angling the hips and shoulders for a more extreme pose from the three-quarter view.

Flip through magazines and look for three-quarter view poses with attitude. Draw them mentally — or on paper if you want! — to experiment with different angles.

Male models usually pose with much less attitude, so modify your angles when using the three-quarter view with guys. When drawing a man in the three-quarter view, follow the same steps you use to draw a woman, but change the shapes for the chest and crotch. You can see a laid-back male in a three-quarter view pose in Figure 5-12.

Figure 5-12: A guy from the three-quarter view.

Getting a good look at the back

Although you won't draw a fashion design from the back every day, you'll use the back view occasionally. A woman's back in fashion illustration is quite beautiful, with sleek lines and shoulder blades that look like angel wings. Outrageous dresses for women with barely there backs, including wedding gowns, cry out for a back view. And a guy's broad back looks hot when he's sporting board shorts.

Drawing the back isn't all that different from drawing the front — they both start with the basic trapezoids and the arm and leg holes.

Follow these steps to create a female torso from the back view:

1. **Draw two trapezoids just like you do for the front view and add the back of the neck as a reference. Draw "angel wing" curves to show the back shoulder blades. (See Figure 5-13a.)**

2. **Add arcs for the arms and the upward arcs for the cheeks of the derrière, as in Figure 5-13b.**

   The imaginary center front line — or in this case, the center back — passes through the derrière cheeks (see the earlier section "Marking the center front and the apex" for more on the center front). Sketch in a head and arms, too, if you'd like.

For attitude, draw the trapezoids at two different angles, remembering to lengthen the shoulder blade on the side that leans closer to the ground because the arm extends in that direction. Figure 5-13c shows a finished sketch of a figure with her shoulders angled. For more examples of how to draw a model's back, head to Chapter 15.

Figure 5-13: The beautiful female back.

a   b

c

A guy's back is broad and trim, at least in fashion illustration. It tapers to the waist, whether you're drawing a surfer or just a really hot shirtless dude.

To draw a guy that's too hot to handle from the back view, follow these steps:

1. **Draw two trapezoids, keeping the waist wide and the shoulders broad. (See Figure 5-14a.)**

2. **Add in longer angel wings that extend about two-thirds of the way down the upper trapezoid. Draw arcs for the arms and small arcs for the buttocks. (Refer to Figure 5-14b.)**

3. **Finish with broad shoulders and a wide neck. (See Figure 5-14c.)**

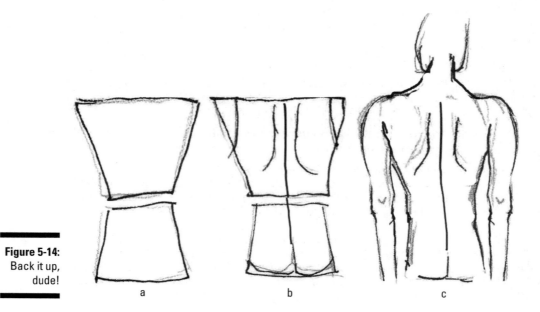

Figure 5-14:
Back it up,
dude!

a   b   c

Chapter 6

Forming Fabulous Arms, Hands, Legs, and Feet

*I*n the world of fashion drawing, arms, legs, hands, and feet give your sketches attitude. For female figures, the arms should be expressive, the hands elegant, the legs long, and the feet shapely and arched. Arms and legs, regardless of whether they're covered or bare, convey emotion and add interest to your fashion look. In this chapter, we fill you in on how to draw arms, legs, hands, and feet that convey movement, grace, and style in fashion drawing.

Styling a Figure with Fashion Arms

Fashion models practice moving their arms to create seductive and graceful poses, alluring and charming poses, and shocking and powerful poses. If a model can't work those arms in different ways, she'll be lost in the modeling industry. Creating great arm attitude is tough enough to do in person, and you, as a fashion illustrator, have the extra challenge of capturing those same attitudes on paper. But don't worry; in this section, we show you how to achieve the same feelings when you draw arms that fashion models express on the catwalk.

You aren't figure drawing; rather, you're styling the fashion figure with your signature drawing lines. Realistic arms aren't the idea here! Check out Figure 6-1 to see how the models' arms (and legs) contribute to the relaxed feel of the drawing.

Arms can add fun personality to your drawing, but don't stray too much from proportional rules! Stand up and let your arms hang down. In general, your hand begins a little below the horizontal line of your crotch with the fingers hitting at midthigh. Keep this in mind as you bend and pose your model's arm. More often than not, beginners make the arms too short rather than too long.

Figure 6-1:
Arms (and legs) add attitude!

In addition to practicing how to draw women's long, slender arms, you can try your hand at men's and children's arms in this section. The good news is that men and children pay much less attention to their arm positions than the ladies do, so male and kid arms are easier to get the hang of.

Thin and sassy: Working with women's arms

Women's arms convey any number of moods and fashion types, from confident and sexy to on-the-go. Female fashion models use their arms to emphasize their bodies and their clothes. A woman may may bend both arms at the elbows, let one arm hang at her side, or raise or extend her arms for a different look. Regardless of how a woman poses her arms, she does so with attitude and style.

No matter what attitude you want your model to send, her arms should be smooth, fluid, and shapely. You don't want any chicken-wing arms here (you know what we mean: those flabby upper arms that flap when a woman waves). You can tell the shape of a woman's arms regardless of whether she's dressed in casual weekend wear or grabbing attention in a little black dress that shows off her arms and shoulders, so make sure to draw your female arms long and lean.

As the arm tapers to an end, don't forget to draw the wrist bone — the marvelous beginning of a fashion hand (we explain how to draw wrist bones and hands later in the chapter). When you first start drawing arms, don't worry about getting the hands right. Let the arm taper off after the wrist bone with a simple line.

The powerful look: Bending both arms

The powerful stance is in, and arms can convey such a powerful feel in fashion drawing. The popular hands-on-the-waist look really brings out the fierceness of a pose.

To create fierce bent arms, follow these steps:

1. **Draw two trapezoids to represent an angled torso, as in Figure 6-2a.**

   Refer to Chapter 5 for info on using trapezoids to draw torsos.

2. **Add armholes on either side. Mark the figure's center front line with a dashed line to keep the body even, as in Figure 6-2b.**

3. **On each side, sketch a bent arm using two lines and a circle to represent the elbow.**

   Each arm line is a little longer than the upper torso. We made the bottom half of the arm slightly longer than the upper half, but you can choose to keep them the same length. When the arm is bent, the elbow falls slightly above waist level.

   The figure's left arm in this sketch extends farther down the body because the model is leaning to her left. Check out Figure 6-2c to get an idea of what your drawing should look like at this point.

4. **Draw cylinder shapes over the lines to create arms, as in Figure 6-2d.**

   Leave the circles between the cylinders to indicate the elbows.

5. **Sketch in a head and outline the woman's torso, arms, and neck, as in Figure 6-2e.**

   Erase the circles, trapezoids, and center front line.

The come-hither look: Mixing bent and straight arms

If you're not going for the powerful look (see the preceding section), you may be looking for a slightly more alluring, come-hither look. To achieve this style, try bending only one arm while keeping the other straight. The straight arm looks fluid and demure rather than fierce and angled. The mixture of the two creates a fun personality.

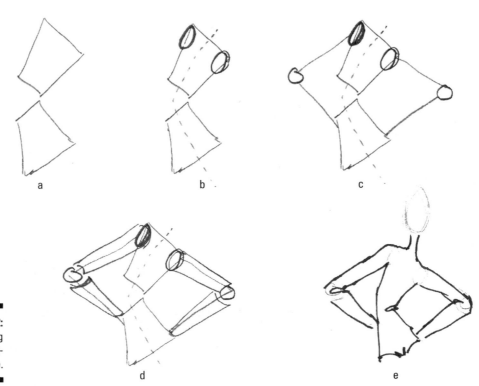

Figure 6-2:
Developing
the bent-
arm pose.

To create a pose with one arm bent and one arm straight, try these steps:

1. **Draw two trapezoids to represent an angled torso, as in Figure 6-2a.**

   Refer to Chapter 5 for info on using trapezoids to draw torsos.

2. **Add armholes on either side. Mark the figure's center front line with a dashed line to keep the body even, as in Figure 6-2b.**

3. **Create a bent arm on the longer side of the torso using two lines and a circle to represent the elbow that connects them, as in Figure 6-3a.**

   The elbow of the bent arm should fall slightly above the waist.

4. **On the other side of the torso, draw a straight arm by connecting two straight lines with a circle, as in Figure 6-3a.**

   Keep the upper arm and forearm lengths about the same, and line up the elbow with the raised hip. (If the hips and shoulders weren't tilted, the elbow of the straight arm would fall at the waist.)

5. **Draw cylinder shapes over the arm lines to create the arms, as in Figure 6-3b.**

   Keep the circles intact between the cylinders to represent the elbows.

6. **Outline the woman's torso, arms, and neck, as in Figure 6-3c.**

   Erase the circles, trapezoids, and center front line.

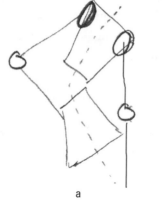
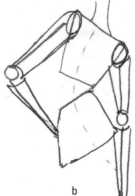

a   b   c

You can also experiment with drawing the bent arm on the short or bent side of the torso and sketching the straight arm on the longer side of the torso. You can see what this pose looks like in Figure 6-4.

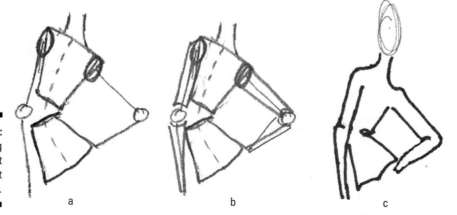

Figure 6-4:
Switching
the bent
and straight
arms.

a   b   c

You also have the option to draw the straight arm so it bends slightly, gracefully following the side of the torso.

Follow these steps to rest a slightly bent arm along the body:

1. **Draw two trapezoids to represent an angled torso, as in Figure 6-2a.**

   Refer to Chapter 5 for info on using trapezoids to draw torsos.

2. **Add armholes on either side. Mark the figure's center front line with a dashed line to keep the body even, as in Figure 6-2b.**

3. **Sketch a sharply bent arm on the longer side of the torso using two lines and a circle to represent the elbow that connects them, as in Figure 6-5a.**

4. **For the slightly bent arm that curves with the body, draw straight lines and a ball for the elbow right along the torso. (See Figure 6-5a.)**

   Keep the elbow at the waist. Sketch in the beginnings of her legs as well.

5. **Draw cylinders over the arm lines, as in Figure 6-5b.**

   The cylinders over the slightly bent arm overlap the torso to show that the arm is lying against the body. Be sure to leave the circles to represent the elbows.

6. **Outline the woman's torso, thighs, arms, and neck, as in Figure 6-5c.)**

   Erase the circles, trapezoids, and center front line.

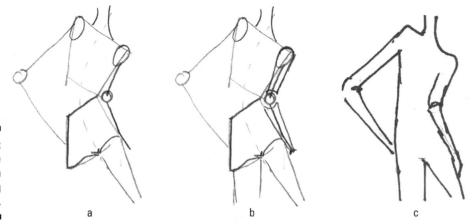

Figure 6-5:
A seductive straight arm rests along the torso.

a   b   c

You can draw both arms straight, but you tend to lose some of the edgy attitude. If you want attitude, you want to bend an arm!

Other fun looks: Raising the arms away from the body

Don't think you've exhausted all your arm options by knowing how to draw a bent arm and a straight arm. Arms can go any which way. A few more fun options include bringing one or both arms above the head or having them cross the body.

Take a look at fashion magazines to get some ideas for arm placement. You often see models with their arms covering their foreheads, resting on their heads, crossing over or in front of their bodies, or lying behind their heads.

To draw a pose with an arm over the head, try these steps:

1. **Begin with a front pose where the torso isn't tilted, as in Figure 6-6a. Include armholes and a neck.**

2. **Add a head. Then draw an arm with an elbow circle raised to head level, as in Figure 6-6b.**

   Place the elbow circle about level with the middle of the head and slightly beyond the width of the shoulder. Angle one line from the shoulder to the circle, and then angle another line that ends at the head.

To show how the arm rests on the head, add a short line to represent where the hand will go.

Note: You can draw both arms bent over the fashion figure's head by following this step for both arms.

3. **Sketch the second arm so it's bent away from the body with the hand resting on the hip, as Figure 6-6b.**

4. **Draw cylinder shapes over the arm lines to create the arms, as in Figure 6-6c.**

   Leave the circles between the cylinders to indicate the elbows.

5. **Outline the woman's torso, arms, neck, and head, as in Figure 6-6d.**

   As you finish the arms, add a small hand resting on the head. Erase the circles, trapezoids, and center front line.

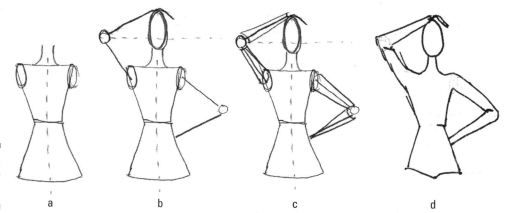

Figure 6-6:
Going over
her head.

a   b   c   d

You can make the arms more interesting by moving them away from the body and leaving the hands free. Think of a hula dancer, for example.

When you have an arm going across the body, it looks more natural to draw both arms going toward the bent side of the torso. To see why, stand in front of the mirror with your body matching the bent torso of Figure 6-7a. Move both of your arms across the body in one direction. Then move them in the other direction. Which side feels less awkward? Bringing the arms toward the bent side of the torso feels better and looks more like a fashion pose.

Here are the steps to draw a pose with one arm going in front of the body:

1. **Draw a tilted torso with armholes and a neck, as in Figure 6-7a.**

2. **Starting with the upper shoulder, draw an arm that goes across the body. Use a circle for the elbow, as in Figure 6-7b.**

   The arm line should tilt down slightly to cover the other shoulder. Place the circle for the elbow in front of the other shoulder.

3. **For the other arm, draw the straight lines and a circle extending away from the body, as in Figure 6-7b.**

4. **Draw cylinder shapes over the arm lines to create the arms, keeping the circles to represent the elbows. (See Figure 6-7c.)**

   Include short lines at the ends of the arms to represent the hands. Draw the head to show the overall balance of the torso.

5. **Outline the woman's torso, arms, neck, and head, as in Figure 6-7d.**

   Erase the circles, trapezoids, and center front line.

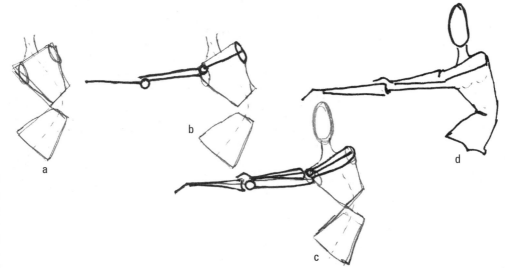

Figure 6-7:
Willowy arms moving across the body.

Sculpting arms for men

When you're drawing a dude's arms, don't aim for Muscle Beach in fashion drawing. Male arms can look toned and terrific without making people's heads swivel in disbelief at their size and shape. Keep in mind that men's shoulders are wider.

To draw attention-getting arms on a man, follow these easy steps:

1. **Lightly sketch a torso with armholes, as in Figure 6-8a.**

   Add the neck to help visualize the upper body.

2. **Draw two bent arms using straight lines and circles for the elbows, as in Figure 6-8b.**

   Keep the height of the elbow a little above the horizontal line of the waist.

3. **Add cylinders over the arm lines, keeping the circles to represent the elbows. (See Figure 6-8c.)**

4. **Sketch in a head and round out some of the perimeter lines around the arms for muscle definition, as in Figure 6-8d.**

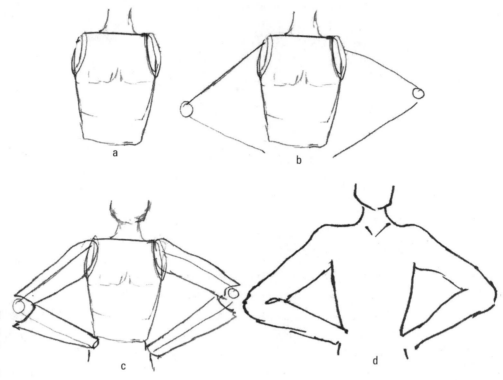

Figure 6-8:
Toned arms
for guys.

Scrawny arms on men often are viewed negatively, but some fashion illustrators go that route for their fashion look. Working out at the gym isn't a priority for these dudes; they prefer a long and lean image. You won't see these guys' arms on parade at the beach; instead you'll more likely find them hidden under a flannel shirt or a hoodie. A much-loved T-shirt is *the* signature statement for this group of guys.

If you want to tackle some long and lean arms for men, use the preceding steps, but when you draw the cylinders in Step 3, draw them thinner and more similar to a woman's arm. Refer to Figure 6-9.

You can draw pipe cleaners for a guy's arms, but you must always draw shoulders. Sloping necklines aren't allowed for guys, so keep the shoulders broad.

Staying simple with children's arms

Kids' arms are short and rounded, and they're always purely functional looking. No kid frets about how his arms look the way teens and adults do. Kids' arms are meant for climbing, playing, and carrying, not for posing or preening.

No cartooning when drawing kids' arms: You're drawing fashion kids who look hip like their fashion-forward parents.

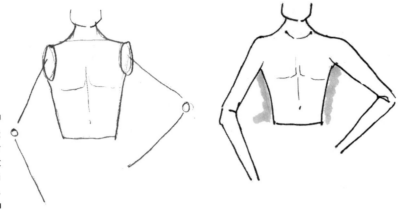

Figure 6-9:
Slender
arms that
work on a
dude.

Here's how to create arms for kids:

1. **Draw a child's torso with a head and armholes.**

   You can read about creating a kid's torso in Chapter 5.

2. **Add short, straight arm lines with circles as elbows, as in Figure 6-10a.**

   Keep the arms relaxed and not necessarily on the hips; kids tend to just let arms fall in a relaxed fashion. Bent elbows fall a little above the waist.

3. **Add cylinders over the arm lines, keeping the circles to represent the elbows, as in Figure 6-10b.**

   Children's arms are shorter in length and rounder in width than adult arms, so keep them chubby and stubby! Refer to Figure 6-10b.

4. **Outline the child fashion figure and erase your initial lines, as in Figure 6-10c.**

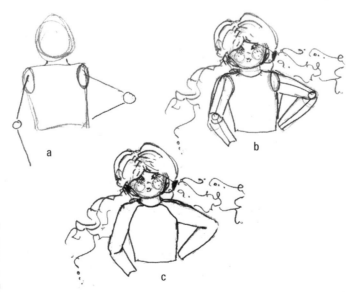

Figure 6-10:
Cute kid
arms.

Handling Hands

You can really have fun with hands in fashion illustration. Gone are the days of always hiding them behind a fashion figure's back or slipping them into pockets. Instead, try some fluid and playful styles. After you master a few classic or playful poses, you can use them for every type of fashion look.

To draw hands in proportion to the rest of your figure, use your head — literally. If you open your hand and place it over your face, you see that your hand is almost the same size as your face. An open hand should not be wider than the oval of your face. When you hold your wrist at chin level, the top of your hand ends a little past your eyebrows. So a hand should be a little shorter than the height of the oval for your head.

Here are a few options for playful poses of fashion hands:

✔ Bent at the wrist holding something, as in Figure 6-11a

✔ Bent at the wrist and resting on a leg, as in Figure 6-11b

✔ Lying as a one-line gesture, as in Figure 6-11c

✔ Bent as a little triangle at the hip, as in Figure 6-11d

For fashion drawing, realism is not required. You can draw obviously fake or unrealistic hands, depending, of course, on what you're accenting! You don't always need to draw each finger and nail; simply draw a few lines to get the point of the hand across.

In the following sections, we get you started on sketching great fashion-forward hands and wrists.

Figure 6-11:
Fun fashion hands.

From arm to hand: Drawing the wrist

Think of the lower part of the arm as the gateway to the hand. The arm is slim and tapering down to the important wrist bone — the arm is the tiniest where the wrist starts.

Don't ignore the wrist bone. If you do, you end up drawing an arm that pours onto the hand without definition. The result is a chunky, unfashionable look.

To make a smooth transition from arm to hand, follow these steps:

1. **Draw the arm from the elbow to the wrist, as in Figure 6-12a.**

   Make sure that the arm tapers in at the wrist.

2. **Add a small curve to show the wrist bone, as in Figure 6-12b.**

3. **Attach the forearm to an upper arm and the rest of your figure, as in Figure 6-12c.**

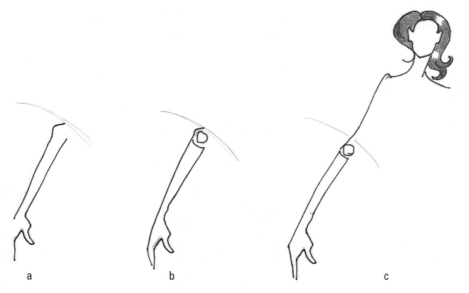

Figure 6-12: Focus on the wrist for an elegant arm.

a   b   c

Lending a lady a hand

When it comes to drawing a lady's hands, we have good news for you: One hand position works for many classic fashion poses. You can use this single pose of the hand for holding a little clutch or a tube of lipstick or for resting the hands on the hips.

Keep drawings of the hands simple and light: no shading or hand creases allowed! Adding shading or lines creates the appearance of an older hand. You want your fashion model to be hip and youthful.

Follow these steps to draw a graceful female fashion hand:

1. **For the palm, draw an oval on the diagonal, as in Figure 6-13a.**

2. **For the fingers, attach a triangle at the top of the oval, as in Figure 6-13b.**

3. **Sketch in a simple thumb, starting it about halfway down the oval, as in Figure 6-13c.**

4. **Create fingers from the triangle shape, rounding out the front of the shape into two long tube shapes, as in Figure 6-13d.**

   Feel free to add a little nail at the end of each finger for drama.

5. **Add the slim wrist with a wrist bone, as in Figure 6-13d.**

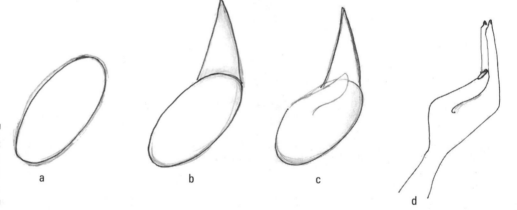

Figure 6-13:
A simple and graceful hand.

After you've finished drawing the fashion hand, turn your paper and look at it from all directions. If it looks like a hand from all directions on the paper, you've done the job well.

Showing strength in a man's hands

Drawing a guy's hands requires a somewhat different approach from drawing a woman's. As with a lady's hand, a guy's hand isn't as realistic as a figure drawing. However, you can't be as fun and flirty as you would be drawing a woman's hand, either. Give the dude's hand a bit more of a squared-off form when you draw it. In fashion illustration, a guy is usually strolling down a runway or city street; he rarely carries fashion extras like women do. So most guys' hand positions are relatively similar from drawing to drawing.

When you draw a man's hand, it should be strong and relatively square. Check out these steps:

1. **For the palm, lightly sketch a loose and simple rectangle, as in Figure 6-14a.**

2. **Add a few curved lines for fingers and begin to round out the palm, as in Figure 6-14b.**

3. **Attach a curved oval shape for a thumb and further round out the hand. Lengthen the wrist and add a wrist bone, as in Figure 6-14c.**

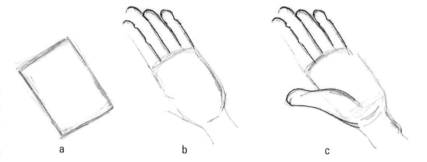

Figure 6-14: Give the man a hand!

a   b   c

When drawing kids' hands, follow the same steps you would for a man's hand, but keep the hand and fingers shorter and stubbier.

Propping Up Your Figures on Fashion-Ready Legs

Legs can make or break a great fashion pose. They add so much personality and attitude. Long legs can turn women into supermodels whose bodies go on forever. For men, legs define masculinity even in the most feminine of outfits. For children, legs portray the innocence of a relaxed child's pose. In the following sections, we show you how to draw fashionable legs for women, men, and children.

Lingering over a gal's long, lean legs

Have you ever seen a fashion illustration where the figure has short, stubby legs? No, and you probably never will — unless you're looking at some kid sketches. Forever-flowing legs are the one feature that all female fashion figures should have in common. If you look at any fashion magazine or illustration, every model has endless legs.

Go to town when drawing a lady's legs; the length of them helps make clothes look great, shoes snappy, and the whole image exciting! Long legs aren't just sexy; they also convey vitality, action, and suppleness. Draw your legs much longer than your torso and head combined. (Flip to Chapter 4 for details on proportions in fashion figures.) Also, don't forget to lightly sketch in the pelvic area — without it, the leg proportions won't fly.

Starting where the jaunty hips end, go long to the foot, and don't be afraid of experimenting with legs that are in impossible positions. Take a look at Figure 6-15, for example; of course the lower leg can't humanly curve like that, but in fashion illustration, this curve brings an edgy look.

In the following sections, we show you how to draw ladies' legs from the front view, the three-quarter view, and the side view.

A front view of the legs

Sometimes you want to show your leading lady from the front view — maybe you want to show off her great top or her fabulous skinny jeans. The front view is the most basic, but it's often effective.

To draw wonderfully thin, long legs on your female fashion figure from the front view, follow these steps:

1. **Draw the figure's lower torso with leg holes, as in Figure 6-15a.**

   Check out Chapter 5 for more on using trapezoids to draw torsos.

2. **For the thigh, start with a straight line that connects to a circle for the knee. For the lower leg, add a slightly curved line that connects to a small triangle for the foot, as in Figure 6-15b.**

   In this pose, the knees are coming together. *Remember:* Legs — especially the lower leg (from the knee down) — can never be too long. For fun, try making the lower leg twice as long as the thigh; but as always with fashion illustration, take this as a fun suggestion, not a rule!

3. **Draw in cylinders over the leg lines, as in Figure 6-15c.**

   As you're drawing the cylinders, make sure you keep them slender and tapered toward the ankle.

4. **Finish your drawing of the fashion figure and erase your initial lines, as in Figure 6-15d.**

Figure 6-15:
Love those
legs!

Legs are the key to making sure a fashion pose is grounded. To keep your figure grounded, always draw one leg or foot directly under the head to keep the figure from looking like she's falling over. Compare the poses in Figure 6-16; the figure on the left-hand side is falling over, and the one on the right is grounded.

A three-quarter view of the legs

Drawing only front poses gets boring sometimes! Add some spice to your figures by changing up the look and going for the three-quarter-view pose. To make your fashion figure look like she's partially turned, hide one of the legs slightly, as in Figure 6-17. You see the knee more on one side. The calf is still visible on both sides, but you can see it a little more on the back leg.

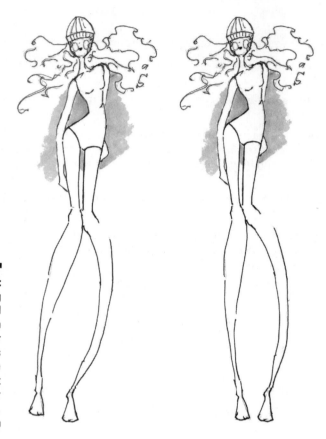

Figure 6-16:
Keeping
the head
aligned with
one leg or
foot makes
the figure
on the right
appear
grounded.

Figure 6-17:
A view of
a partially
turned leg.

Follow these steps to draw legs in a three-quarter view pose:

1. **Draw a figure's lower torso from the three-quarter view.**

   Check out Chapter 5 for details on how to draw torsos in the three-quarter view.

2. **Sketch in the lines for the legs, crossing one over the other, thus partially hiding one leg.**

   Bend one leg so you can get a view of both legs, as in Figure 6-18a. And don't forget the circles to represent the knees. Keep your leg proportions in check, with the lower legs perhaps twice as long as the upper legs.

3. **Draw cylinders over the leg lines to finish the legs, keeping the circles to represent the knees.**

   For the hidden leg, draw only the part of the cylinder that's visible. Make sure your cylinders for both legs are slender and tapered toward the ankle, as they are in Figure 6-18b.

4. **Outline your final drawing and erase your initial lines, as in Figure 6-18c.**

Figure 6-18: A three-quarter view of totally toned legs.

a   b   c

A side view of a lady's legs

To mix things up, you can take a side approach to your lady's legs. Side views are great for showing off the derrière and creating killer fashion poses! Take a look at Figure 6-19, which shows how the front view of the leg compares to the side. Notice on the front view, the thigh connects to the knee and then to the lower leg with a curve below the knee for the calf muscle. From the side view, the knee curves on one side of the leg, and the calf curves below the knee on the other side.

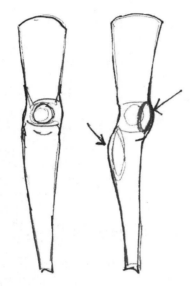

Figure 6-19: The front view compared to the side view of the leg.

To create legs from the side in a fun walking pose, follow these steps:

1. **Draw the lower torso and leg lines with circles to represent the knees. (See Figure 6-20a.)**

   From the side view, only one leg hole shows on the lower torso (refer to Chapter 5 for information on drawing torsos from the side). The leg stepping forward bends at the knee, and her other leg follows a graceful curve from thigh to foot.

2. **Draw cylinders over the leg lines, keeping the cylinders thin but shapely and tapered toward the ankle. (See Figure 6-20b.)**

3. **Finish your figure and erase your initial lines, as in Figure 6-20c.**

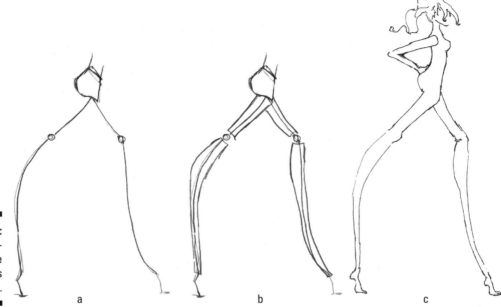

Figure 6-20:
A high-fashion side view of legs in motion.

a b c

Singing praises about sexy men's legs

Let's hear it for the boys! A dude's legs can look pretty fine in Bermudas, cut-off jeans, bike shorts, or a bathing suit — including the infamous Speedo.

Many of the same tips that apply to women's legs (see the preceding section) apply to men's legs — well, except for the fact that male thighs are denser looking and the calves are more developed. So sorry, guys: no miniskirts for you!

Men's legs can be too long! For guys, try to keep the length of the legs similar to the length of the torso and head combined. The thigh and calf can be close in length. Here are some other guidelines to keep in mind as well (check out Figure 6-21 to see what we mean):

✔ Define the thighs with strong lines and curves.

✔ Form the calves using shading techniques. (Check out Chapter 3 for details on shading.)

Drawing children's legs

In fashion drawing, children's legs are chubbier and less sculpted than men's and women's legs.

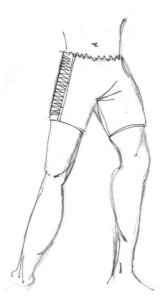

Figure 6-21:
Fit-looking
male legs.

Here's how to draw children's legs:

1. **Draw the lower torso for a child. Add in lines with circles for the knees and triangles for the feet, as in Figure 6-22a.**

   Keep the top and bottom of the legs about the same length.

2. **Add very round cylinder shapes for chubby thighs and calves, as in Figure 6-22b.**

3. **Finish the look with rounded curves by the knees and ankles, as in Figure 6-22c.**

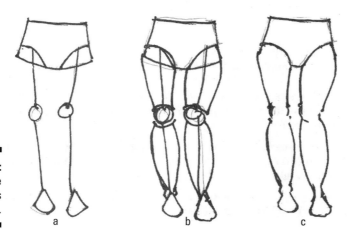

Figure 6-22:
Adorable
children's
legs.

a   b   c

Putting Your Best Fashion Foot Forward

A mini golden rule is that you must know what a foot looks like before you can even begin to draw a shoe. Chapter 3 provides a short refresher on the basics of drawing feet, and the following sections provide some detailed pointers. After you know the basic shape of a foot, you can draw everything from classic sandals and loafers to outlandish boots and heels. When you're ready to draw shoes, flip to Chapter 13.

Being sweet with tiny fashion feet

Let's face it: Real fashion models have big feet. They're super tall and couldn't possibly walk, run, or leap with tiny ones. But in fashion illustration, you *never* draw feet as big as boats. In fact, some fashion illustrators draw teensy feet on impossibly tall fashion creatures; that's extreme fashion drawing to the highest power! You can see a delicate foot in Figure 6-23.

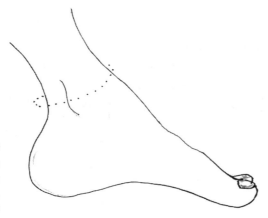

Figure 6-23:
A dainty
fashion foot.

Here's how to draw a simple foot:

1. **Start with three shapes: Draw a flat triangle for the toes and ball of the foot, a square for the middle part of the foot, and a circle for the heel. (See Figure 6-24a.)**

2. **Outline the bottom of the foot by first going around the circle for the heel. Curve slightly upward under the foot for the arch and finish the bottom with a slight curve under the toes, as in Figure 6-24b.**

3. **Outline the top of the foot with a smooth line that comes up from the toes to the ankle, as in Figure 6-24c.**

Figure 6-24:
The basic
shapes of
the foot.

A bit of foot knowledge can take you a long way when you're ready to draw shoes, boots, and even simple flip-flops. Keep these points in mind:

- ✔ All feet have heels, so don't ignore them when drawing feet from the side.

- ✔ An arch in the foot gives it a more appealing look. In fact, the higher, the better for female feet. Head to the next section for more on drawing sky-high arches. Men don't generally wear high heels, so their arches don't need to reach for the sky.

- ✔ Don't get obsessed with rendering toes; stylize them instead.

Playing with the Barbie arch

Remember the shape of Barbie's foot? She has the highest and most perma-nent arch in the history of dolls. Barbie is *made* for high, high heels, and so are many female fashion figures. A roller coaster of a line is perfect for draw-ing feet with the Barbie arch look.

To create a high arch for dainty lady feet, follow these steps:

1. **Draw a rolling curve for the heel, arch, and ball of the foot, as in Figure 6-25a.**

2. **Lightly sketch a slanting line for the top of the foot, as in Figure 6-25b.**

3. **Sketch a tiny curve for the big toe, as in Figure 6-25c.**

   Don't forget the nail polish!

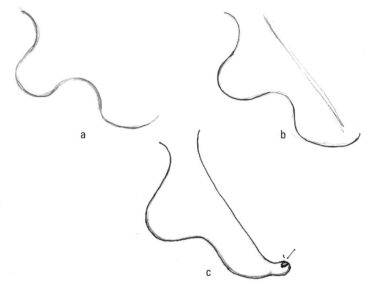

Figure 6-25:
Barbie
arches
forever.

Sassy, simple fashion foot poses

Fashion stances change over the years, but here are some foot poses that are popular today:

- **Baby-doll pose (Figure 6-26a):** This stance is the most popular. In the baby doll pose, women's fashion feet usually turn in to show off whimsical-looking clothes.

- **Walking pose (Figure 6-26b):** Feet can look confident striding down the runway.

- **Ballet pose (Figure 6-26c):** The third position in ballet, with toes turned outward and heels overlapping, provides feet with a regal look.

- **The come-hither stance (Figure 6-26d):** This pose, with one foot facing forward and one to the side, beckons you to check out a fashionista's outfit and accessories. She screams high fashion.

For men, a few simple rules always hold true: Men *never* turn their feet inward for a cute pose, and their feet turn slightly outward when they walk. However, don't make a guy's feet turn out like a duck's. You can check out a typical guy stance in Figure 6-27.

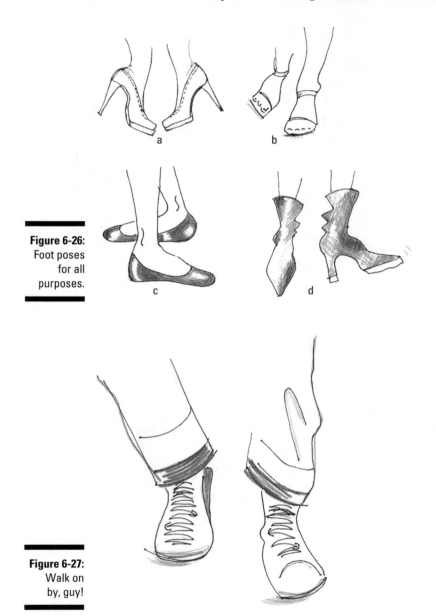

Figure 6-26:
Foot poses
for all
purposes.

Figure 6-27:
Walk on
by, guy!

For children, keep the feet shorter in length and put them in fun poses with detailed footwear. Try turning the toes together in Mary Janes, keeping the toes forward when sketching fun cowgirl boots, or drawing larger athletic style shoes from a three-quarter view with the laces untied! See Figure 6-28.

Figure 6-28:
Cute foot
poses for
kids' shoes!

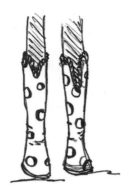

Chapter 7

Putting Your Best Face Forward

Faces are fun stuff. Drawing faces in a fashion illustration lets you create a character who can be anything from elegant and arrogant to scruffy yet stylish. Faces help play up the mood you want to create with your illustration. Each facial feature is special in fashion style.

In this chapter, we show you how to draw fashion faces with all the details that add just the right touch of style to your fashion illustration. We explain how to choose the right view for your look, and then we run through eyes, noses, mouths, and ears.

Fashion illustration isn't about drawing portraits with proper features; it's about drawing figures with stylized faces.

Choosing the Right View for Your Face

Before you can start on a fashion face, you first have to draw a head with a face grid (see Chapter 3 for details). When you're ready for your face, you can adjust the guide lines on the face grid to reflect various views of the face as it slowly turns. When you have a profile, for example, the center front line moves all the way to the side.

If you want to draw a face from the front view, flip to Chapter 3, where we give you the basics of drawing a head with a face grid. Other than keeping the fashion figure head small, there's not much difference between drawing a forward-facing head on a figure drawing and drawing one on a fashion model.

Of course, you can't always draw faces that look straight ahead in the front view. Nor would you want to, when you have so many fabulous angles to choose from! The following sections show you how to perfect your figures' faces, whether you're going for a three-quarter view or a profile. Throughout the rest of this chapter, we focus on individual features: eyes, nose, mouth, and ears.

Subtle and sassy: Drawing faces in the three-quarter view

A face in a three-quarter view is more subtle than the front view. When a face is seen from the three-quarter view, it lends some mystery to the fashion figure.

Here's how to draw a face in the three-quarter view:

1. **Start with an oval like the one in Figure 7-1a.**

   Use your face grid for feature placement. The vertical line marks the center front of the face. The horizontal line that appears halfway down the oval marks the eye level.

2. **To turn the face, move your center front line slightly to the right, as in Figure 7-1b.**

   Moving this line moves the figure's facial features — eyes, nose, and mouth — slightly to the right as well. Curving the guide lines slightly adds dimension.

3. **Map out the placement of the eyes, nose, and mouth, as in Figure 7-1c.**

   Notice that the side of the head facing you is more pronounced; the far side of the face slides to the back with less obvious features so that the fashion figure's left eye is barely visible. As the head turns, you also start to see the back of the head as well as where the ear will eventually be.

Figure 7-1:
Creating
a three-
quarter view
face in three
steps.

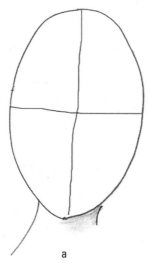
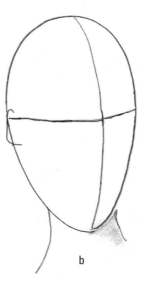
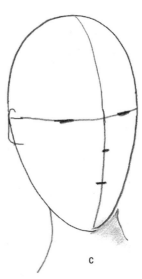

a   b   c

You're your own best model when studying facial features. Try this exercise: Look at yourself in the mirror and slowly turn your head to your right side. Notice how your features change and fall into various three-quarter positions. One side of your face becomes more noticeable as the other recedes. Pay attention to models in photographs and how their heads turn to further explore various views of the face.

Perfecting profiles

Profiles are used frequently in fashion drawing because they convey an elegant, haughty look.

You can create a perfect profile for women, men, and children by following these steps (we show a woman's profile in Figure 7-2 and a child's and man's profile in Figure 7-3):

1. **Start by drawing an oval and a face grid, as in Figure 7-2a.**

2. **Sketch in the forehead, eye, nose, and lips from the side view, as in Figure 7-2b. Draw the top and back of the head, curving in as you approach the neck.**

   Place the eye slightly above the center horizontal line and the nose a little below it. The nose in a profile view is just a slanted angle shape.

   Draw the lips in profile outside the oval, about halfway between the middle horizontal line and the bottom. The top lip curves up toward the nose, and the lower lip curves down toward the chin. Keep the lower lip slightly fuller than the upper lip. The lips protrude slightly from the face.

3. **Form the chin, making sure you dimple in the skin just under the lip, as in Figure 7-2c.**

   Keep the chin more rounded for women and children, and present a square look for the guys. See Figure 7-3 for a man's profile.

4. **Add the ear by sketching in a *C* shape around where the guide lines cross. Lightly sketch in the jaw by continuing the line from the chin to the ear, as in Figure 7-2d.**

   The top of the ear lines up near the eyes. (You can read more about creating eyes in the next section.)

   A woman's jawline generally angles up toward the ear. A man's jawline is flatter, which gives him a rugged look.

Figure 7-2: A female profile.

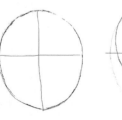
a

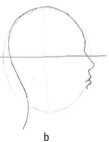
b

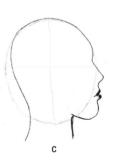
c

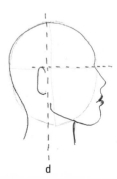
d

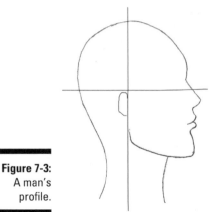

Figure 7-3:
A man's
profile.

Expressing Yourself with Those Eyes

Eyes really are the windows to the soul. The expression in the eyes is the first thing that people look at in real life as well as in fashion illustration. Eyes instantly express a person's mood and can convey a haughty, happy, or distant look. There's no end to the looks you can give your fashion creations through their eyes. Eyes should never be boring!

When you're drawing eyes, you often have to pay attention to many factors, including eyelids, brows, and lashes. Eyes can convey realism or fantasy, depending on how large you choose to draw them. Eyelashes can go on forever or be the only thing you see with closed eyes. There are no hard and fast rules about eyes!

Marianne likes to keep her faces very simple so she can spend the majority of her time working on her clothing designs. Lisa has more of a detailed approach because she likes to create a personality in the face along with her clothing designs. Either approach works great for fashion drawing. The following sections explain a simple approach to eyes and then lead into more-detailed eyes.

Considering the many looks of eyes

Fashion heads can have no faces at all or extremely detailed faces with makeup. Simple eyes can be little more than quick marks that give viewers an impression of eye placement, just so they understand that the model has a face.

Here's how to create simple eyes from the front view:

1. **Start by drawing an oval with a face grid, as in Figure 7-4a.**

   Add a neck for a nice effect.

2. **Draw the eye(s) on the horizontal guide line and about halfway between the center vertical line and the edge of the face.**

   The eye shape dips down in the front and then curves up and over the little pupil. It ends in another little pointed shape, as in Figure 7-4b. To create a bit of shine, the pupil is a crescent shape rather than a full circle. We've included close-ups of the eye shape off the grid to show the shape more clearly.

3. **Add some long, dramatic eyelashes, always pulling and curving to the outside corner of the eye. (See Figure 7-4c.)**

   The eyes can look messy or fake; the point of simple eyes is to quickly throw an eye on the face.

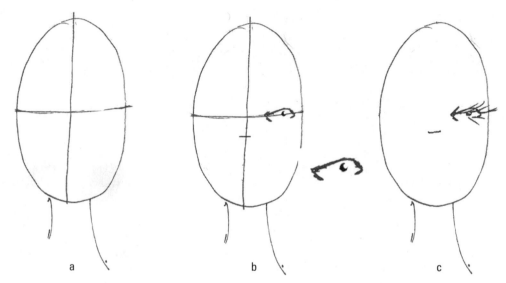

Figure 7-4: The simple fashionable eye.

a   b   c

Here's how to draw a more-detailed eye:

1. **Start with a circle to represent the iris (the colored part of the eye), as in Figure 7-5a.**

2. **For the pupil, draw a small circle in the center of the iris. Fill in the pupil with black, leaving a small white area for shine, as in Figure 7-5b.**

3. **For the outside of the eye, draw an almond shape that cuts off the top third of the iris circle and extends past the circle, as in Figure 7-5c. Add detail inside the iris circle, such as lines radiating out from the black pupil.**

   Keep the inside corner of the eye (the side by the nose) small and pointed, and keep the other side of the eye wider. Draw a tiny circle at the inside corner of the eye.

4. **Erase the top of the iris circle that extends above the almond shape and then shade the inside of the iris slightly. For the lower lashes, add small curved lines around the bottom lid to the corner of the eye. (See Figure 7-5d.)**

5. **For the upper eyelid, add a line that follows the same curve as the almond shape; lightly shade in the upper eyelid. Add lots of curved eyelashes on the top part of the eye, extending farther as the lines near the outside corner. (See Figure 7-5e.)**

6. **Finish the look with an eyebrow, as in Figure 7-5f.**

We show you how to draw eyebrows in the section "Defining jazzy eyes with brows."

Figure 7-5:
A detailed
fashion eye.

     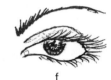

a   b   c   d   e   f

REMEMBER

With all the different ethnicities of the world and all the expressions faces can portray, eyes can have a million different looks. If you're interested in discovering more about eyes, check out *Figure Drawing For Dummies,* by Kensuke Okabahashi (Wiley), and study cartoon drawings and styles such as Anime.

Here are some examples of a few more types of eyes:

✔ Eyes can be angled, sloping up or down with as much eyelid as you want to show. Get the angled look by tilting the almond shape of the eye, as in Figure 7-6a.

✔ Eyes can be rounded and wide, with the bottom line missing for a very youthful look. Accomplish this by rounding out the top of the almond shape and erasing the bottom line, as in Figure 7-6b.

✔ Eyes can be long and thin with hardly any eyelid and small amounts of the iris showing. Achieve this look by straightening out the top of the almond shape, as in Figure 7-6c.

TIP

For inspiration, we encourage you to people-watch and look at photos. Faces include so many incredible, subtle variations! And eyes, of course, are the focal point of the face (which may be a good reason to cover them up in some of your drawings — so they don't detract from the clothes!).

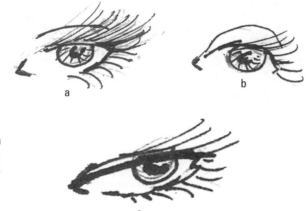

Figure 7-6:
A variety
of fashion
eyes.

Defining jazzy eyes with brows

Eyebrows can say so much about a figure; they really help define your eye and add expression. High, arched, and penciled-in eyebrows are super-haughty looking, and thick, straight brows can give your fashion model a serious look. Thick brows also fit a less-manicured masculine look.

When giving your fashion women eyebrows, you can try one of the following different looks:

- Draw an arched brow with only one pencil line above the eyelid, as in Figure 7-7a. You can draw the arch as high as you like. This look is reminiscent of the historical and current styles in which women plucked their eyebrows and drew them in. Think movie stars from the '30s.

- Draw a high arch above and following the curve of the eyelid, as in Figure 7-7b. This line is more angled and gives the face a sultry, confident look. The arch is about as high as the eye is wide. You can make this line thin or thick.

- For drama, draw the same high arch but extend it a bit lower to form a tear shape near the inner corner of the eye, as in Figure 7-7c. This look creates a dramatic face.

Experiment with high and low arches; varying the height of the arch creates a completely different personality. You can also experiment with smooth, rounded arches versus angled, pointy arches. A rounded arch tends to make the face look young, and a pointy arch gives the face a more mature look.

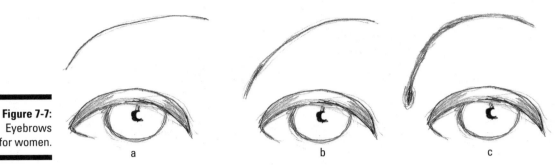

Figure 7-7: Eyebrows for women.

Men need super-cool eyebrows too! You can give your fashion man a more masculine brow in this way:

1. **Draw a very slight curve above a guy's eyelid, as in Figure 7-8a.**

   Follow the shape and length of the eyelids to get the perfect man brow. Most guys don't pluck or wax, so you don't need much of an arch.

2. **Fill in the curve with a series of short crisscrossed lines that create the eyebrow, as in Figures 7-8b and 7-8c.**

   A masculine brow can be more trimmed, too, so you can also make the brow more solid — it's all about the look you want to create!

Figure 7-8: Eyebrows for men.

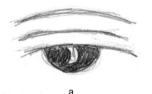 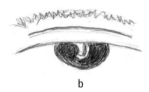 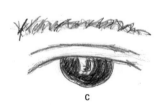

Children's eyes tend to be smaller and rounder than adult eyes. Round out the child's eyebrow to match the look of the eye. Keep the eyebrow fuller for children than for adults (although if you're drawing teen or pre-teen girls, they may have already started plucking and defining their eyebrows).

Lashing out with attitude

Eyelashes are a fashion frill, especially for women, but men and children can use them, too; otherwise, their eyes may have that not-quite-finished look.

Here are some rules to remember when drawing fashion lashes (these rules all apply for women, men, and children):

✔ Vary the length of the lashes to avoid the centipede look. Figure 7-9a shows what lashes look like if you don't vary them. Kind of buggy, huh?

✔ Eyelashes are longer at the outer corner of each eye. Check out Figure 7-9b to see what we mean.

✔ For an extra "wow" look, make the upper lashes much longer at the outer corner of the eyelid. See Figure 7-9c to see lashes with pizzazz.

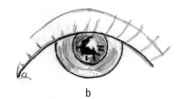

a b

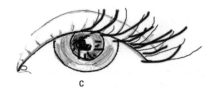

c

Figure 7-9:
Eyelashes
add a
finishing
touch.

Tackling eyes from different angles

You'll often draw eyes from different angles, depending on the look that you're going for. Each angle involves a different set of steps. We explain how to sketch eyes in a three-quarter view and profile view in the following sections. Drawing eyes for a forward-facing view is pretty straightforward — just combine the steps for eyes, brows, and lashes in the preceding sections.

Trying out three-quarter-view eyes

The key to drawing eyes in the three-quarter view is not drawing both eyes the same size. Because the model's head is turned away from the viewer, the eye that's farther away looks slightly smaller than the eye that's closer to the viewer. That's the effect of perspective. You also don't generally fully see the eye that's more distant from the viewer. Take a look at the child's face in Figure 7-10 to see what we mean.

Figure 7-10:
The view
of the eyes
changes
when a
model's
head turns.

In addition to drawing two different-sized eyes, you can emphasize the turn of the head by making the eyelashes longer at the outside of the eyes.

Here's how to draw the eye in a three-quarter view:

1. **Draw an oval for the face and sketch a face grid, turning the face as in Figure 7-11a. On the right side of the oval, indent the oval a bit at the eye socket.**

   Keep the horizontal line in the center and the vertical line off-center. When you move the center line, imagine that the face is turning; therefore, the side away from the viewer will show the eye coming off the side of the face. For the eye socket, start with an indentation inside the circled area of Figure 7-11a.

2. **Draw the eyes. The eye closest to the viewer is a regular full eye. The eye on the side turned away is less wide and comes to the edge of the face. Extend some lashes for a dramatic effect, as in Figure 7-11b.**

   To draw the three-quarter view eye, start with a rounded almond shape, as in Figure 7-11c. Cut through the almond shape to draw the upper eyelid, leaving more space for the eyeball than the eyelid. Draw the iris with a few lines for shading and then blacken the pupil while leaving a space white, as in Figure 7-11d. Finish with some long eyelashes on the top and bottom of the lids, as in Figure 7-11e.

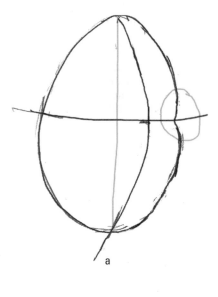

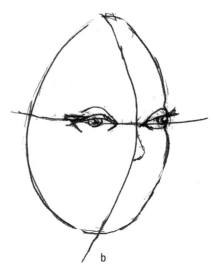

Figure 7-11: The view of the eyes changes when a model's head is turned.

Using the profile view for your figure's eyes

An eye seen from a profile view doesn't look much like an eye from the front view. From the side, you see only half of the eye and how it's set into the head.

To draw an eye in profile, follow these guidelines:

1. **Draw a triangle, as in Figure 7-12a.**

2. **For the iris, add an oval on the vertical side of the triangle, as in Figure 7-12b.**

3. **Sketch in an eyelid that runs parallel to the top line of the triangle. Check out Figure 7-12c to see what we mean.**

4. **Extend lashes from the outer points of the triangle, at the top and bottom of the oval. (See Figure 7-12d.)**

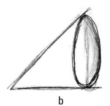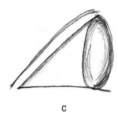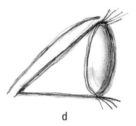

Figure 7-12: The eye in profile.

a   b   c   d

Adding flair with closed eyes

Sometimes you can add flair simply by drawing eyelids and lashes. In the following sections, we give you a couple of fashionable closed-eye looks.

Coy, downward-looking eyes

You can make fashion figures look a little coy by having them look down toward the ground. Drawing downward-looking eyes is a good way to add some personality to your figure's face.

Drawing a coy model is easy because you don't have to draw a detailed eye; all you need is a closed eyelid and lashes. Try these steps:

1. **Draw an upward arc for the eyelid and gently shade in the lid with your pencil to give it volume. (See Figure 7-13a.)**

2. **Add lashes to the outer corner of the eye, as in Figure 7-13b.**

The downward-looking eye can double as a wink. Just draw one eye open and the other eye closed.

Figure 7-13:
A coy eye is
a cute eye.

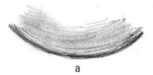

Eyes closed in laughter or happiness

You can also add flair to your figure's eyes by going for a happy, laughing look. The eyeball doesn't show when you draw a laughing or smiling eye. To fully convey the model's joy, make sure to draw a smiling mouth, too (we get to mouths later in "Setting Down Mouths That Speak and Smile").

To create a happy look, follow these steps:

1. **Draw a downward arc for the eyelid, as in Figure 7-14a.**

2. **Sketch in lashes on the outer corner of the eyelid, as in Figure 7-14b.**

3. **Add an eyebrow that follows the same shape as the eye, as in Figure 7-14c.**

   Make sure the eyebrow follows the direction of the smiling eye.

Figure 7-14:
Smiling
eyes convey
a happy
mood.

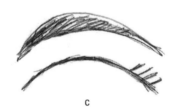

Keeping Noses Simple

Keep noses under control in a fashion illustration. The idea is to create a great-looking nose without going overboard with too many shapes and shadows. You're not illustrating an anatomy textbook, and the nose isn't an area you want to stress. Oh, and realistic-looking nostrils aren't at all fashion forward!

You really want to create a nose that *isn't* noticed; if it grabs attention, you've probably overdone it! Use fewer lines when drawing a nose to keep it from looking too heavy-handed. Use light shadowing to enhance your line work, but don't overdo the top of the nose with your lines and shadowing — a minimal look is a must.

In the following sections, we show you how to get a great-looking nose every time.

Blessing your fashionista with an elegant nose

Female fashion noses breathe class and refinement. The sweet girl-next-door button nose is nothing to sneeze at, but it doesn't fit a woman of high fashion.

Here's how to draw a simple fashion nose from the front view:

1. **Draw an oval for a face and a face grid, as in Figure 7-15a.**

2. **Divide the bottom half of the face into thirds and mark them with dashed lines, as in Figure 7-15b.**

3. **For the nose, draw two little slash lines in the center of the upper dashed line.**

   Fashion noses are much shorter than real noses. Figure 7-15c shows what this type of nose looks like after you erase your guide lines.

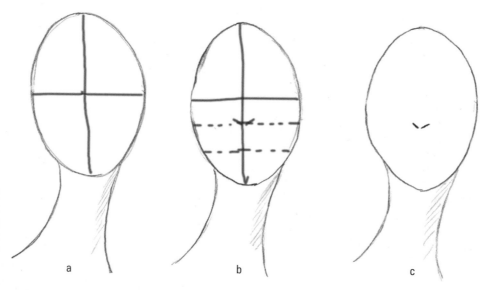

Figure 7-15: Elegant noses don't need lots of detail.

a   b   c

Giving your guy a strong nose

A masculine nose is drawn in thick, strong lines. Boldness works well for the masculine nose, but you're not going for the big schnozz look here; even though it's bold, a masculine nose is still elegant.

Try for a strong yet tapered style when drawing a masculine nose. Here's how:

1. **Sketch a man's eyes and brows. Draw a slightly curved line starting right between the eyes and running down to where the tip of the nose begins, as in Figure 7-16a.**

2. **For the bottom of the nose, draw a couple of *L*-shaped marks slightly above the top of the upper lip, as in Figure 7-16b.**

Add nostrils by making the bottoms of the *L*s a little darker.

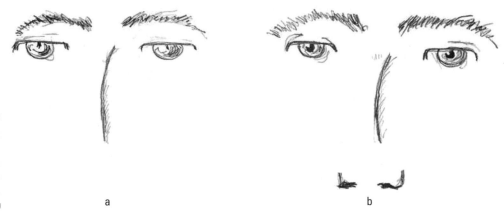

Figure 7-16:
You can be
bolder when
drawing the
male nose.

a   b

Creating a cute kid nose

Kids' noses are simple and cute. Don't get realistic or detailed; otherwise, their little faces will be overwhelmed. These simple solutions provide you with a perfect child's nose (if you decide to include a nose at all):

- ✒ Use a small sideways *V,* as in Figure 7-17a.

- ✒ Draw a small *V* shape to show the tip of the nose. Use this shape for the *bottom* of the nose, not for the line of the nose, which you can leave out on youthful faces. See Figure 7-17b to check out what this nose looks like.

- ✒ Go for a simple upward arc. You can see this cute nose in Figure 7-17c.

The fave face grid for a child is the same for an adult: The eyes are vertically centered and the bottom half of the face is divided into thirds, with the nose taking up the top third. A child's overall face shape is rounded and not as long, so the features look closer together.

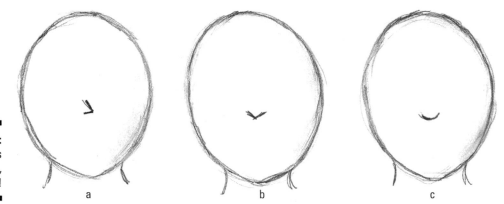

Figure 7-17:
Kids' noses
are cute,
cute, cute!

a   b   c

Taking in the nose from other views

Because your figure won't always be looking straight ahead, mastering the nose from a three-quarter view and a profile view is important. We give you the lowdown on these noses in the following sections.

The nose in three-quarter view

A three-quarter view nose is angled to the side. The nose from this view can be tricky to draw, so our best advice is to keep it simple and clean.

To draw the nose in three-quarter view, try these steps:

1. **Draw a head with a face grid but shift the vertical line to the right side of the oval, as in Figure 7-18a.**

2. **Draw two dashed lines that divide the lower half of the face into thirds. The nose point goes on the upper dashed line, as in Figure 7-18b.**

3. **End with a short horizontal line heading to the left side to depict the bottom of the nose, as in Figure 7-18c.**

   For women and children, the nose is a little more curved rather than pointy. Check out Figure 7-18d for ways to illustrate the nose for women and Figure 7-18e for a child's nose. Sometimes the slight differences in appearance come from the length of the top line of the nose: The longer the line, the more masculine it tends to look.

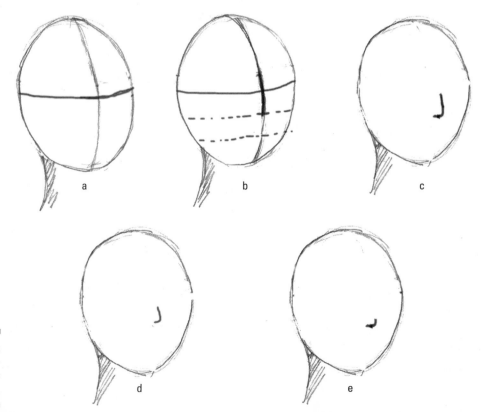

Figure 7-18:
The three-quarter view nose.

a   b   c

d   e

In profile

Noses in profile can be pointy and simple; rounded and simple; or either pointy or rounded with some nostril detail and shading. No matter which style you like, all these noses begin with two simple lines that meet up somewhere away from the face. The distance away from the face is up to you, the designer!

Follow these steps to achieve a perfect profile nose:

1. **Draw a line that angles away from the face, and draw another line that's a slight downward curve back toward the face. When you put these lines together, they create a nose in profile.**

   Figure 7-19a shows the placement of the nose: The top of the nose starts around the eye level line, and the nose finishes about a third of the way down the bottom half of the head.

   Figure 7-19b shows the basic lines that make up a simple nose. The distance you bring the nose away from the face on the angle is the distance you bring back the curve underneath. Notice that the top of the nose line lines up with the end of the lower curve.

2. **For a nose with a rounded look, simply round out the point where the angled line meets the curve, as in Figure 7-19c.**

3. **To add detail, simply draw in a *C*-shaped curve above the open end of the lower curve. For the nostril, draw another little curved line above the lower curve but closer to the point of the nose, as in Figure 7-19d.**

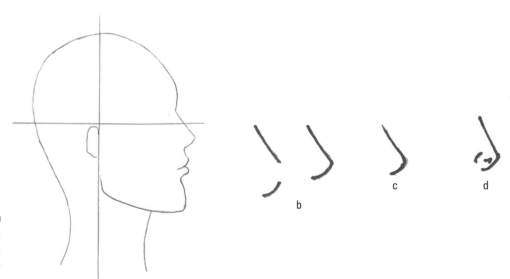

Figure 7-19:
Drawing a nose in profile.

Setting Down Mouths That Speak and Smile

You can often read a person's mood just from the set of her mouth, and the same is true in fashion illustration. Certain mouth shapes are in style at different times; for example, full lips are popular in the fashion world these days. But don't limit yourself to one style; lips can come in shapes from classic to rosebud to diamond shaped.

Like other parts of the face, fashion mouths aren't rendered for realism but rather as a series of lines and shapes that create a unique fashion feeling. Expressive-looking mouths in fashion illustration convey moods and attitude for women, men, and children.

For most fashion illustrations, drawing teeth gives an overly toothy look that distracts from fashion stylization. If your model is smiling or has her mouth open, just leave a white space in the open mouth with no shading or lines to indicate teeth. Don't worry that leaving the mouth empty will make your figure look toothless; if you play up the shape of the open lips, the lack of teeth won't even be noticed.

In the following sections, we show you how to become a master of mouths, whether you're drawing women, men, or children.

Trying the classic feminine pout

A woman's mouth can take so many different shapes — from full to thin to diamond shaped — but you can't go wrong with the classic shape in Figure 7-20.

To practice the traditional feminine mouth shape, follow these steps:

1. **Draw a short horizontal line to establish the opening of the mouth, as in Figure 7-20a.**

2. **Sketch in the lower lip as an upward arc, as in Figure 7-20b.**

3. **Draw the top lip with two peaks on each side of the center to add form. You can see the peaks in Figure 7-20c.**

   Keep in mind that the lower lip is almost always fuller and deeper than the top lip.

For placement of the lips, look at Figure 7-18b. The bottom half of the face is divided into thirds, and the lips go on the lower dashed line.

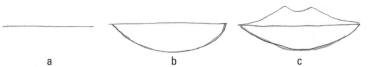

Figure 7-20:
Female
lips speak
volumes!

Marianne loves to draw faces as simply as possible! Here are some modifications you can make for a simple yet fashionable mouth:

- Use only a few lines for the lips. Figure 7-21a shows a slightly pointed top lip, a curved line for the opening between the lips, and a deep curve for the lower lip. Below the drawing is a sketch of circles you can use to help you create the shapes of the lips.

- For more of a pout, the top line can have a gentler curve, and the center line can be a short dash; the bottom lip is only a slight, pointy curve, as in Figure 7-21b. The heart shape below the illustration shows how you can establish this shape.

- Figure 7-21c shows Marianne's favorite simple lips. The top part of the lip is a short, pointy line that's wider than the bottom lip. The bottom lip is a short curve.

- You can draw just a simple little dot or line to show that lips are supposed to be there. This mouth is great for a very simple style of face.

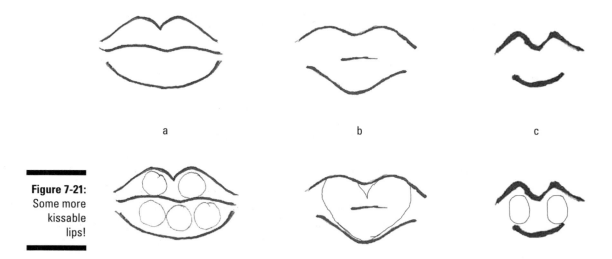

Figure 7-21:
Some more
kissable
lips!

Sketching a manly mouth

Women's mouths tend to be curvier and fuller than men's mouths, so most fashion illustration males have a straight-lipped look. However, you can feel free to try out some other options to suit the look you're going for.

To draw a male mouth for a fashion illustration, follow these steps:

1. **For the opening of the mouth, start with a simple horizontal line with a slight dip in the center, as in Figure 7-22a.**

2. **Draw the lower lip as an upward arc. Shade slightly under the lower lip, as in Figure 7-22b.**

3. **Add the upper lip, but keep the curves to a minimum, as in Figure 7-22c.**

   Make sure the lower lip is fuller than the upper lip.

4. **Add two little lines at the corners of the mouth, one at each side. (See Figure 7-22d.)**

   Keep the lines short; longer lines create an older-looking mouth.

5. **Add light shading on the lips, as in Figure 7-22e.**

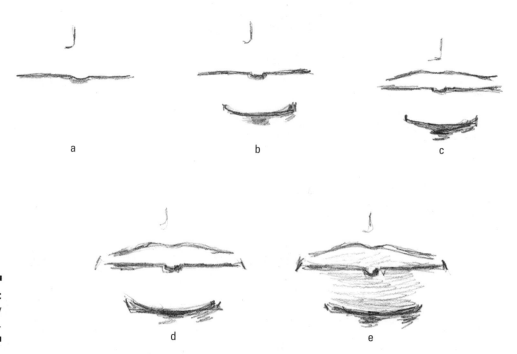

Figure 7-22:
A manly
mouth.

Try experimenting with fewer lines and less detail to play with other male lip looks. Keep in mind that male lips curve less than female lips.

Making sure your kids aren't too mouthy

Kids' mouths are quite simple because they are what they are. Kids don't apply lipstick every day and fret about new colors, nor do they worry whether their lips are too full or too thin. In general, a kid's mouth is small and not particularly well formed — except for the rare rosebud shape that's usually found on babies. Go for a simple look when drawing kids.

Kids' features are usually mapped out closer together than adults'.

Follow these steps for a simple kid mouth:

1. **Draw a circle for a kid's face and add in the face grid, as in Figure 7-23a.**

2. **Sketch in some dashed horizontal lines that divide the lower half of the face into thirds, as in Figure 7-23b.**

   The opening of the mouth goes at the lower dashed line.

3. **Draw the opening of the mouth as a pair of downward curves that meet at a dip in the middle. Draw the bottom of the lips as a slight upward curve, as in Figure 7-23c.**

   Erase the face grid and your other guide lines.

Figure 7-23d shows a style of drawing not only lips but faces in general. Leaving the face grid on the face is something that you see on fashion illustrations every once in a while and in quite a few examples in this book.

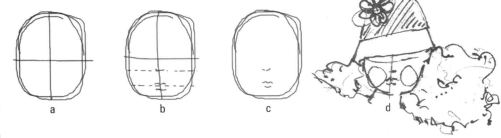

Figure 7-23:
Drawing a child's mouth.

a   b   c   d

Looking at lips from different perspectives

Just like eyes and noses, lips look different when drawn from the three-quarter or profile view. The following steps explain how to draw lips for women with modifications for men and children.

Here's how to draw three-quarter lips for women (the placement of the lips is the same for women and children):

1. **Sketch an oval for the head and draw a face grid with the vertical line off-center. Use a couple of dashed horizontal lines to divide the lower half of the face into thirds, as in Figure 7-24a.**

2. **Draw the woman's eyes, nose, and lips along the horizontal lines, as in 7-24b.**

   We discuss drawing eyes and noses in "Tackling eyes from different angles" and "Taking in the nose from other views."

   The opening of the mouth sits on the lower dashed line. To draw the lips in a three-quarter view, divide the lips in left and right halves. Draw the half closest to the viewer as usual, with the upper lip as a downward arc and the lower lip as half an upward arc, as in Figure 7-24c.

Draw the other half of the lips the same as the first half, but keep the curved top shorter and narrower. Make sure the bottom half is a small curve, as in Figure 7-24c.

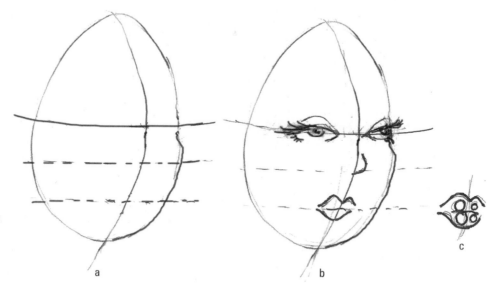

Figure 7-24:
The three-quarter lips.

Here's how to draw lips in a profile view:

1. **Draw a sideways triangle that points to the right. Draw a dashed horizontal line that cuts the triangle in half, as in Figure 7-25a.**

2. **Add two curves at the left side of the triangle, making the top curve narrower than the bottom, as in Figure 7-25b.**

3. **Erase the left side of the triangle and trace over the dashed line with a solid line to separate the lips. (See Figure 7-25c.)**

Figure 7-25d shows another look in which the upper lip is slightly more forward than the lower lip, reflecting a realistic view of how the front teeth go just in front of the lower teeth.

Figure 7-25:
The lips in profile.

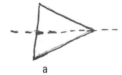
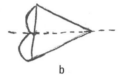

a   b   c   d

Stylish and Subtle: Playing Down Ears

You don't want to draw anything other than a graceful ear in your fashion illustrations. Fashion ears shouldn't be big and floppy, and they shouldn't stick out on your fashion head. Fashion ears are often no more than a place to hang a pair of elegant earrings.

You don't want to play up ears on women or men, but you do have a bit of a leeway with the kids. Until a child is about 12, the ears tend to naturally stick out a bit more.

Ears are one of the easiest features to master, because they pretty much look the same no matter whether you're drawing women's, men's, or children's. You don't even have to change what you draw for the different views — front view, profile, and three-quarter view. Check out the following sections for more information.

"C-ing" a simple ear for beauty

You can draw women's, men's, and children's ears using a simple *C*, whether the model's face is forward, in profile, or at a three-quarter view. To draw a fashion ear properly, slant the *C* slightly instead of placing it upright. Here are the guidelines to follow:

- Use a capital *C* for a woman's ear, as in Figure 7-26a.
- Use a double capital *C* for a man's ear, as in Figure 7-26b. Draw one *C* and then draw a smaller *C* inside the ear for definition and a masculine look.
- Use a lowercase *c* for a kid's ear, as in Figure 7-26c.

The rule of thumb for ear placement is that the top of the ear begins on the side of the face just below the eyebrow line, and it ends just about at the bottom of the nose. This golden rule of fashion helps you keep the face in proportion.

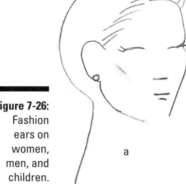
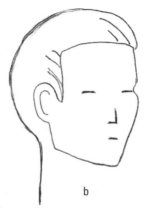

Figure 7-26: Fashion ears on women, men, and children.

a

b

c

Allowing ears to peek through long hair

Do you ever see ears when your fashion figure has long, thick hair? Not really. However, if your lady has long hair and is in motion, you may need to draw ears. Hair moves when the model does (but not as a solid mass), which allows the ears to peek through. Drawing strands of hair running across the ears, leaving the earlobe visible, creates the right sense of movement. Draw the ears in the same way if the hair is pinned up with a few tendrils tumbling down the neck.

To draw long hair that partially covers the ear, follow these steps:

1. **Draw a fashion face with *C*-shaped ears like those in Figure 7-27a.**

2. **Sketch in hair with lines covering part of each ear, as in Figure 7-27b.**

    Let the earlobe show through the hair.

Figure 7-27:
Ears can
peek
through
hair.

a   b

Chapter 8

Guaranteeing Good Hair Days

Although clothes and accessories take precedence, hair still serves an important purpose in fashion illustration. Hairstyles convey a certain mood or tone; wild curly hair goes better with a boho look than with a ballroom look, for instance. On the other hand, you may want to play against the labels and draw a smooth, elegant chignon on a model wearing jeans and a T-shirt.

In this chapter, we arm you with the skills you need to draw any type of hair on any style of fashion model by showing you how to draw several common hair types and popular hairstyles for women, men, and children. This chapter provides you the chance to play around with hairstyles you know you couldn't pull off in a million years but always wanted to try!

Locks 101: Getting the Basics on Drawing Fashion Hair

Great-looking hair is a fashion essential — even in a fashion illustration. If your drawing doesn't have natural yet exciting-looking hair, the hair will detract from the overall impact of your drawing. And unstylish hair can date your drawing in a nanosecond. As a trendy fashion illustrator, you definitely don't want people thinking your art is outdated.

Keep up with current hairstyles by reading fashion magazines and using the Internet for research. We recommend *Vogue, Bazaar,* and *Nylon* for traditional magazines. Explore www.style.com when you go online.

Hair shouldn't be the main focus in fashion illustration. It should convey a mood without overpowering the most important part of fashion illustration — the clothes and accessories. To create gorgeous hair and avoid the mistakes found in lesser fashion drawings, keep these three basic hair facts in mind:

> ✔ **Hair grows out of the head.** This point may sound obvious, but many people tend to draw hair that's contained within the original oval they sketch for the head. Hair grows out of and extends beyond the head.

✔ **Hair falls across the face and head.** Again, this fact may sound obvious, but many illustrators draw hair coming from the outside oval of the head. Hair grows from your forehead, temples, and the sides of your head, so it covers part of the oval that makes up the face.

✔ **The hairline follows the natural contours of the head.** A delicate oval head shape requires a hairline that's somewhat different from the hairline of a big guy with a square head.

The following sections explain the knowledge and skills you need to give your fashion illustrations a solid hair foundation, including getting your hairline and parts right. (Of course, you can't really expect to draw hair without having to draw a head. If your head drawings need work, flip to Chapter 7.)

Keeping things natural with a curving hairline

Hair grows out from the *hairline,* which forms over the forehead and temples. Everyone's hairline is different, but it always follows the natural contour of the forehead. Like the hairstyle in general, the hairline shouldn't be a focal point on a fashion illustration; it should look natural. A hairline that's too low looks Neanderthal, and one that's too high leaves too much empty forehead. To mimic a person's natural hairline, use a gentle curve that follows the shape of the head. Keep in mind that fashion figures are known for having elegant and high foreheads.

Here's how to draw a curving hairline on a front-facing figure:

1. **Draw a head, as in Figure 8-1a.**

2. **Sketch out facial features on your face, as in Figure 8-1b.**

   If necessary, use a face grid to help you place the eyes and other features in the right places. Lisa always starts with the eyes. If you need some help with facial features, check out Chapter 7.

3. **Mentally divide the space between the eyes and the top of the head into thirds. A little more than a third of the way down, draw the beginning of a curving hairline. To outline the hair area, add another line above the head line, going down and around the sides of the head.**

   This is how you cut into the face area and add hair to the outside of the original sketched oval. Figure 8-1b shows what this looks like with chin-length hair.

   Be careful where you start your hairline. Allow some distance between the top of the head and the start of the hairline; otherwise, you'll have a fashion figure with scanty hair.

   To show the outline for an updo, draw the hairline curve to meet the top of the ears and round out the bottom of the hair a little blow the ears, as in Figure 8-1c. The curve tapers and narrows as it approaches the ear. It should meet at the top of the ear and shouldn't ever go over the ear.

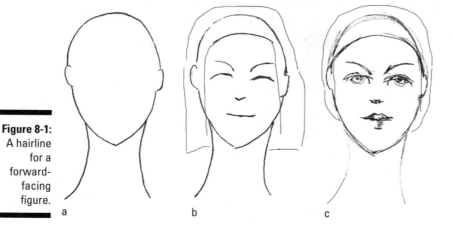

a   b   c

If your fashion figure is in profile, follow the preceding steps but continue the curve of the hairline to the top of the ear and then behind the ear on the neck. Fill in the hair at the side and back of the head and behind t the ear, as in Figure 8-2.

You see more of the back of a fashion figure's head when looking at a profile, which means you have to include more hair in your fashion figure profiles.

Figure 8-2:
A profile
view of a
hairline.

Delivering a good parting line

A part is a line that determines the hair shape and direction in which the hair falls. Every hairstyle starts with a part (or lack thereof); you can't begin to draw a hairstyle until you establish whether your model will have a side part, a middle part, or no part at all. Part placements, like hairstyles, convey differ-ent looks that may be more appropriate for a particular fashion style.

You can part hair in tons of different ways (some of which are pretty extreme), or you can avoid parts completely. If you stick with the following three parting styles that are commonly used in fashion illustration, your figures will always look stylish:

- ✔ **Hair pulled back into a topknot with no part:** Even though you don't use a part with this option (see Figure 8-3a), it's a classic model hairstyle. This is a great casual look that keeps hair off the shoulders and shows off clothes beautifully.

  A fashion figure's topknot can be deliberately styled to have stray wisps of hair escaping the updo for a modern "I just threw this together" look.

- ✔ **Hair parted down the center:** A center part, as in Figure 8-3b, works for long or short hair.

- ✔ **Hair parted to one side:** A side part (see Figure 8-3c) is sexy yet sophisticated. It works for long or short hair.

Parting hair for men is the same as parting hair for women. You can go with a center part, a part off to the side, or no part (as in brushed forward or backward).

To draw a part, first draw a fashion figure's head, adding a hairline across the forehead (see the preceding section for details). Then follow these guidelines:

- ✔ **For a center part:** Draw a center line that goes from the middle of the top of the head down to the curve of the hairline.

- ✔ **For a side part:** Draw a line that's slightly off center that goes from the middle of the head down to the curve of the hairline.

Refer to Figures 8-3b and 8-3c to see how a center part and a side part turn out in a final drawing.

After you've chosen which part to use (or to skip one altogether), you're ready to think about your model's crowning glory: the actual hair. In the next section, we tell you how to draw straight and curly hair. Later in this chapter, we give you all sorts of ideas that allow you to combine hairlines and hair types to create knockout hairstyles for women, men, and kids.

Figure 8-3:
To part or
not to part.

a   b   c

Curly, Straight, and Shiny, Oh My! Drawing Different Types of Hair

Even though hair isn't the main focus of a fashion illustration, it adds to the overall look and can portray a certain style. However, you don't have to follow any specific hair rules. If you prefer wild-looking hair on your prim and proper fashion model, go for it! Our only suggestion is to break the rules only after you have your fashion drawing foundation in check.

Hairstyles shouldn't distract from the fashion elements (clothes), but your model's hair also shouldn't be boring. Drawing great hair adds to the fashion mood, especially for an editorial look. The sections that follow show you how to create curly and straight hair on your models and how to add shine to your models' hairstyles.

Creating curls

Curly hair looks lively in fashion drawings! Wheather it's for men or women, letting the curls do their own thing creates a fun and playful look. Curls can go anywhere from the red carpet to a college dorm to the basketball court. You have two options for drawing your fashion figures curly hair. You can go with wild-looking tight curls or loose curls with lots of waves.

For a more wild-looking crop of tight curls, follow these steps:

1. **Draw a head, complete with the basic facial features mapped out and the central part of the hairline started. (See Figure 8-4a.)**

   Refer to Chapter 7 for the how-to on drawing heads and mapping out facial features. And check out the earlier section "Keeping things natural with a curving hairline" to determine your hairline.

2. **Using the side of your pencil, start by drawing several loose zigzag lines, beginning at the center of your figure's head and working downward, as in Figure 8-4b.**

   Make sure to sketch in some hair next to the neck to represent the hair at the back of the head. For the best type of zigzag line, use both the side as well as the point of your pencil to show texture.

3. **If you want more dimension and volume, simply add more zigzag lines and use a range of dark and light lines. Add a curl coming down from the part to soften the look, as in Figure 8-4c.**

   Don't make the zigzag lines even, or your hair will appear lifeless. Vary the lengths of the zigzags, and don't be afraid to overlap your lines. End the hair between the chin and the shoulder line.

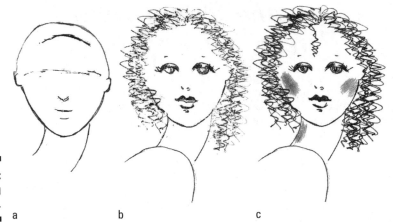

Figure 8-4:
Drawing
tight curls.

a   b   c

For a loose, wavy curls, follow these steps:

1. **Draw an oval with a face grid in three-quarter view and add a curve to the back of the oval to represent the back of the head, as in Figure 8-5a.**

   Refer to Chapter 7 for the how-to on drawing heads and mapping out facial features.

2. **Using a thin squiggly line, map out an irregular shape that shows where you'd like the hair to lie. Keep it away from the original oval and head for volume. Create a side part that starts on the forehead and goes to the top of the sketched circle. (See Figure 8-5b.)**

   This type of hair can be huge! Feel free to take up space outside the head while also cutting into the original oval shape. To create a sense of movement, don't connect all the squiggly lines.

3. **Erase the lines from the face and back of the head. For texture, add a few dots with the squiggly lines to outline of the hair. Add a few short lines by the side part on the head, as in Figure 8-5c.**

4. **Finish the drawing with various types of wavy lines inside the hair outline. Add some tight curly lines and some loose wavy lines, including both short and long and thick and thin lines. (See Figure 8-5d.)**

Figure 8-5:
Letting wavy
hair hang
loose!

a   b   c   d

Achieving straight, voluminous hair

Long, straight hair looks sleek, which can be a plus for all types of designs, ranging from formal to casual for women and men. Make sure you master long, flowing straight hair.

Even the straightest hair doesn't lie flat. Toss in some long curved lines as well; these add body to your fashion figure's hair and make it appear more realistic.

To draw straight hair on your figure, follow these steps:

1. **Sketch a head, complete with the basic facial grid and the hairline mapped out, as in Figure 8-6a.**

   Refer to Chapter 7 for information on drawing heads and mapping out facial features. And see the earlier section "Keeping things natural with a curving hairline" to place your hairline.

2. **Start a side part at the top of the head above the model's left eye. Use a few long, slightly curved lines to wrap over the forehead to the other side of the head, as in Figure 8-6b. Draw a few slightly curved lines down the side of the face and over the top of the shoulder.**

   You can start erasing part of your original hair outline.

3. **Finish the look by adding a few shorter, darker lines by the ears and forehead, complementing the original lines, as in Figure 8-6c.**

   Keep the lines long and sparse. You can draw hair with a less-is-more attitude.

Figure 8-6: Include some curved lines in your straight hair for a more realistic look.

a　　　　　　　　b　　　　　　　　c

Twinkle, twinkle, big star: Making your fashionista's hair shine

Add shine to your fashion figure's hair when you want it to really gleam — which can be anytime you draw hair. After you've drawn a head with the basic facial features and hairline mapped out (see Figure 8-7a), you can create shine in two ways. Here's the lowdown on both:

- **Line technique:** For the line technique, simply draw lines and leave blank areas on the paper to create shine. Figure 8-7b shows what we mean.
- **Shading approach:** For the shading approach, use the side of your pencil as well as the eraser to vary the shading of the hair. Shade the hair vertically with a pencil and then drag your eraser in a horizontal line across it to create highlights, as in Figure 8-7c.

You can read more about creating shine in Chapter 3.

Figure 8-7: Making hair shiny.

a   b   c

Exploring Wonderful Hairstyles for Women

Gone are the days when women stuck with the same hairstyles for life (most of the styles quite conventional and usually similar to whatever style they wore in high school). The global reach of different cultures has widened the hair horizons for women — and for your fashion figures. Fashion is about change, so you can explore a variety of hairstyles.

To make the most of your female fashion figures, you need to be able to draw short hair, long hair, simple hair, fancy hair, and everything in between. No matter what hairstyle you choose when drawing your fashion figure, make sure it's the right accent for the mood you're aiming for. We show you some common styles in the following sections.

Short and sassy styles

Shorter hairstyles can convey a cutting-edge look if they're super short, or they can express more of a mom-around-town look if they resemble a classic bob. You have two options for short cuts: short and shorter. Both make strong fashion statements, but the bob works best for the sophisticated suburban look, and the super-short cutting-edge styles work better for the hipper crowd as well as for African-American women, who may wear curly hair cropped quite close to the head. We walk you through the process of creating both short hairstyles in this section.

First up is the more traditional short bob. Here are the steps:

1. **Draw a head with the basic facial features mapped out and a lightly sketched hair outline that goes around the back of the neck, sides of the face, and top of the head, as in Figure 8-8a.**

   Follow the shape of the top of the head and include some space next to both ears.

2. **To add bangs, draw a slight curve across the forehead starting at the top of one ear and ending at the top of the other ear, as in Figure 8-8b.**

3. **Fill in the hair by drawing lines of varying lengths, using both the point of the pencil and the side, as in Figure 8-8c.**

   For texture, replace the smooth line at the ends of the hair with jagged lines.

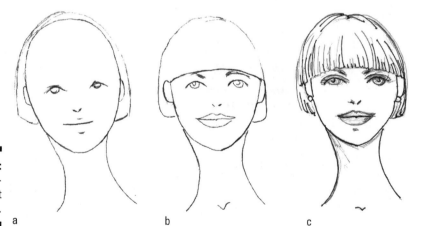

Figure 8-8:
The sophisticated but cute bob.

a   b   c

If you want the edgy look of the super-short hairstyle, follow these steps:

1. **Sketch a head with the basic facial features mapped out and a hairline started, as in Figure 8-9a.**

2. **Outline the overall shape of the hair, extending a little beyond the face, as in Figure 8-9b.**

3. **Draw a series of short vertical lines whose roots follow the curve of the hairline. Shorten the lines as you approach the ears. (See Figure 8-9c.)**

Vary the length of the lines, using both the pencil point (for dark lines) and the side of the pencil (for lighter lines) to create depth.

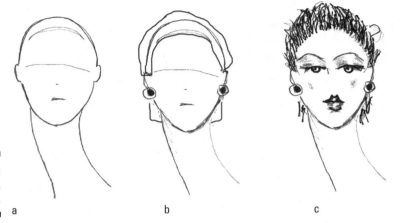

Figure 8-9:
The short, hip cut.

a   b   c

Shoulder-grazing tresses

Hair that hovers slightly above the shoulder on a model is a fashion designer's dream because you don't have to worry about tumbling locks distracting the viewer from the clothing. Opt for a neat, clean, shoulder-length style that looks hip yet tailored when you're drawing a classic and sophisticated look. Part the hair down the center or on the side.

Follow these steps to draw a classic shoulder-length cut:

1. **Draw an oval with a face grid. Add a neck, as in Figure 8-10a.**

2. **Add the hairline and outline of straight shoulder-length hair. Give the hair a side part, as in Figure 8-10b.**

   Follow the head shape for the hairline. Draw curving lines that wrap around the head to the level of the ears and then add straight lines ending just above the shoulder. Sketch in your facial features.

2. **Draw parallel lines that extend from either side of the part to indicate hair direction. For depth, add parallel lines behind the ears and at the ends of the hair, as in Figure 8-10c.**

   Include a few loose strands of hair for interest.

3. **Use the side of your pencil to shade in the hair. Leave a few light areas for shine, as in Figure 8-10d.**

Figure 8-10:
Mastering
the
shoulder-
length look.

a   b   c   d

Long and lustrous locks

Long hair is a gorgeous way to accent all clothes in fashion. Your drawing may show hair streaming over the outfit for a more editorial look, or it may show hair pushed off to the side to reveal a special collar. Drawing long hair isn't that different from drawing shoulder-length hair; you just have to extend your pencil lines to the middle of the back and arm or to the waist.

Try drawing long hair using the following steps:

1. **Sketch out a woman's head and neck in profile. Outline the shape of the hair, as in Figure 8-11a.**

   Draw a curved line that goes toward the ear above the forehead. Draw a curved line outside the head that mimics that head shape and goes down to the level of the ears. Continue the curve outward to just past the neck, and then curve inward for long hair — the overall shape of her hair resembles an *S*.

2. **Add curved lines of varying lengths and thickness to follow the shape of the hair, as in Figure 8-11b.**

3. **Add some thicker and darker lines for depth, as in Figure 8-11c.**

   More lines make for a darker shading effect.

4. **To create a head of long, full, and lustrous hair, continue adding more lines, including some darker lines and some lines that are a little wavy. (See Figure 8-11d.)**

Sweeping updos

What better way to show off a great gown, a long pair of earrings, and a lovely necklace than with a fabulous-looking updo? The good news is that you can draw an updo in much less time than it takes to have your own hair styled in an updo (and you won't have to use tons of bobby pins or hairspray, either).

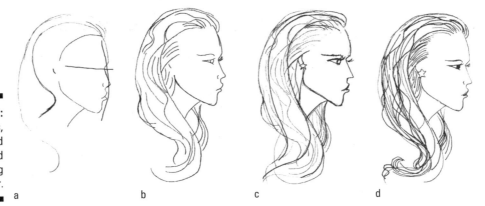

Figure 8-11:
Long lines,
waves, and
shading add
up to long
hair.

a   b   c   d

To create a formal updo, follow these steps:

1. **Draw a face in profile. Sketch in an updo hair shape using thick and thin curved lines that are longer in the middle of the 'do, as in Figure 8-12a.**

   By drawing a side view, you can show both the front and the back of the style.

2. **Fill in the hair using short lines near the hairline and longer lines of varying lengths that extend upward, as in Figure 8-12b.**

3. **Add shading for drama, as in Figure 8-12c.**

   Hair is usually darkest at the nape of the neck as well as where the hair folds up over itself when styled.

   Don't forget to add shine to your updo! Flip to the earlier section "Twinkle, twinkle, big star: Making your fashionista's hair shine" for details.

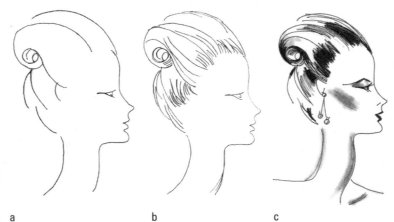

Figure 8-12:
The updo.

a   b   c

When drawing updos, think everyday ponytails, buns, French twists, half up and half down, and more — the varieties are endless! Take a look at any runway show or spreads in magazines such as *Vogue,* and you're bound to see some creative updos. You can add accessories and be as creative as you like when designing your fashion figures' hair.

Creating Dude 'Do's That Aren't Duds

Although men usually have fewer choices in hairstyling than women, you still have to master the main male hairstyles. The next sections show seven masculine 'do's, ranging from classic to trendy.

Keep in mind that men also have another hairy area to consider: the face. In a few of the sketches, we simply added some shading in around the lips or in the chin for a five o'clock shadow look. If you want to add something as dramatic as a beard, follow the steps for short hair on the head, but add it to the chinline rather than the hairline.

Sporting the classic look of short hair

There's no doubt about it: Short hair is still a classic style for men in suits, particularly in the corporate world. Short hair is a perfect complement to more traditional-looking fashions.

Here's how to give your male fashion figures a head of short hair:

1. **Sketch a square-jawed head shape for a guy, complete with the basic facial features and a hairline mapped out, as in Figure 8-13a.**

   Refer to Chapter 7 for how-to instructions on drawing heads and mapping out facial features. You can read more about hairlines in the earlier section "Keeping things natural with a curving hairline."

2. **Using a series of short, straight lines and a few curved lines, map out a short style with the hair ending at the top of the ears. (See Figure 8-13b.)**

   Make sure the short lines follow the grain of the hair.

3. **Add shading for depth and shine, as in Figure 8-13c.**

   For info on adding shine to your man's 'do, check out the earlier section "Twinkle, twinkle, big star: Making your fashionista's hair shine."

Figure 8-13:
Short hair and business clothing go hand in hand.

a

b

c

The African-American man's hair

Ethnic hair can have lots of texture or curl. African-American men also frequently sport the plain bald look.

To draw an African-American man's hairdo from the front:

1. **Sketch a square-jawed face for a guy, complete with the basic facial grid, as in Figure 8-14a.**

   Refer to Chapter 7 for how-to instructions on drawing heads and mapping out facial features. You can read more about hairlines in the earlier section "Keeping things natural with a curving hairline."

2. **Add in facial features and some shading around the lips for a manly five o'clock shadow. Then complete your hair look.**

   • **The bald look:** Square off the top of the head slightly for a bald look, as in Figure 8-14b. Add a few lines for the skin of the forehead to add dimension to the look.

   • **Short hair:** To add short hair, map out a hairline that starts by the ears and curves around the forhead. Make sure the forehead of the hairline has a *U* shape, as in Figure 8-14c. Add some shading with the side of your pencil to add color and texture, as in Figure 8-14d.

   • **The Afro:** Using a thin, squiggly line, map out a helmet-like shape around the face covering the ears and some of the forehead. You can decide the size of the Afro by how far out you want the outer perimeter lines of the hair to extend. Finish the look by adding short and long thin squiggly lines throughout the inside of the Afro. (See Figure 8-14e.)

Figure 8-14:
The bald,
the short,
and the fro.

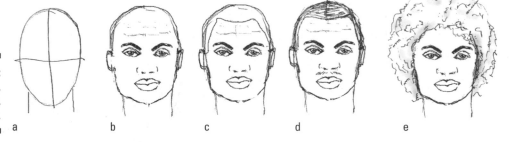

a   b   c   d   e

Drawing an African-American man from the side gives you a better view of fun hairdos such as the Afro or cornrows. Of course, Afros can also be seen from the front, but braids are difficult from that view, and who wouldn't want to show off beautiful cornrows!

To draw an African-American man sporting some great styles from the side:

1. **Sketch a long, narrow oval with a curve connected to it for the back of the head. Add in a facial grid, as in Figure 8-15a.**

2. **Add in facial features in profile, including a square jawline and an ear above the jaw lined up with the eyes. Then add your hairstyle:**

   • **The bald look:** Round out the back of the head for a smooth bald look. Add in some shading with the side of your pencil to lightly show a barely-there hairline from the back of the neck, around the ear, and up and around the forehead. (See Figure 8-15b.) The trick is to keep the hairline very light!

   • **The Afro:** Use a thin squiggly line and map out a a curve around the back of the head adding as much room as you want the Afro to fill. Continue the line from the neck up the side of the face covering the ears and resting on the forehead. Add some thin, long and short squiggly lines for texture. (See Figure 8-15c.)

   • **Cornrows:** Draw a pair of thin, sqiggly lines that follow the shape of the ear. Wrap the pair of lines around the ear. Continue making rows until the last set of lines is the profile of the head, as in Figure 8-15d. Finish the look by drawing texture on the pairs of lines for braids, as in Figure 8-15e. See Figure 8-15f for the steps for creating braids: Start with the pair of squiggly lines, draw *x*'s over the pair of lines, and finish with light shading on the outside of the squiggly lines.

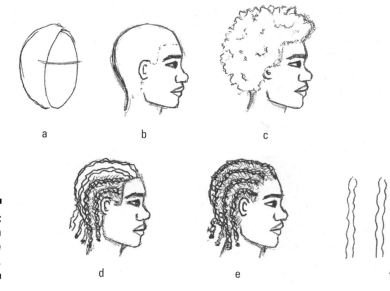

Figure 8-15: Styling from the side view.

a   b   c

d   e   f

Taking the free-spirit approach with longer locks

Longer hair on a man is a fashion statement that screams liberation and free spirit. Most men with long hair are trying to make statements about themselves, and "buttoned-down office guy" isn't the statement they're reaching for. A long hairstyle goes particularly well with fashions designed for surfer dudes; students; outdoorsy granola-eating, tree hugging hikers; and band members. Some have sleek, straight hair, and others sport a wavy or curly top.

If you're comfortable drawing long hair on female fashion figures, you're in luck: The only difference between long hair on men and women in fashion is the shape of the head. Men's heads tend to be larger with more of a square shape.

Here are some specifics to help you achieve the right long-haired look on your male fashion figures:

1. **Draw a square-jawed head for a more masculine look, and then map out the basic facial features. (See Figure 8-16a.)**

   Check out Chapter 7 for guidance on drawing facial features and heads.

2. **Sketch in a side part and an outline of where you would like the hair to fall. (See Figure 8-16b.)**

   Let one side of hair fall across the forehead and cover the eye

3. **For a shaggy look, add short and long lines in various shades to the ends of the hair, the parted area, in the front across the eye, and in the back toward the top of the head. Create dimension by leaving a little shadow at the top of the hair and along the sides, and leave white space to provide shine, as in Figure 8-16c.**

   End the hair below the chin on one side, and make the hair on the other side chin length.

Figure 8-16: Long hair is a match for casual, free-spirited clothing.

a   b   c

The smooth operator: Smoothing back your man's mane

Hair that has been smoothed back with gel or some other product has a sophisticated look, which makes it great for white or seersucker suits (think piano bars, summer lawn parties, and the classic movies of the '30s and '40s). Use a profile view to show off the slick and gracious style. From the front view, slicked-back hair sometimes gives your guy a bald look — not every hairstyle works well with every view.

To create a mysterious male look (without having to buy gel or pomade), follow these steps:

1. **Sketch a male profile with a hairline to show the full benefits of smoothed-backed hair. (See Figure 8-17a.)**

   Refer to Chapter 7 for details on drawing facial features and heads. You can read more about hairlines in the earlier section "Keeping things natural with a curving hairline."

2. **For the hair, follow the shape of the head; curve all your lines away from the forehead or toward the nape of the neck, as in Figure 8-17b.**

3. **Taper the hair at the back and the side of the head for an elegant, more-controlled look. Add some shading and leave some white places for shine, as in Figure 8-17c.**

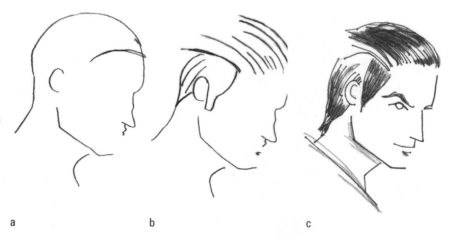

Figure 8-17: The smoothed back, sophisticated look.

a   b   c

Be careful not to make smoothed-back hair look too shiny and oily; otherwise, it looks too stiff and '50s-like.

Adding a spiked and trendy coif

Spiky, trendy hair is the typical look for a *metrosexual* male — a man who's really into creating a hip image for himself. This hairstyle pairs well with urban and club attire as well as anything that's super trendy.

When you give a male fashion figure metrosexual hair, make sure his face looks relatively young. This trendy style is typically found among guys in their 20s to 30s.

Here's a rundown of how to create this hairstyle on your male fashion figures:

1. **Draw a man's head in a three-quarter view with chiseled facial features mapped out. Place a hairline above his eyes, as in Figure 8-18a.**

   The distance from his eyes to his hairline should be about the same as the distance between his eyes and his mouth. Flip to Chapter 7 for information on drawing facial features and heads.

2. **Lightly sketch in the hair shape, as in Figure 8-18b.**

3. **Use many clusters of short, vertical, straight lines to cover the head for style. Use shading for depth toward the hairline and the ears, and leave some white space. (See Figure 8-18c.)**

   Not every strand of hair has to be drawn, and white space doesn't always indicate shine. Hair can be very stylized with white spaces that give the hair dimension and movement.

Figure 8-18:
Stick with trendy attire when you give a fashion figure a spiky hairstyle.

a   b   c

Being young, hip, and emo

Some guys like to look sensitive, brooding, and emotional, and their hair reflects their moods. For these guys, long, slightly disheveled hair is the way to go; however, they achieve their messy look in a deliberate way. Their hair often flows across one eye in a dashing fashion.

Try out these steps when you mean for your male model to convey a moody attitude:

1. **Draw a guy's head, complete with basic facial features mapped out with the hairline starting just above the eyebrows. Add a few lines under the ears to map out the length. (See Figure 8-19a.)**

   Chapter 7 provides information on drawing facial features and heads.

2. **Sketch the hair shape lightly and close to the head shape, stopping it just above the shoulders, as in Figure 8-19b. Draw some hair tucked behind the ear on one side.**

3. **Add some hair going across one eye. For texture, draw a few lines near the center part, below the ear, and by the shoulders. Add shading in the hair around the ear and toward the back of the head for dimension. (See Figure 8-19c.)**

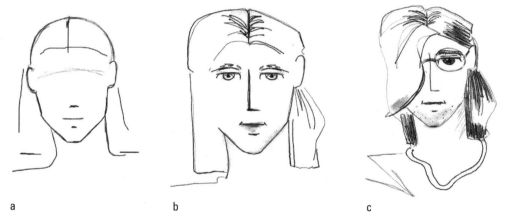

Figure 8-19:
A moody young man.

a   b   c

Keeping It Simple for Kids' Hairstyles

You rarely see a kid with a fantastic 'do. After all, their main agenda is playing, and a parent's goal is keeping kids' hair easy to care for and style. So when you draw fashions for children, make sure your figures have simple hairstyles. We introduce you to the two main kiddie hairstyles in the sections that follow.

Sticking with the short and sweet look

A short cut is every parent's dream, and it helps showcase your children's fashion designs. A short cut on a girl tends not to go much past the ears; a short cut on a boy usually crops in pretty close to the head.

Nobody's hair lays like a helmet around the face. Add a few stray hairs on top of the head for a cute effect.

Here's how to draw a girl's short cut:

1. **Draw a circle for a kid's head, as in Figure 8-20a.**

   Most children's faces run on the round side, so a circle with little definition works best.

2. **Sketch a curved line a little more than halfway up the circle across the forehead for bangs, as in Figure 8-20b.**

3. **Draw the hair visible behind the ears, ending just below the ears. Also add lines for the part. (See Figure 8-20c.)**

   Make the ends slightly uneven so they resemble hair and not a helmet. Keep in mind that hair with bangs doesn't have a true part, so draw a few lines downward and curving at the crown of the head to indicate that the bangs fall from that point.

4. **Darken the lines at the crown using a pencil point, and add dimension and value by using your pencil to shade. Add shine by leaving some white space. (See Figure 8-20d.)**

   You can read about adding shine in "Twinkle, twinkle, big star: Making your fashionista's hair shine."

Figure 8-20: Making cute girl hair.

 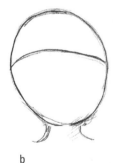  

a   b   c   d

Here's how to draw a boy's short cut:

1. **Draw a circle for a boy's head, as in Figure 8-20a. Add a face grid and facial features. Draw a the hairline curving up from the ears and peeking over the nose. (See Figure 8-21a.)**

2. **Add jagged lines and blank spaces across the front of the hairline and along the outer perimeter of the hair, especially on the sides. Add a few broken pointy lines on the inside of the hair, as in Figure 8-21b.**

Holding back hair in ponytails, pigtails, and braids

Ponytails, pigtails, and braids are great for keeping hair out of a child's eyes, and they also throw in a dash of fun that works for fashion designs. All these hairstyles belong to the same family. The hair is tied back differently in each style, but they all work with any little girl's outfit.

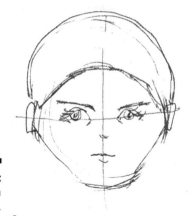

Figure 8-21:
Diggin' a
boy's style.

a

b

Always use a center part for pigtails and braids. You can read more about parts in the earlier section "Delivering a good parting line."

To add a ponytail to your child's fashion figure, follow these steps:

1. **Draw a child's head and add a hairline.**

   Keep the hairline slightly higher than an adult's hairline; children tend to have larger foreheads and heads in proportion to their bodies. Most children's heads run on the round side, so a circle with little definition works best.

2. **Curve the hairline on her forehead to her ears. Draw a line above her head — the distance between this line and her eyes should be almost the same as the same distance from her eyes to her chin. Use parallel lines to show that the hair is pulled up from the sides to form a side ponytail toward the top of the head. (See Figure 8-22a.)**

   After you've tied or clipped the hair up and back, hair flows from the tie or clip in an uncontrolled way, as in Figure 8-22b.

3. **Add shading around the hairline of her forehead and the ponytail holder. Darken a bunch of lines around the ponytail holder and the ends to add dimension to her hair.**

For downward pigtails, try out these steps:

1. **Draw a child's head.**

   Most children's heads are rounded, so a circle with little definition works best. Draw the head from the front to show the pigtail action.

2. **Start with a center part, bring the hair down over the ears, and secure both sides with a tie or clip. (See Figure 8-22c.)**

3. **From the bottom edge of the tie or clip, draw a series of parallel curves for hair that reaches above the shoulders. Add shading and darker lines around the center part and where the hair bunches up around the tie or clip, as in Figure 8-22d.**

Figure 8-22:
Keep kiddie
hair back
with flair.

Here's how to draw tiny braids:

1. **Draw a child's head. Sketch a series of zigzag lines and loops and curves for a curly look, as in Figure 8-22e.**

   Most children's heads are rounded, so a circle with little definition works best. Draw the head from the front with a center part so the braids show in all their glory.

2. **Add dark and light lines with loose and tight loops. Add a few braids by using two to three lines of tight loops on top of each other, moving together away from the head. Draw a bead at the bottom of each braid, as in Figure 8-22f.**

After you master these pulled-back looks, you can adapt them in so many ways. You can place the pigtails higher on the head rather than closer to the chin, or you can pull braids up into a ponytail. Kids can have fun hairstyles — experiment!

Part III

Dressing Your Fashion Figure

The 5th Wave   By Rich Tennant

"I'll just wait for the knock-off."

In this part . . .

Time to get dressed! In this part, you try your hand at drawing everything from pants and shirts to ball gowns. Then add outerwear for every season. As in real life, you finish with the shoes, the hats, and, of course, the bling!

Chapter 9

Slipping into Shirts and Sweaters

....

....

Sooner or later, fashion figures need to cover up. A shirt is part of most people's everyday wardrobe — you rarely draw a fashion illustration without one! Styling for shirts, blouses, tees, sweaters, and other tops may change each season, but the basic structure stays the same. In this chapter, we reach for the top and show you how to create the perfect look from the waist up. (If you need a review on drawing torsos, flip to Chapter 5.)

When you want to draw tops for boys or girls, we recommend you follow the instructions we give for a guy's piece of clothing and scale it down to kid size. Women's pieces generally have more shape to them to show off a woman's curves, something that's not necessary or appropriate for youngsters.

Topping It Off: Basic Shirts for Everybody

Blouses, sweaters, and T-shirts come in so many fantastic styles that having to choose one is like being in a candy store — where do you start? As always, you start with the basic shapes and add the details that top off any look (check Chapter 2 if you need a refresher on basic drawing techniques).

In the following sections, we show you how to draw a basic shirt for anyone of any age. Then we show you some details.

Drawing the basic shirt

Whether dressed to the nines for formal events, relaxing around the house on the weekend, or playing in the park, men, women, and children all wear shirts. From runways to rodeos, all shirts have certain elements in common. For example, every shirt has some type of opening for the head, body, and arms. However, the fit and the finish can vary as much as you'd like. Master the basic shirt and then have fun adding the finer details.

To begin with a simple shirt with set-in sleeves, the most common type of sleeve, follow these steps:

1. **Lightly sketch a torso from the front view.**

   We use a woman's torso for this example.

2. **To create the neckline, draw a small curve going from one side of the neck to the other, labeled as A and B in Figure 9-1a.**

   Use a darker pencil to draw the shirt over the figure's body. Curve the neckline around the sides of her neck to show how the shirt disappears over her shoulders.

3. **Draw straight lines that come down from her underarms and end a little below belly button level, as in Figure 9-1b.**

   This creates a loose-fitting shirt; if you'd like your shirt tighter, draw the lines closer to the body and hug the curves.

4. **Connect the side seams at the bottom with a slightly curved line for the hem. (See Figure 9-1c.)**

   Don't draw the line straight across, or your shirt will look stiff and lifeless. By adding a slight curve at the sides of the hem, you show how the shirt falls around the hips.

5. **Starting at the neckline, trace over your model's shoulders and go down the arm, stopping where you'd like to end the sleeve, as in Figure 9-1d.**

   Draw your sleeve line slightly over the actual shoulder and keep the look a little loose, not stiff.

6. **Draw the part of the sleeve on the underside of the arm, starting at the top of the shirt's sides. End the line slightly farther down the arm than the line for the upper sleeve, as in Figure 9-1d.**

   Allow the under-the-arm part of the sleeve to fall slightly away from the arm.

7. **Connect the upper and lower sleeve lines with a line that goes across the arm and wraps behind it at the ends, as in Figure 9-1e.**

8. **Finish with an armhole seam, a slightly curved line that goes from the top of the shoulder to the line that begins at the underarm. (See Figure 9-1f.)**

This simple shirt also works for guys and kids. You can modify the shape of the sides to create a looser fit for men and children.

Adding shirt details

In fashion drawing, you're either copying something that's already been designed — drawing something you see on the street or runway — or designing a garment as you draw. Either way, you'll discover endless style variations, more than we could ever show in this book. We show you what you need to know most, but remember that there are many more shirt types for you to copy or create! The difference is in the details.

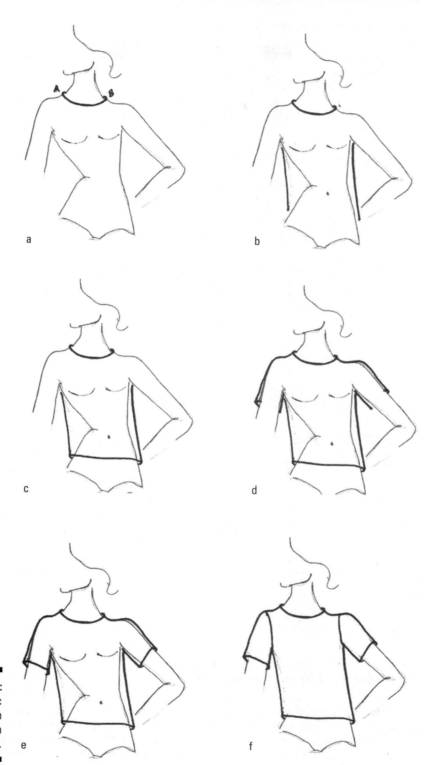

Trying out topstitching

Topstitching, thread stitched on the fabric that's visible from the outside of the garment, adds much of the detail in shirts. Topstitching on shirts is mostly decorative; when you draw pants, you may also use topstitching, but it can be decorative or functional (to attach pockets, for example; Chapter 10 has details on pants and topstitching). On shirts, you commonly see topstitching around the neckline, the hems of the sleeves, and the bottom hem of the shirt.

Draw a basic shirt and then add the topstitching in the following manner:

1. **Draw in two rows of small dashed lines around the hem of each sleeve, following the curve of the hem. (See Figure 9-2a.)**

   Shirts almost always have two rows of topstitching here because of the type of stitch used to finish the sleeve.

2. **Move to the bottom hem of the shirt and draw a row of dashed lines following the curve of the hem, as in Figure 9-2a.**

3. **Finish the shirt by drawing a row of dashed lines around the neckline, following the curve of the neck, as in Figure 9-2b.**

Figure 9-2:
Adding the
topstitching.

a   b

Knit and woven fabrics: Stretching your knowledge of shirt construction

Different fabrics lend themselves to different styles of shirts. One way you can distinguish a dressy shirt from a knock-around tee is by the fabric each shirt is made of — the fabric choice leads to different methods of construction. We know you may not be actually sewing your designs, but someone *will* be. And then a model will have to put on your garment, so keep the construction aspects in mind.

Here are some examples of how fabric can affect construction:

- **A shirt made of knit fabric stretches.** *Knits* are made by looping a continuous strand of thread or yarn back on itself. If a shirt stretches, you just pull it over your head. There's no need to put buttons and a *front placket* (the type of opening used for shirts that open at the center front) on a stretchy shirt . . . although a knit shirt may have them! You need fewer lines to draw knits, and they may have a less fitted look.

- **Shirts made from woven fabrics usually don't stretch.** *Woven fabrics* are made by interlacing two sets of thread at right angles. If the fabric doesn't stretch, then you can't pull it over your head, so you need to give your model another way in and out of it, such as a zipper or buttons. The fact that you can just draw it on her without her lifting a finger is immaterial! Garments made of woven fabrics also have seams to improve the fit.

  Most shirts made from woven fabric open in the front, because an opening on the back of the shirt would be hard for your model to put on — not that that stops some fashion designers from creating such designs. Shirts made from woven fabrics can have a variety of collars or just simple necklines.

You don't use a specific type of drawing line for knits and another for woven materials — a trained designer's eye can pick out clues about the fabric from the seam placement and fit.

In a drawing, showing exactly what type of fabric your model is wearing isn't always easy. You can give other hints about the type of fabric through details such as texture and draping (how the fabric hangs on the body) — see Chapter 14 for more information.

Designing shirts for different looks

How a shirt is cut and put together can completely change the look. For example, a shirt with an opening down the front is generally dressier than a pullover shirt. And the cut of the armholes, sleeves, and cuffs can make a shirt look casual or dressy. A puffy, flowing sleeve has a dressier look than the straight sleeve of the tee or a sleeve with the ribbed type of cuff you normally see on sweatshirts. But make the shirt out of silk and put a long row of buttons on the cuff, and you've created a dressy shirt. The varieties are endless!

You can also use the following elements to put a certain stamp on a shirt:

- **Yokes:** *Yokes,* which you often see in Western style shirts, are seams that create fit and style in the chest area by the shoulders, as in Figure 9-3a. Yokes can appear on the front or the back of a shirt or blouse, and they're suitable for women's or men's shirts.

- **Gathering:** *Gathering* is any part where fabric is bunched together. Sometime it's on necklines, sleeves, or hems, as in Figure 9-3b. You most often find this detail on women's tops.

- **Lacing:** Any type of shirt can have lacing. It can be functional, such as to make the top super tight, or it can just be for looking cool. Figure 9-3c shows the front of a lace-up corset. We suppose you can put lacing on a man's shirt and go for the Renaissance look, but lacing is generally found on women's clothing.

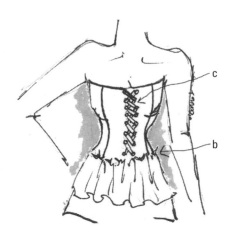

Figure 9-3:
Gathering
up some
details.

Putting Together the Tee

Ah, the T-shirt! The most common piece of clothing in almost everyone's closet or dresser drawers (or on the bedroom floor). Throughout the years, the T-shirt has made its way from the gym teacher's wardrobe to the high-fashion runway and back again! The tee is easy to draw, and it lends itself to all kinds of fun prints. Guys, women, and kids practically live in them.

In the following sections, we show you how to turn the basic shirt into a T-shirt for either women or men. Then we show you how to modify the tried-and-true tee to create similar tops.

Fitting the girl to a tee

When drawing a girl in a T-shirt, following the curves of the body is important. A woman's tee usually has at least a slight curve to hug a woman's hourglass shape to indicate the shirt is designed for the female sex.

Here are the steps for drawing the basic girl tee:

1. **Start with Steps 1–8 in "Drawing the basic shirt."**

   T-shirts can be tight or loose on the body. To make the shirt tight, follow the woman's torso shape closely. To make it loose, keep the lines farther away from her body.

2. **Draw the collar by adding a curved line slightly below the curved neckline, as in Figure 9-4a.**

3. **Draw short parallel lines to add ribbing to the collar, as in Figure 9-4b.**

   These lines connect the two curved lines of the collar.

4. **Finish by adding two rows of topstitching lines to the sleeve hem and to the bottom hem, as in Figure 9-4c.**

Figure 9-4: Tighten up a tee for women.

a   b   c

To modify a woman's T-shirt, try changing the neckline:

✔ **Draw a *V*-neck.** Instead of drawing a curved line at the neck, draw a *V* with the top of the *V* starting on either side of the neck. The lines should meet at a point in the top third of the woman's chest under her chin.

✔ **Go daring with a deep scoop neck.** Draw a curved line more in the shape of a *U* on the chest. This neckline allows you to show some skin or accessorize with a fun necklace.

Making casual tees for guys of every size

A T-shirt on a guy is a statement about casual living — and sometimes about his favorite sports team or band. These easy-to-wear, often-rumpled items of clothing are often picked off the floor in the morning and pulled on.

Here are the main differences between girls' and guys' tees (see Figure 9-5 for a guys' tee):

✔ A guys' T-shirt usually hangs straighter because guys don't have curves.

✔ Guys' tees are less likely to have fancy details. Sports logos are more like it.

✔ A guy's neckline is usually a simple curved neckline or shallow *V* shape rather than a deep scoop.

✔ Although some guys go for a tighter fit, most guys, especially kids, wear their tees loose.

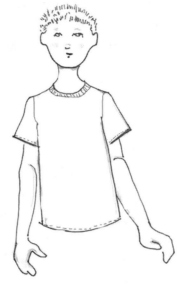

Figure 9-5:
Boys love
T-shirts,
too!

Trying tank top variations

Tank tops are basically T-shirts without sleeves. The shirt sits on the shoulders in a variety of ways. Men may wear tank tops around the house and under dress shirts, but women aren't shy about running around in tank tops in public.

Tanks are easy to draw, because they're nothing more than the basic shirt without the sleeves. You can vary the tank top details in the same way as tees, with different necklines and detailing:

- ✔ **Spaghetti straps (Figure 9-6a):** Thin straps connect the front and back of the tank over the shoulders. Camisoles are a variation of this type of tank top.

- ✔ **A-shirt (Figure 9-6b):** These shirts are form-fitting and have wider straps that go over the shoulders. They're often lightly ribbed.

- ✔ **Halter top (Figure 9-6c):** The straps on these tanks meet behind the neck. They may tie, cross, or connect at the back of the top, revealing your fashion figure's back.

- ✔ **Strapless (Figure 9-6d):** These tops are often held in place by strong ribbing that runs the length of the bodice. Their staying-up power may be reinforced with an elastic band that rings the inside top edge and makes the top almost stick to the wearer's skin. There's also a whole world of boning and underlining, but that's a whole book on its own!

Tanks usually have a tighter fit than T-shirts.

Figure 9-6:
Tank tops
come in
many cuts.

Taking sports jerseys beyond the stadium

Boys, girls, and adults everywhere wear sports jerseys. They can look just like a simple tee with a team name and number splashed across the front and the back (cheesy polyester is the norm, so give your fabric a bit of shine). You can also create terrific rugby shirts, which feature bold stripes and great cotton quality.

Here's how to complete the sports jersey look:

1. **Draw the top half of a boy and start the jersey with a *V* neckline, as in Figure 9-7a.**

2. **Draw a horizontal line across the chest, hitting the bottom of the *V*. Then draw in the side seams by following the body and draw the hem across the bottom of the waist. (See Figure 9-7b.)**

3. **Draw sleeves that end at the elbow. Don't forget to draw armhole seams from the top of the shoulder to the underarm. (See Figure 9-7c.)**

4. **For a finished look, add a stripe above the hem of each sleeve and large numbers on the front, as in Figure 9-7d.**

Figure 9-7:
Sports jer-
seys are fun
for both kids
and adults.

Putting on a Polo

Polos are shirts made out of knit fabric, which means they stretch and are quite comfortable to wear. They're like T-shirts but dressier. The neckline on the polo has a collar and a placket with several buttons. Men, women, and kids all sport polos, often with a manufacturer's logo and sometimes with a pocket on one side. Because guys wear polos more often than women do, we tell you how to draw theirs first, and then we describe how to make the same shirt work for women.

Polo players for guys

Polo shirts, especially ones that feature the right logo, were once known for being part of the quintessential preppie look. Now men wear polo shirts for a casual-dress look anywhere. This look goes from high-end restaurants to the grocery store, from the office to a pre-game party. One of the few places you'll feel quite out of place in a polo? An extremely hip urban club.

Think of a polo as a good T-shirt with a collar. The cotton is also heavier and of a better quality.

Here's how to draw the classic polo look for a guy:

1. **Draw a top half of a guy, as in Figure 9-8a.**

2. **Map out a square shape for a polo shirt and draw in the side seams, following the sides of the body. (See Figure 9-8b.)**

   Add a couple of folds at the waist where the fabric rests on the hips.

3. **Draw the collar and neck hole by adding a triangle on each side of the neck with a *V* shape between them. Draw short sleeves and add the shoulder seams, as in Figure 9-8c.**

4. **Soften the collar triangles by curving the lines a bit to follow the shape of the shoulders and neck. Add two or three buttons at the neck on the right side of the *V* and finish with topstitching on the hem of the sleeves and bottom of the shirt. (See Figure 9-8d.)**

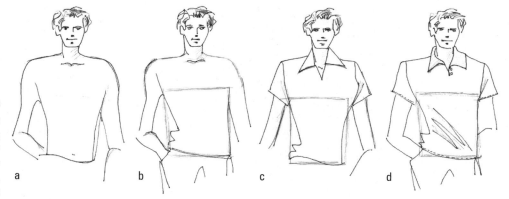

Figure 9-8: Polo shirts work for many occasions.

a   b   c   d

Women's polos

Women's polos can sport the same collar type as a man's polo but may also include a more feminine-looking collar and placket. The fit is also tighter on a women's polo.

Here's how to draw a women's polo shirt:

1. **In this three-quarter view, start with Steps 1–7 for drawing the basic shirt but don't draw the neckline.**

   You can find these steps in the earlier section "Drawing the Basic Shirt."

2. **Draw one side of the neck hole and placket, as in Figure 9-9a.**

   Draw a line coming from behind the neck and around to the front of the body, pivoting at the center front and going directly down a few inches, about halfway to the breast line.

3. **To start the collar, draw a short line from the neck to the curve of the shoulder, as in A in Figure 9-9b. Opposite line A, at the point where the neckline meets the center front line, draw a short diagonal line away from the neck.**

4. **Draw a slightly curved line that connects line A to the diagonal line you drew in Step 3. (See Line B in Figure 9-9b.)**

   This completes half of the collar.

5. **Turn the center front line into a rectangle and draw three buttons on it, as in Figure 9-9c.**

6. **Finish the other side of the collar the same way as the first, connecting the lines that wrap around the neck. (See Figure 9-9d.)**

7. **Finish the rest of the shirt with topstitching at the sleeve hem and bottom hem of the shirt. (See Figure 9-9e.)**

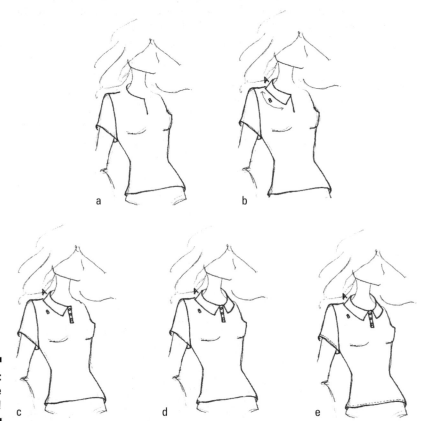

Figure 9-9:
Ladies love polos, too!

Dressing Up the Button-Down Shirt

The button-down shirt hangs in everyone's closet these days. For guys, it's standard dress in many offices, and it's a staple in nearly every woman's wardrobe. Little boys wear a button-down with a tie on dress-up occasions, and little girls may wear one under a dressy jumper or with a skirt. In the following sections, we show you how to draw female and male versions of this fashion must-have.

Drawing the classic Lady Blouse

We call the women's button-down a *Lady Blouse* because every woman, teen, and little girl has one in her closet. These shirts are for everything from interviews to school concerts or the first meeting with the boyfriend's parents. They're also the perfect accompaniment to a standard business suit.

Follow these directions to draw the Lady Blouse:

1. **Sketch a light drawing of a woman's top half, as in Figure 9-10a.**

2. **Draw a curve for the neckline, as in Figure 9-10b.**

3. **Add two small inverted triangles for the collar. Draw a slightly off-center line that goes down the front, as in Figure 9-10c.**

   Extend the curve and collar around the back of the neck to create a sense of depth. Put the line for the shirt's front opening a little to the right of center, because the buttons will go on the left side of the line in Step 6.

4. **For the armhole seams, draw slight curves from the underarms to the shoulders. For each side seam, draw a line that follows the side of her torso and finishes by her hip, as in Figure 9-10d.**

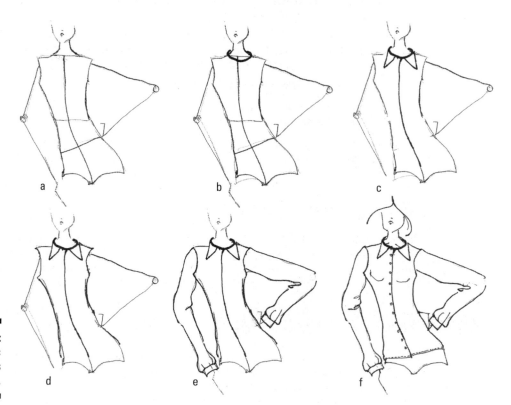

Figure 9-10: The classic blouse is hip.

5. Draw sleeves for each arm and add cuffs, as in Figure 9-10e.

6. Finish the shirt by adding buttons on the left side of the center front opening and topstitching at the hem, as in Figure 9-10f.

The dress shirt: Nailing the corporate look for guys

Collar styles may change a tad, but the guys' basic button-down shirt never changes. Wide, brightly colored stripes make this shirt more casual, whereas a crisp white shirt or subtle pinstripes embody corporate America. (For info on drawing stripes, see Chapter 14.) Dress it up with a blazer and tie (see Chapter 11) or go dressy casual by leaving the top button undone.

Here's how to draw a men's button-down shirt:

1. Draw the top half of a guy, as in Figure 9-11a.

2. Map in the curve of the neckline and a *V* shape, as in Figure 9-11b.

   You get a *V* shape because the top button is undone.

3. Place buttons down the center front and draw a line left of the buttons, as in Figure 9-11c.

4. Follow the body as you draw shoulder, armhole, and side seams. Draw a line that connects the points of the collar to the curved neckline, creating a triangle shape on each side. (See Figure 9-11d.)

5. Add sleeves and a bottom hem, as in Figure 9-11e.

6. Finish with cuffs, another seam line next to the buttons, and topstitching, as in Figure 9-11f.

   Include a pocket on the front of the shirt if you like. You can also add a top button to the left and a buttonhole on the right.

Going casual in flannel

The flannel shirt is back big-time. Boys love 'em, the more worn-in the better. What really makes this shirt casual-looking is the plaid, so brush up on your line techniques in Chapter 3 of this book. Follow the same steps as when drawing a man's dress shirt (as in Figure 9-11) and then add the pattern.

Don't even *think* about tucking a flannel shirt into a pair of pants. Let it all hang out!

Figure 9-11:
Dress shirts
personify
style.

Here's how to draw the plaid flannel shirt on a boy:

1. **Draw the top half of a young boy, as in Figure 9-12a.**

2. **Map out the shirt, beginning with the neck hole, and add two triangles for a collar. Draw loose fitting sleeves over the boy's arms, as in Figure 9-12b.**

   Even though flannel shirts are made of a casual fabric, they have the structure of a dress shirt, so remember to add the cuffs.

3. **Draw in two long rectangles for the front of the shirt, as in Figure 9-12c.**

   If your model is wearing his flannel shirt over a T-shirt (as ours is), you can leave a bit of space between the rectangles to make the flannel shirt appear open. If he has the shirt buttoned, draw the rectangles so they're touching at the center front line.

4. **Add buttons and use the side of your pencil to draw the plaid pattern, as in Figure 9-12d.**

   If the shirt is open, draw the buttons on the right side of the right rectangle. If the shirt is buttoned, draw the buttons to the right of the center front line.

Figure 9-12:
Boys love
flannel
shirts.

a

b

c

d

Many times, the plaid pattern on shirt pockets doesn't line up with the pattern on the main body of the shirt. Designers often have fun and turn the plaid on an angle for a twist! Check out Chapter 14 for more on drawing plaids and other patterns.

Stepping Out in Snappy Sweaters

Sweaters are great layering pieces that keep your model warm and fashionable all at once. Some sweaters open from the front, and others go on over the head. Sweaters are always made of some type of stretchy material, so you can draw them either pretty tight without a lot of seam lines or really loose and baggy but still without a lot of seam lines.

Common elements of sweaters include a ribbed neckline (similar to the T-shirt), ribbed cuffs, and a ribbed hemline. Although you may joke about the printed sweaters of the '80s, adding in lines for texture gives visual cues that your model is wearing a sweater.

Drawing a simple sweater

Men, women, and youngsters all pull on sweaters when the weather turns chilly. When drawing sweaters, you really just draw a long-sleeve version of the basic shirt and add a few details to show that your model is wearing a sweater and not a long-sleeve tee.

Here's how to draw a sweater:

1. **Start with Steps 1–7 for drawing the basic shirt. On Step 5, draw the sleeve to the end of the arm, as in Figure 9-13a.**

   See the earlier section "Drawing the basic shirt" for basic shirt info. You can draw a sweater as tight or loose as you'd like. Women's sweaters, like women's tees, most often follow the lines of a woman's body. Men's and children's sweaters should be less form-fitting.

2. **Add a cuff to the end of each sleeve by drawing two curved lines. Add ribbing to each cuff by connecting the curves with short straight lines, as in Figure 9-13b.**

3. **Add a ribbed neckline by drawing a curve parallel to the neckline and connecting the curved lines with short, straight lines, as in Figure 9-13c.**

   You can experiment with the shape of the neckline. We show you some variations in the next section.

4. **Add a ribbed hemline by drawing a curved line parallel to the shirt's bottom and connecting the lines with short, straight lines. (See Figure 9-13d.)**

5. **Throughout the sweater (except for the ribbed areas), finish with dots and short lines to indicate some texture from the yarn. (See Figure 9-13e.)**

Adding some style to the basic sweater

Fashion wouldn't be nearly as interesting if designers didn't add some pizzazz to the basic sweater. Details such as colors, textures, cuts, and embellishments catch the eye and help people express their personalities. Keep reading for some great ideas for jazzing up your sweaters.

Figure 9-13:
A woman's
sweater
follows her
curves.

Varying necklines

Sweaters come with a variety of necklines. Here's a sample of sweater necklines to draw on your fashion figure:

- **Scoop neck (Figure 9-14a):** This neckline is a bit wider and deeper than the neckline you draw for a basic shirt (the crew neck). Your curved line should drop onto the chest a bit and start and end more toward the outside of the shoulders.

- **V-neck (Figure 9-14b):** The *V*-neck is one of the easiest necklines to draw. Start outside of the neck and draw two diagonal lines that meet about a third of the way down on the chest. If you feel daring, go for a deeper *V*.

- **Turtleneck (Figure 9-14c):** Turtlenecks make long fashion necks look even longer. Draw a line from the neckline halfway up each side of the neck and just outside of the neck. Connect these two lines with a slightly curved line across the neck.

- **Cowl neck (Figure 9-14d):** This loose, drapey collar takes some practice. Wrap lines around the neck, starting from the shoulder of each side. The trick is to keep the lines different lengths and make sure they don't connect in the center.

- **Crew neck (Figure 9-14e):** This is the same neckline you use when drawing the basic shirt.

- **One shoulder only (Figure 9-14f):** Used on lighter sweaters, the one-shoulder neckline starts at the midpoint of one shoulder, scoops across the upper chest, and ends at the outer edge of the opposite shoulder. Sometimes designers add a spaghetti strap to the wider side of the neckline to help hold the sweater in place.

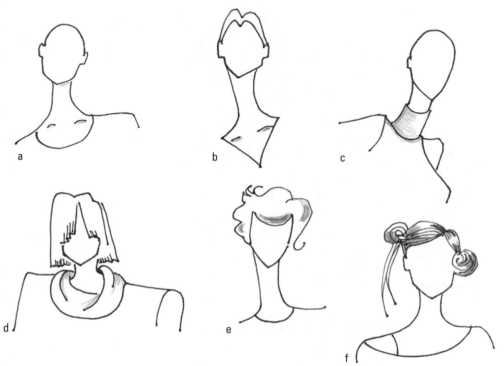

Figure 9-14: Sweater necklines galore.

Sweater trimmings: Incorporating the cute factor

The cut of a sweater may not change, but the cute trimmings for a youthful appeal do. Many of the details we describe here originally appeared on children's sweaters, but before long, designers were stealing the ideas for juniors' and women's sweaters as well. Change the look of your sweaters by trying some of the ideas in Figure 9-15; after all, reinventing what's been done before is what fashion is all about.

- Big buttons (Figure 9-15a)

- Flared sleeves (Figure 9-15b)

- Scalloped neckline and cuffs (Figure 9-15c)

- Cap sleeves (Figure 9-15d)

Figure 9-15:
Changing
the details
can com-
pletely
change the
look of a
sweater.

Creating cool cardigans

Today's cardigan comeback has expunged the earnest librarian look. You can embellish cardigans with playful-looking buttons, a cluster of sequins, and more. Drawing the cardigan is just like drawing a button-down shirt, but you can skip the pointed collar and the cuffs on the sleeves (see the earlier section "Dressing Up the Button-Down Shirt" for the how-to of sketching button-downs). Both men and women as well as kids may don a cardigan. Men's versions usually have a *V* neck, whereas women's cardigans tend to have a *V* neck or rounded neckline.

Try these variations in your cardigan:

✔ Sequins (Figure 9-16a)

✔ Spiffy looking buttons (Figure 9-16b)

✔ Short sleeves (Figure 9-16c)

✔ Long length (Figure 9-16d)

Figure 9-16:
Cardigans
with all the
trimmings.

Fashioning sweatshirts

Sweatshirts are a variation on a sweater. Sweats are made of different material from sweaters but the follow the same lines. You see *hoodies* — sweatshirts with an attached hood — everywhere and on everyone.

How do you distinguish a sweatshirt from a sweater in your drawings? Skip the texture lines that represent yarn and make the ribbing at the cuffs, neckline, and hem narrower. You can also add pockets or a logo, school name, or team name across the front.

Draw sweatshirts baggy for men and kids; women's sweatshirts often have some shape to them, but they fit loosely on the body.

Here's how to create the always-popular hoodie:

1. **Draw a boy down to his waistline and start the hoodie with a shallow**
   V **neck, as in Figure 9-17a.**

2. **Add the inside of the hood by drawing a curved line that starts at one side of the neckline and goes over the head to the other side. (See Figure 9-17b.)**

   Make sure to keep this line loose, away from the face.

3. **Draw the top of the hood by adding a line above the line you drew in Step 2. Start from the sides of the head, flare out slightly, and taper to a point at the center top. (See Figure 9-17c.)**

   Don't make the top of the hood too pointed.

4. **Draw the sleeves to the hand. Include cuffs and armhole seams that go from the top of the shoulder to the underarm, as in Figure 9-17d.**

   Don't forget to draw in deep folds at the elbows.

5. **Finish with a front pocket that has topstitching at the top and bottom. (See Figure 9-17e.)**

You can vary the hoodie by adding a logo, a front zipper, or strings attached to the hood.

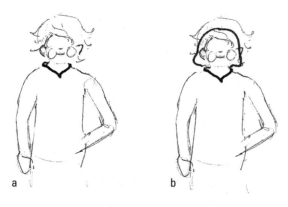

a   b

Figure 9-17: Everyone wears hoodies.

c   d   e

Chapter 10

Presenting Perfect Pants

- -

In This Chapter

▶ Drawing pants and getting the details down

▶ Putting pants on women

▶ Creating great pants for guys

▶ Drawing pants and overalls for kids

- -

*E*veryone wears the pants these days, in styles from sweats to business dress. Classic khakis and jeans remain popular for men, women, and kids. However, cuts and styles change every year, so stay current with trends. Details are key! These details include things like belt loops, zippers, and topstitching. In this chapter, we explore the wide (and sometimes wild!) world of pants.

Mastering Pants One Line at a Time

Pants are pretty simple: They start around the waist and follow the legs down to the vicinity of the feet . . . although in today's fashion, they can also start somewhere around the middle of the derrière and end anywhere from just below the knee to the ground! They can't be called *pants* if they don't have two legs, but the pant legs can hug the body or flow outward and can end above the ankle or drape the floor. The *pants* designation may also encompass shorts, which end, well, anywhere south of the derièrre!

Pants need detail to make them stand out. When illustrating pants, focus on the details such as pockets and topstitching as well as different leg lengths and widths. Think of shorts as pants that end around the knee — anything you can use to illustrate pants also works for shorts.

In the following sections, we show you how to draw a basic pair of pants (or shorts) and how to enhance them with eye-catching details.

Putting the basic shape in place

Conveying a pair of fashion pants takes about eight lines. To draw not-too-tight, not-too-loose pants, follow these steps:

1. **Draw the lower half of your figure using a front grounded pose, as in Figure 10-1a.**

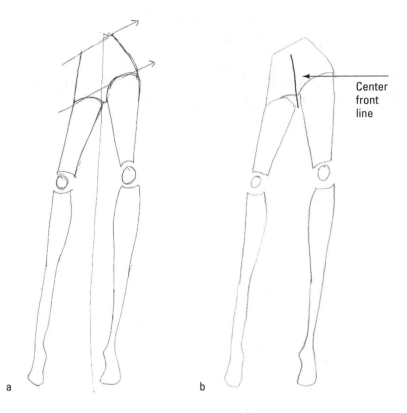

Center
front
line

Figure 10-1:
Pants start
with a fash-
ion pose.

a   b

Refer to Chapter 4 for info on how to draw a grounded pose. Use pencil
so you can erase the lines.

2. **Draw a straight line at the center front, as in Figure 10-1b.**

   If you're drawing a midline waist, start the center line below where the
   belly button would be and end it just past the crotch. If you're drawing
   low-rise or high-waisted pants, adjust the length of your center front line
   accordingly. Use pen for this step, because the center line will be part of
   your final drawing.

   Almost all pants have a center front line; it's a law of nature for sewing.
   It's rare for *bifurcated garments* (a fancy name for pants or shorts) not to
   have a center front seam. You're used to looking at the body straight on,
   but people also have a third dimension from the front to back that needs
   some sort of seam. Example garments that may not have a center front
   seam include pants with *really* stretchy material, such as the maternity
   pants in Figure 10-9a, and the *sailor pants,* which button on two sides, as
   in Figure 10-9b.

3. **Draw a slightly curved line around the waist, putting the waistline
   where it fits the pant style best (see Figure 10-2a).**

   In basic fashion pants, the waistline should fall a little below the bellybutton. The *true waistline* falls slightly above the bellybutton, but few
   people actually wear their pants there. For a high-waist look, go above
   the bellybutton. For low-rise pants, place the waistline as far below the
   natural waistline as you want to go.

4. **Add straight lines down the outside of the legs to the spot where you want the pants to end. (See Figure 10-2b.)**

   Decide how tight or loose fitting you'd like the pants to be. Tight pants follow the leg lines closely; loose pants follow gravity and fall away from the body to the floor.

5. **Draw the inseam lines (on the inside of the legs), starting from the bottom of the center front line and ending at the bottom of the pants. (See Figure 10-2c.)**

6. **Connect the inner and outer lines of the pant legs at the hem with a line just above each foot. (See Figure 10-2d.)**

   The shape of the hemline depends on the type of pants. For example, if the pant legs fall to the floor, they pile up around the foot. If they're tapered or tight, they may curve up and around the ankle.

7. **Draw your front fly (a *J* shape made out of topstitching) and other details such as pockets, belt loops, a waistband, and topstitching at the hem and across the pockets, depending on which type of pants you're drawing. (See Figure 10-3a.)**

   We give you the skinny on drawing these details in the following sections.

8. **Erase your pencil lines, and now you have pants! (See Figure 10-3b.)**

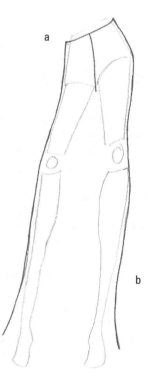
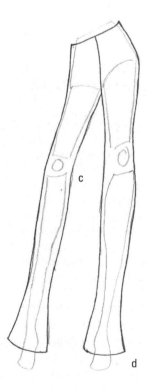

Figure 10-2:
Drawing basic pant legs.

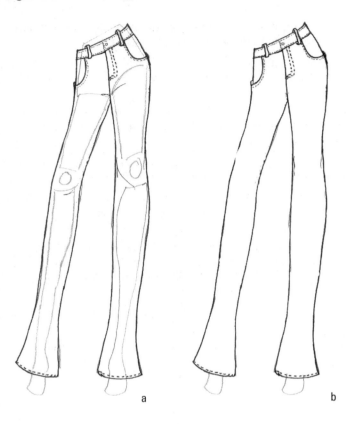

a   b

Working on the waistband and belt loops

Drawing the waistband and belt loops takes just a few simple steps. The complication factor comes from the variety of ways you can design the look. You can alter the number of belt loops, the location of the topstitching, the placement of the button, how many buttons you use — the options are endless!

To find inspiration for the details you can add to pants, pull out a couple of your own pairs of pants and study them on a flat surface for a few minutes. Notice the center front line and how the button is off to one side of it. The fly does not open at an angle, which is how so many people try to draw it!

Drawing a traditional waistband

Practice drawing a basic waistband that has two belt loops in the front this way:

1. **Start the waistband by drawing two curved horizontal lines parallel to each other, as in Figure 10-4a.**

   The belt loop lines go on top of the waistband, so draw these curved lines in pencil first. When you're finished with the drawing, you can go over it with a pen and erase the pencil lines.

2. **Connect the lines with short perpendicular lines on both sides. Draw the center front line, a straight line directly down the center that extends below the band. (See Figure 10-4b.)**

   The inseams will extend from the center front line when you draw the pant legs.

3. **At the end of the center front line, draw a little *z* shape to designate the crotch.**

4. **Add a button to the right of the center front line and draw a short horizontal line coming off the button for the buttonhole. (See Figure 10-4c.)**

   The placement of the button on either the right or left side of the center front line has no *real* rule. For men's clothing, you usually place all buttons — regardless of whether they're on shirts, jackets, or pants — on the right side (so the buttons are on their right when they're wearing the garment unbuttoned). For women's clothing, buttons are typically placed on the left side. However, it's become a trend in the apparel industry to put all buttons on pants, especially jeans, on the right side.

5. **At this point you can leave the waistband simple with only the button, or you can add belt loops. We chose to add a few belt loops in Figure 10-4c.**

   If you want to add belt loops, follow the next set of instructions.

Figure 10-4:
Detailing your waistband.

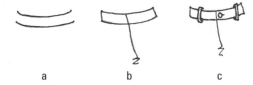

a   b   c

Mastering the basic belt loop

Here's how to draw belt loops:

1. **Start with a long, narrow *c* shape. (See Figure 10-5a.)**

   Whether you're drawing on the left or right side of the center front line determines which direction the opening of the *c* faces: The opening should be toward the center front line. In Figure 10-5, we're drawing a belt loop to the left of the center front line. To the right of the center line, you'd draw a backwards *c*.

2. **Add a short, straight, horizontal line at the top of the *c* and another at the bottom of the *c*. (See Figure 10-5b.)**

   These lines should be opposite the opening of the *c*.

3. **Connect the ends of the two lines with a vertical line. (See Figure 10-5c.)**

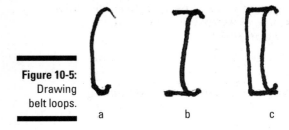

a   b   c

Figure 10-6 shows an example of a waistband with the button on the left, four belt loops, and lots of topstitching (for the lowdown on topstitching, check out the later section "Taking on topstitching"). There's no rule on the number of belt loops on a waistband. It's typical to have two in the front and three in the back, but you may see as many as four in front and three in back. It's all up to the designer.

Figure 10-6:
Keep your
pants on
with a
waistband,
button, and
belt loops.

Stretching your skills with an elastic waistband

Some pants don't feature belt loops. The cut of the pants may curve over the hips and fit snugly at the waist; this style may not have any waistband. Other pants stay up because they have an elastic waistband that stretches to fit. Sweatpants usually have elastic waistbands, and they may even include a drawstring.

Here's how to indicate an elastic waistband:

1. **Draw two curved, horizontal, squiggly lines, as in Figure 10-7a.**

2. **Connect the ends of the squiggly lines with short, vertical lines. Add lines going up and coming down from both curved lines to indicate gathering.**

   Vary the lengths of the gathering lines, as in Figure 10-7b.

3. **Finish the pants with a center front line, the crotch z line, and some side seams. Sometimes elastic-waist pants have drawstrings, so draw those, too, if you like. (See Figure 10-7b.)**

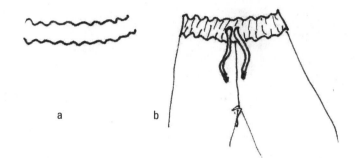

Figure 10-7:
An elastic
waistband.

a   b

Focusing on the fly

Great design is important, but so is practicality! When drawing pants, ask yourself, "How do I get into these pants?" Most of the time, you're going to go with the fly front. However, drawing a fly may not be as easy as it sounds. Communicating seam lines on a garment is important, and seams of the fly front are confusing!

Here's a simple way to show the all-important fly:

1. **Starting toward the bottom of the center front line, draw a short, dashed, curved line that goes to the right of the center front line and up to the waistband, creating a *J*, as in Figure 10-8.**

The *J*-shaped line of the fly must be dashed because it represents stitching. A solid line would represent a seam, and every designer knows there's not a seam there. The solid center front line must be centered, or your model will appear asymmetrical.

The fly can go to the left or the right of the center line. Today's fashion trend is to place almost all buttons, including the button on the fly, on the right side. But like most fashion rules, this rule is made to be broken. Some fashion designers follow the traditional placement of men's buttons on the right, women's on the left. If you place the fly to the left of the center front line in your drawing, use a backwards *J* shape.

2. **Draw a second dashed line right next to the first one.**

Together, these two lines represent two rows of topstitching.

Not all pants have a front fly opening, but always think about how the person is getting in and out of the pants. If there's no front fly, then the fabric must be really stretchy (think leggings or maternity pants; see Figure 10-9a) or must have an elastic waistband. Sailor pants are another example of pants without a traditional fly front; they have a front panel that buttons on the sides, as in Figure 10-9b. Dressier pants may have a hidden side zipper (also called an invisible zipper) that keeps the front of the pants smooth.

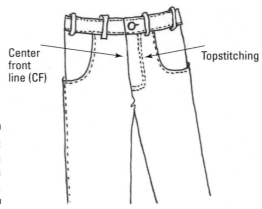

Figure 10-8: Topstitching indicates the fly.

Center front line (CF)

Topstitching

Figure 10-9: Alternative ways of fastening pants.

a   b

Putting in pockets

Pockets play a key role when you're drawing pants. Some are easy to see from the outside (usually in jeans), and others are sort of hidden in the side seams (you can't really illustrate these; just draw a hand hiding in them). Here's a list of the variety of pocket styles (check them out in Figure 10-10):

- ✓ **Stitched, rounded pocket:** Almost always used as front pockets, these usually appear in pairs, stay flat on the body, and have a row or two of topstitching on the inside edge. The right front pocket on a pair of jeans often includes a little coin pocket peeking out above the opening.

- ✓ **Back pocket:** Back pockets go on the back of pants, especially jeans. Back pockets feature a flat topstitched pattern of some sort and lay flat on the body.

- ✓ **Safari pocket:** Safari pockets, which you generally see in men's pants, have a flap on top, a button or snap closure, folded fabric (or pleats, indicated by the two vertical lines) to give extra room in the pocket, and topstitching around the perimeter to attach the pockets to the pants. They're not flat, and from the side, the safari pocket looks similar to the cargo pocket. The safari pocket is often found on the side of men's pants.

- **Cargo pocket:** Cargo pockets are popular in men's pants and have made their way onto women's pants as well. They feature a rounded fold in the body, a flap with a button or snap (sometimes invisible under the flap), and topstitching around the perimeter. They're usually located on the sides or back of the pants.

- **Flap pocket:** *Flap* refers to a piece of material that covers the opening on the pocket. A flap can be paired with any type of pocket that doesn't already include a flap as part of its design, thus creating a flap pocket. Flap pockets usually include a button or snap to keep the flap closed.

- **Side-seam pocket:** A side seam pocket is generally invisible from the outside of the garment. It's visible simply as a slit in the side seam. You may see topstitching around the pocket on the seam line.

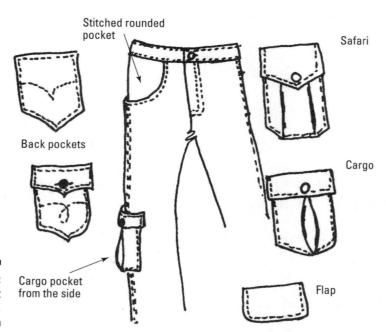

Figure 10-10: Pocket details.

Stitched rounded pocket

Safari

Back pockets

Cargo

Cargo pocket from the side

Flap

Taking on topstitching

Topstitching, which is thread stitched on the fabric that can be seen from the outside, can add the detail that distinguishes one pair of pants from another. Topstitching can have both a functional and decorative purpose. When it's used functionally on a pair of pants, topstitching attaches pockets or a zipper (on a fly front) to the pants or strengthens a seam. When it's used decoratively, topstitching creates a design on pockets or down a pant leg, adding visual interest to an otherwise plain stretch of fabric. Some pants and shorts have hardly any topstitching, whereas others are full of it.

This is what topstitching looks like:

- **Dashed lines:** These individual lines can be any length within reason. The dashes represent the thread used to create the topstitching. (See Figure 10-11.)

- **Multiple dashed lines:** Pants, shorts, and especially jeans often have more than one row of topstitching. You may see topstitching in pairs or in triple rows down the sides or the inseam of the legs due to the type of seam used to construct that area.

Play with the length of the dashed lines, the number of rows of lines you place next to each other, and the color of the dashes to add some pizzazz to your pants. If you're drawing with colored pencils or markers, you can add your topstitching in a different color than the color you used to draw the outline of the pants. For example, if you draw a pair of black jeans, add gold or silver topstitching.

Figure 10-11:
Topstitching
adds detail.

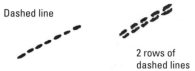

Dashed line

2 rows of
dashed lines

Take a look back at Figure 10-10 to see the ways topstitching can jazz up the pockets on a pair of jeans. But don't limit topstitching to the pockets; imagine all the other places you can use it. Topstitching looks good in the following places:

- Around the top and bottom of the waistband
- On the front fly
- Down the sides
- Outlining the pockets
- On the pockets for added detail
- Around the hem (see Figure 10-12)
- Across the yoke (see Figure 10-19 in the section "Checking it out from the back")

You also find topstitching on garments other than pants — shoes, shirts, and coats all look a little nicer with topstitching detail.

No hemming and hawing over stylish hems and cuffs

Even the bottoms of pants should look sharp in fashion illustration. To accomplish this, use curved lines to wrap the bottom of the pants around the ankle, foot, or calf (or thigh if you're drawing shorts). The type of pants you're drawing determines the kind of hem you draw. Hems can reflect the following cuts (see Figure 10-12):

✔ **Skinny-leg pants:** These types of legs are like a second skin on the leg. Their hems usually hit at the top of the foot and can create a slouchy look.

✔ **Wide-leg pants:** Wide leg pants start either loose or fitted around the waist and hips; the leg becomes wide around the thighs and usually stays wide all the way to the floor.

✔ **Straight-leg pants:** These pants are tailored to the body (not too tight and not baggy). After they hit the knee they continue to fall straight to the foot.

✔ **Flared-leg pants:** These pants can be loose, fitted, or tight on the upper body, but from the knee down, they flare out in a bell shape as they hit the foot.

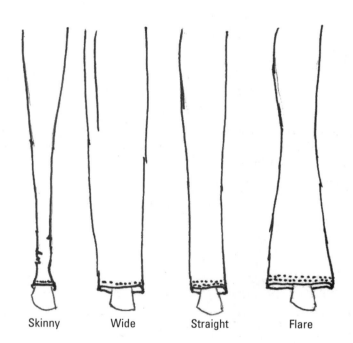

Figure 10-12: Types of pant leg cuts.

Skinny   Wide   Straight   Flare

Here's how to draw a hem with topstitching and a cuff:

1. **Draw a leg from the knee down, as in Figure 10-13a.**

   In this drawing, we show both a female front view (on the left) and male side view (on the right). In this example, we give the girl skinny pants and the man straight-leg pants.

2. **Draw the bottom half of the pants from the knee down.**

   For skinny pants, the line of the pants follows the shape of the leg, as in Figure 10-13b. For straight-leg pants, draw a line coming down straight from the knee and another one that falls from the top of the calf muscle, as in Figure 10-13c.

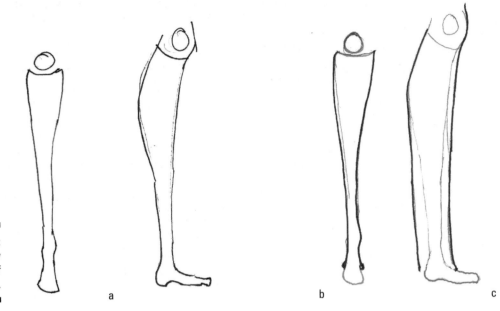

Figure 10-13:
Pants follow
the curve of
the leg.

a   b   c

3. **Draw a curved line up and over the foot where you want your pants to end, connecting the two sides of the pant leg that you drew in Step 2. (See Figure 10-14a.)**

4. **Add topstitching.**

   Keep in mind most hems have one or two rows of topstitching. We also added a side seam for the man's pants leg. (See Figure 10-14b.)

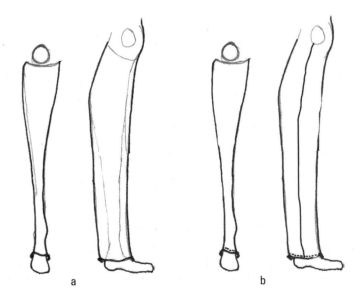

Figure 10-14:
Topstitching
adds inter-
est to hems.

a   b

You may prefer your pants to end in cuffs rather than a simple hem. Here's how to draw cuffs:

1. **Draw a leg from the knee down.**

2. **Draw the bottom half of the pants from the knee down.**

   Stop the pant lines on the inside and outside of the leg a little before the spot where the cuff will fall, as in Figure 10-15a.

3. **Add two curved horizontal lines that wrap around the ankle or calf.**

   You determine how wide the cuff is by how far apart you draw these lines. The lines that form the bottom of the cuff should extend outside the rest of the pant, as Figure 10-15b shows.

4. **Connect the top and bottom of the cuff with short vertical lines and then add topstitching. (See Figure 10-15c.)**

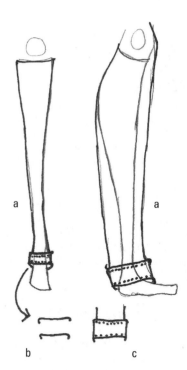

Figure 10-15:
Finishing the
cuff.

Shorts can have cuffs, too, as you see in Figure 10-16.

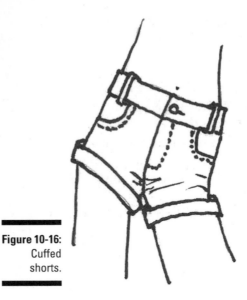

Figure 10-16:
Cuffed
shorts.

Rounding Out a Women's Pants Wardrobe

From jeans to khakis to leggings, pants are a staple in every woman's wardrobe. Whether they're denim with holes or silk for a night on the town, pants are here to stay!

Women's pants are fun to draw, and the varieties are endless. The waistlines, length, and fit are constantly changing. Designing pants can be such fun when you think about the placement of pockets and topstitching, along with the height of the waistline and length of the hem. You get a feel for some of these variations on the basic pants in the following sections.

Pulling on a pair of skinny jeans

What woman *doesn't* own a pair of jeans? The range of styles goes from tighter-than-tight to baggy-beyond-belief. *Skinny jeans* are aptly named: They're tight and tapered down to the ankle. *High-waisted, low-rise,* and *boyfriend jeans* (which have few curves and often have some holes and a rolled-up cuff) are also well-named descriptions of hot styles for jeans — see Figure 10-17. The creative details make the differences in jeans. When you're drawing jeans, pay attention to the front fly opening, and be sure to include tons of topstitching.

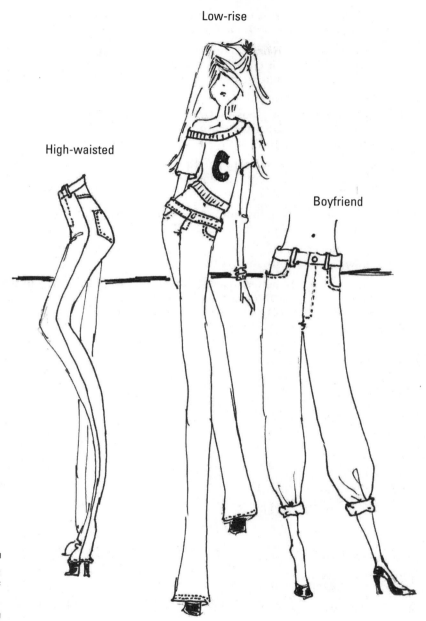

Low-rise

High-waisted

Boyfriend

Figure 10-17:
A variety of
jean styles.

Skinny jeans look great tucked into high boots or paired with super-high stilet-tos. Draw a great pair of skinny jeans this way:

1. **Draw the lower half of your figure using a front grounded pose. Add the center front line and waistline of the pants.**

   To draw this, complete Steps 1 through 3 from the earlier section "Putting the basic shape in place."

2. **For skinny jeans, draw lines for the side seams and inseams by following the shape of the legs exactly. (See Figure 10-18a.)**

   Skinny jeans need to be tight. If one leg is bent at all, add in a few bendy lines to show the fabric bunching. These lines communicate how tight the jeans are. See Chapter 14 for more info on drawing folds in tight clothing.

3. **Draw the hem of the jeans by wrapping the hemline around the ankle. Add in the topstitching lines following the hemline. (See Figure 10-18b.)**

   Skinny jeans can be different lengths. Some styles end right below the ankle, and some are very long and bunch or gather below the ankle at the top of the foot.

4. **Draw the waistband, including the center front button, belt loops, topstitching, and pockets. (See Figure 10-18c.)**

   Refer to the earlier sections under "Mastering Pants One Line at a Time" for how to draw these details.

5. **Draw the front fly by using at least two rows of topstitching in the *J* shape, starting at the waistband and going down the center front line. (See Figure 10-18d.)**

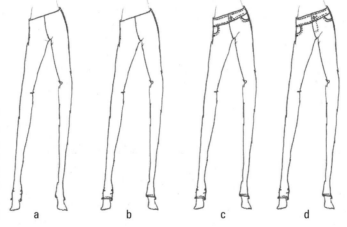

Figure 10-18: Skinny jeans hug every curve of a woman's body.

a   b   c   d

Jeans are all about detail. When you're drawing jeans, include the following:

- ✔ **Lots of topstitching:** Depending on the view of the legs (front, side, three-quarter, back), include topstitching lines on the outside seams and/or inseams of the pants. Most of the time, you see topstitching lines only on the inseam, but fashion is always changing!

- ✔ **Pocket rivets, which add to the authentic look of jeans:** *Rivets* are those little metal circles you see on all jeans to help keep the pockets strong.

Loving those leggings

Once worn only for exercise, leggings have more than crossed into the mainstream. You can dress them up or keep them super-casual; it's your call. You can show off your fashion figure's shape if you pair leggings with a skinny T-shirt, or you can toss a flirty little dress over them. If you love to draw high boots for a fashion look, then leggings, which hug the leg like a second skin, are the perfect pants accompaniment.

Leggings are easy to draw:

- ✔ Follow the shape of the legs, with the fabric hugging the legs, as in Figure 10-18b.

- ✔ If you need to show the waistband of the leggings, draw an elastic waistband. You can skip the belt loops and fly front.

- ✔ Leggings don't need detail, so finish with a simple hem and no topstitching.

Checking out the backside

Pants, especially jeans, are one thing from the front but another story from the back. Pocket placement and details such as darts and yokes are crucial in sketching designer looks!

Darts and yokes feature prominently in the back design of pants. *Darts* are short folds in fabric that are sewn together on the inside of the garment to create fit over curved areas of the body (think the chest and derrière for women). On the outside of the garment, they're usually drawn as short lines — you can see them on some pants on the back, around the top of the derrière to the waistband. *Yokes* likewise shape a garment, but they also give extra support to the piece. You often find yokes across the back of a shirt or between the waistband and legs of a pair of jeans, as Figure 10-19 shows.

Try drawing a pair of jeans with a yoke from the back:

1. **Start by drawing a back view of your fashion figure.**

   Refer to Chapter 4 if you need a refresher on the back view.

2. **Draw the waistband, belt loops, and center back line, as in Figure 10-19a.**

   Choose the style of your jeans, pants, or shorts. How high do you want the waist? How many belt loops?

3. **To create the yoke, draw a wide, shallow *V* below the waistband, as in Figure 10-19b.**

4. **Directly above the *V*, draw a row of topstitching. Finish the pant legs and complete the hem. (See Figure 10-19c.)**

   The row of topstitching is part of the yoke seam most of the time, although you can break this fashion rule, too, if you want.

5. **Add the back pockets (with topstitching) and draw some creases to indicate the knee bends.**

The pockets are placed on the derrière below the yoke. Add creases in the pant legs to indicate the knee bends.

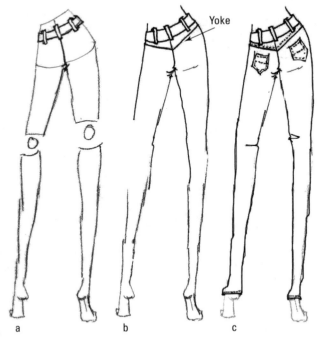

Figure 10-19: Pockets are the first hint that you're looking at the back of a pair of pants.

a   b   c

Putting on dressy pants

Dress pants, flowing pants, and the oh-so-new high-waisted pants are just a few ways to rock it at work or take on the town. Figure 10-20 points out the details that transform a regular pair of pants into an elegant pair of pants suitable for a business meeting or a dressy evening event.

To achieve an elegant high-waisted look in pants, begin with a front or three-quarter pose and draw a basic pair of pants (follow the steps under "Putting the basic shape in place"). However, modify the following areas to create elegant pants:

✔ **The waistband (Figure 10-20a):** In dress pants, waistbands are often higher and wider than on traditional pants. Here's how you can modify waistbands:

- **Higher waistlines:** Elegant pants usually have waistlines that begin around the bellybutton or higher.

- **Wider waistbands without belt loops:** Of course, like anything in fashion design, there are exceptions to this rule.

✔ **The pant legs (Figure 10-20b):** Dress pants usually feature wide legs, which often have wide cuffs. Elegant pants tend to have a *flowy* feel because they're usually made out of lighter weight material than pants such as jeans or khakis. They may be pressed with creases down the center front of each leg; sometimes the crease is only pressed around the hem, and other times it goes all the way up to the thighs.

✔ **The zipper (Figure 10-20c):** Many elegant pants have a side opening and zipper. For this look, simply draw the center front line without a fly, and if you're using a three-quarter view, show some topstitching around the side seam for the length of the zipper.

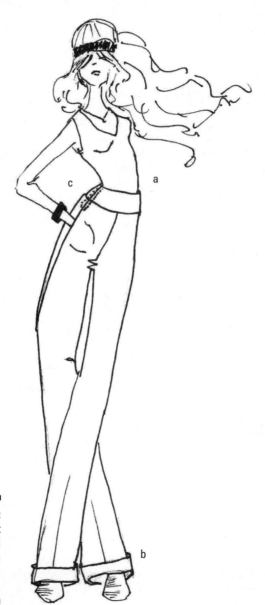

Figure 10-20:
Elegant pants add impossible length to a body.

Use the side or three-quarter view when you want to show the side zipper.

You can minimize or leave off some details when sketching elegant pants. File these next points under "less is more." (Refer back to Figure 10-20 to see what we mean.)

- **Just a little topstitching:** Elegant pants do contain some topstitching, usually around the waistband or hem, but it's usually very tiny and a done in a color that blends in with the fabric.

- **No visible pockets:** Most of the time, you don't see pockets in elegant pants. If pockets exist, they're hidden in the seam or as slits in the back on the derrière. Illustrate the hidden side seam pocket by drawing a hand disappearing into a pocket.

Slipping into sweatpants — so easy

Trends in fashion have allowed sweats to move outside the house, often rocking some wording on the rear or down the leg. Some sweatpants have elastic cuffs, and others hang loose. An interesting point about drawing sweatpants is that you draw the front and the back by following the same steps — no pockets or flies to worry about here! You can add a drawstring to the front or a fun word on the rear to add some interest to the look.

Here's how to draw open-legged sweatpants (see Figure 10-21):

1. **Draw a fashion figure from the back view.**

   Remember to include a center back line.

2. **For the elastic waistband, draw a pair of matching curved, squiggly lines. Add short vertical lines to indicate gathering.**

3. **Draw the side seams and inseams of the legs down to the top of the foot.**

4. **For the hem, draw a line connecting the side seam and inseam.**

   Don't bother with topstitching. Sweatpants fabric doesn't usually unravel, so the hems of the pants aren't finished.

5. **For a trendy look, add a short word across the derrière or down the leg.**

   If you're showing the front of a pair of sweats, you can add a drawstring at the waistband.

Figure 10-21:
Sweatin' it
out from the
back.

Here's how to draw sweats with elastic bottoms:

1. **Draw a fashion figure from a side view and give her an elastic waistband.**

2. **Draw the pant legs, side seams, and inseams of the legs, keeping the pant legs loose and bubbling out a little before being tightened at the calf or ankle. (See Figure 10-22a.)**

3. **At the bottom of each pant leg, draw a wide cuff with squiggly vertical lines to show the elastic of the cuff. Add some lines that come up from the cuff to show the fabric bunching slightly, as in Figure 10-22b.**

4. **Add letters going down the leg for a varsity look. (See Figure 10-22c.)**

   The side of the leg is a good place for a long word, like a school or team name.

Follow the same steps for dressing men and kids in sweats. Men and kids love sweatpants, too — just *try* to get a young kid to put on something else so you can wash the sweats! Sweatpants are great for cold weather, sports, sleeping, and more.

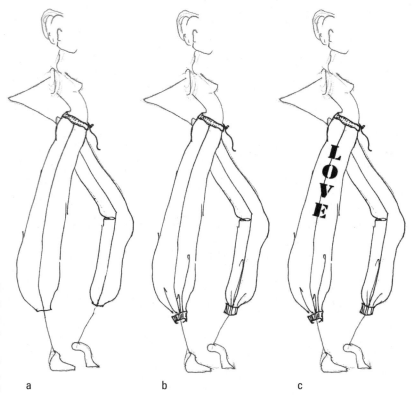

a   b   c

Drawing the Man's Must-Have: Pants for Guys

A man's gotta have pants. We don't know many guys who wear skirts on a regular basis — or ever — but that's not as boring as it may sound. You can create dozens of different looks for men's pants. A well-dressed guy turns heads. Fit is important when you're going for a tailored look, and for students, the style is all about going slouchy. Either way, you're allowed to have fun with guys' fashion pants.

Men's pants differ from women's mostly in the fit and in the subtle details such as the pocket locations and the length of the center front fly. In the following sections, we show you how to draw three popular styles of men's pants.

Going casual with cargo pants

Guys of all ages love cargo pants. Who wouldn't love the comfortable, casual look of cargos — not to mention all the extra places for carrying keys, wallets, and cellphones! Cargo shorts are just cargo pants cut off right below the knee.

To dress your guy in rockin' cargos:

1. **Start with a guy in a front pose.**

   Or if you really want to show off the features of cargo pants, draw a three-quarter or side pose; these poses allow you to show the pockets on the side of the pants.

2. **Draw a basic pair of pants with a waistband, belt loops, topstitching, and a fly, as in Figure 10-23a.**

   Follow Steps 1 through 8 from "Putting the basic shape in place."

3. **Add cargo pockets to the side of each pant leg, with the tops of the pockets about midway between the waist and knee. (See Figure 10-23b.)**

   Refer back to the section "Putting in pockets" earlier in the chapter and to Figure 10-10 to get an idea of how to draw a cargo pocket. You can add more than one cargo pocket on each leg.

4. **Finish the pants by adding a few lines around the knees and hems to show the baggy look of the pants. (See Figure 10-23b.)**

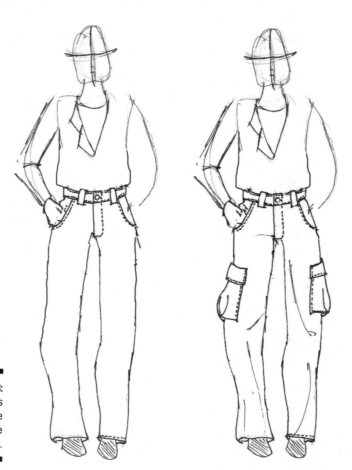

Figure 10-23: Cargo pants put the focus on the pockets.

Achieving a formal look with dress pants

Most men have at least one pair of dress pants in their closets. Some men have dozens. Draw a pair of dress pants just like you would a basic pair of pants (see the "Putting the basic shape in place" section earlier in this chapter); then add the details that differentiate dress pants from casual pants:

- ✔ **Hidden side seam pockets:** A hand slipped inside the pocket shows that a pocket is present — skip the topstitching here.

- ✔ **Pleats in the front:** Between the fly and the pockets, draw a couple of short, slightly curved lines extending down from the waistband. These lines should be no longer than the length of the fly.

- ✔ **Tab closures:** Trendier pants may not have pleats (this pleatless style is called a *flat front*) or belt loops; such pants may have a tab closure instead of the traditional button fly. To draw a tab closure, simply add a solid, vertical line on the waistband off to one side of the center front line, opposite the *J* shape of the fly.

- ✔ **Creases down the center front of each leg:** The crease is more prominent from the hem to just above the knee.

- ✔ **Cuffs:** Dress pants often have cuffs. See the earlier section "No hemming and hawing over stylish hems and cuffs" for how to draw these details.

To distinguish dress pants from other types of pants, include at least two or three of these details — see a couple of variations in Figure 10-24. Of course, your fashion model's shirt and shoes also help the viewer know that he's dressed for a more formal occasion.

Dressing guys in jeans and khakis

Everywhere you look, you see guys in jeans. Relaxed-fit jeans, which are worn at casual workplaces and serve as a weekend uniform for relaxing and partying, are a guy's classic pant. You draw khakis similarly to jeans — the main differences are the fabric used and the smaller topstitching lines in khakis. If you're not drawing in color, distinguishing between the two is hard.

Men's jeans and khakis have the same lines and similar detailing as women's. The difference comes down to the fit.

Men have boxier bodies, so guys tend to wear their pants relaxed and straight leg. Keep the waistband relaxed and located slightly below the bellybutton with the pant legs going straight down.

Figure 10-24:
The difference is in the details for formal pants.

Here's how to get the guy's jeans or khakis to look right:

1. **Draw the lower half of a guy in a grounded three-quarter pose.**

2. **Draw the pants, following Steps 1 through 8 from "Putting the basic shape in place."**

   Focus on the fit. Keep the side seam and inseam lines straight or somewhat baggy for a relaxed look, as in Figure 10-25a. If you're drawing khakis, put less emphasis on the topstitching.

To get the emo tight-jean look, draw the waistband lower on the hips and make the side seams follow the shape of the legs. Include all the same jeans details but make the hem of the pants tight around the ankle. (See Figure 10-25b.)

Figure 10-25:
Relaxed
and skinny
jeans.

a   b

Creating Pants for Girls and Boys

For kids' pants, almost all the same rules apply for drawing any of the specified pants for men and women. The rules for women work for girls, with differences in the curves of the body; girls tend to have a boxier shape rather than a small waist and wide hips. Boys' pants are just a shorter version of men's pants; boys and men have the same squarish shape, so the rules that apply to men's pants also hold true for boys' pants. For both girls and boys, the length of legs is closer to the length of the torso than on adults. In the following sections, we discuss some details specific to kids' pants and show you how to draw a pair of overalls.

Finding differences in the details

You include the same details in children's pants as you would for the adult versions, such as center front seams and topstitching, but you can go a little bolder with children's designs. Keep in mind that children's clothes tend to be in bright colors, so keep your markers handy!

Here are a few suggestions for bringing out the kid in your illustrations:

- **Patches (Figure 10-26a):** Patches are both decorative and functional and are a common part of children's clothing. Patches are sewn, ironed, or glued on in high-wear places such as the knees, legs, and pockets.

- **Ruffles for girls (Figure 10-26b):** Adding ruffles to places such as hem of shorts or pants and even to the derrière of girls' clothing instantly says "kids"!

- **Holes in the knees (Figure 10-26c):** Both boys and girls tend to be hard on their clothing, especially in the knee area; therefore, you often see pants that already have holes in them as a fashion statement.

Figure 10-26: Adding details to kids' pants.

Covering up kids with overalls

Overalls are a staple in almost all toddlers' wardrobes. The pants are durable, washable, and cute! Plus, they keep the shirt (and the kid underneath) a little cleaner than a regular pair of pants does. The great news is that drawing overalls is easy.

Follow these simple steps to create classic overalls:

1. **Start by drawing a three-quarter view of a toddler (sneak back to Chapter 4 for guidelines on how to draw kids).**

2. **Draw a pair of jeans, as in Figure 10-27a.**

   Use Steps 1 through 8 from "Putting the basic shape in place" and add details such as topstitching. Remember to scale down the size for a child's body. You don't need a button for the center fly on overalls; instead, there's usually topstitching in a square or *X* shape. Most overalls don't have a front fly.

3. **Starting at the waist, draw a trapezoid covering the chest. (See Figure 10-27b.)**

   The size of the trapezoid, or bib, is up to you.

4. **Add straps that go over the shoulders and buckles at the top corners of the bib, as in Figure 10-27c.**

   Buckles can be a tough feature to draw. Follow the larger example in Figure 10-27c or look online for examples of these closures.

5. **Finish with a pocket on the front bib and a button on the waistband above the side pocket. (See Figure 10-27d.)**

   Add a kid-friendly design on the front of the pocket or draw something peeking out of the pocket — maybe a frog or a half-eaten candy bar.

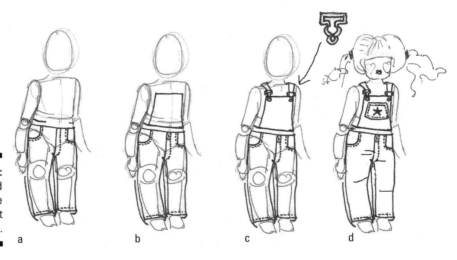

Figure 10-27: Kids and overalls are a perfect pairing.

a   b   c   d

Chapter 11

Getting All Dolled Up: Evening Wear

In This Chapter

▶ Slipping into super gowns

▶ Puttin' on the tux

▶ Dressing up the kids

*I*f you don't get to glam it up and hit the hotspots often enough in real life, enjoy the fact that fashion illustration and glitzy nightlife are made for each other. One of your female fashion creations can don a great-looking shimmery number, a short poufy skirt, or that little black sheath that always knocks 'em dead. The guy in the dapper tux you draw can make women swoon. And don't forget the kids. Lots of little girls love to dress up, and fashion drawing allows you to go all out! As for the little guys? In real life, most of them avoid wearing anything they can't get dirty, but on drawing paper, you're the boss and can make them wear jackets and ties. In this chapter, we show you how to have fun with evening fashion.

Need to complete the evening look? See Chapter 13 for info on accessories and Chapter 8 for tips on hairstyles.

Glamming It Up in Gorgeous Gowns

Most fashion illustrators love to draw fancy dresses and create a glamorous mood. With gowns for women, just about anything goes, and as a fashion artist, you get to go to new and exciting places with your pencil.

Certain views really lend themselves to glamorous gown illustrations. Gowns often have wonderful back features, while three-quarter views are the epitome of a glamorous red carpet look. Front and side views offer great opportunities for using exaggerated poses that show off the drape of the fabrics.

When it comes to dress designs, fabric is crucial! It takes just the right elegant, sheer fabrics to create the flowing, drapey looks that sparkle and shine in evening wear. (Check out Chapter 14 for tips on how to draw such fabrics.) In the following sections, we show you how to use all your fashion-drawing tools to create red-carpet style.

Dressing up the basic shapes

Just about every basic shape comes into play when you're drawing gowns and dynamic dresses. The variety of dress designs are endless, including strapless, backless, and every type of neckline and sleeve. The sheer variety can be intimidating, but you have nothing to fear; in this chapter, we break down various designs into simple shapes to make it easy for you. Experiment with the following:

- A triangle is a sure-shot to map out the shape of a flared skirt. (See Figure 11-1a.)
- Cylinder and square shapes make for a great tube-shaped, tight-fitting dress or skirt. (See Figures 11-1b and 11-1c.)
- Use the heart shape when drawing a bustier or strapless dress with a sweetheart neckline. (See Figure 11-1d.)
- A *V* shape works perfectly for a backless dress. (See Figure 11-1e.)

Figure 11-1:
Basic shapes give you a lot of dress options for a night out.

a b c d e

Mastering the must-have little black dress

Every woman should own an LBD (little black dress), and every fashion artist should be able to draw at least one version of this wardrobe staple. This dress is your fashion lifesaver for any event. Lisa's mom sent her off to college with one, and it came in handy even though she was a rather sloppy art student at the time.

The little black dress is all about the simplicity of the cut. Forget the sequin action and showy embellishments here.

Here's how to master the little black dress:

1. **Draw a full front pose of a woman; add a wide neckline for a simple fitted dress. (See Figure 11-2a.)**

2. **Follow the sides of her torso as you draw the side seams for this form-fitting dress. End the seams several inches below her crotch. (See Figure 11-2b.)**

   Think of a cylinder shape that curves with her body.

3. **For the hem of her dress, connect the side seams with a curved line across the model's thighs. (See Figure 11-2c.)**

   Be sure to wrap the sides of the hem behind her legs.

4. **Color in the dress with a black marker. (See Figure 11-2d.)**

   Be sure to leave a few areas of the dress white to add some dimension.

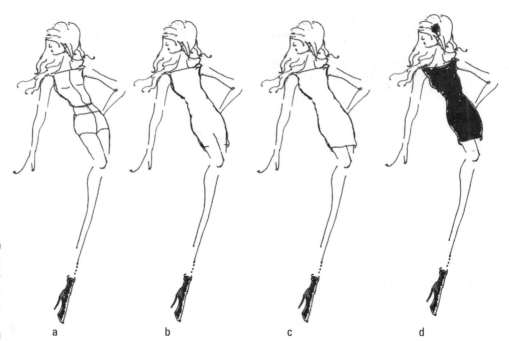

Figure 11-2:
Simplicity makes the black dress classy.

a   b   c   d

Shaking up the look with a cocktail dress

The little black dress (see the preceding section) comes in many styles, fabrics, and even colors — think red, midnight blue, or the complete opposite, white. When the LBD is no longer little or black, it's generally referred to as a *cocktail dress*. Fashion artists can really go to town creating different looks for this type of dress.

Create a cocktail-dress look by starting with a simple cylinder. Modify and embellish different parts of the cylinder with various shapes to suit the mood, the event, or the latest trends. Consider the following alterations:

- ✔ Change the cylinder length to alter the hemline or length of the dress.

- ✔ Narrow or widen the cylinder depending on the closeness of the fit. You can also flare the cylinder at the bottom for a flared hemline.

- ✔ Modify the top of the cylinder for different necklines such as a scoop, *V*-neck, square, or sweetheart neckline.

- ✔ Add straps or sleeves to the top of the cylinder for a spaghetti-strap or cap-sleeve look.

- ✔ Add an indentation, seam, or change the fabric to indicate different waistlines such as an empire waist, natural waistline, or drop waist.

- ✔ Add details such as ruffles, gathering, sequined appliqués, lace inserts, beading, or pockets!

By altering the basic cylinder, you can emphasize different parts of the body or send a subtle message. Here are various cocktail dresses:

- ✔ A dress with cap sleeves and a straight neckline shows off the bust (see Figure 11-3a).

- ✔ An off-the-shoulder dress draws attention to the face and shoulders (see Figure 11-3b).

- ✔ A short-and-strappy number gives your model a fierce look (see Figure 11-3c).

- ✔ A long and tight gown that ends at the ankles plays up a sexy and mysterious look (see Figure 11-3d).

Looking sleek in a sheath

Although the simple sheath has been around forever, it never goes out of style. Necklines can scoop or point, depending on the designers or the season. Choices of fabric vary. However, two things about the *sheath* never change:

- ✔ The sheath's cut is narrow.

- ✔ The neckline and hemline are the focal points.

This dress is very flattering, especially for long, lean fashion models. Your fashion figure will thank you!

Figure 11-3:
Mixing up
different
styles of
cocktail
dresses.

a   b   c   d

Here's how to draw a sheath:

1. **Draw a female fashion figure. (See Figure 11-4a.)**

2. **Sketch a cylinder to map in the dress's shape around the fashion figure, as in Figure 11-4b.**

   The sheath usually ends right above the knee.

3. **Call attention to the waistline by cinching in the cylinder on both sides of the waist to create folds, as in Figure 11-4c.**

4. **Draw armholes for a sleeveless look, add the neckline, and add a few more lines for folds in the waistline. (See Figure 11-4d.)**

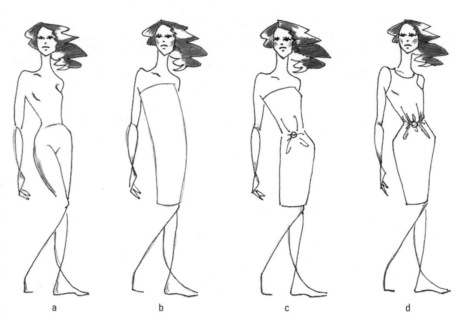

Figure 11-4:
With the sheath, stay close to the body and focus on the natural waist.

a   b   c   d

Creating breathtaking ball gowns

Nothing is lovelier than a ball gown that fills the doorway as a woman enters the room. Ball gowns tend to be over-the-top with huge skirts and fitted tops. Folds and folds of fabric and dreams of charity balls and galas all play their part in the look.

You draw a ball gown in two parts. First focus on the bodice, and then add the stunning skirt. Try your hand at ball gown–bodice design by following these steps:

1. **Draw the front torso of a woman.**

2. **Using the torso as a guide, draw the gown's neckline and armhole(s).**

   Here we draw a one-shoulder, tight-fitting upper half of a dress. For the neckline, draw a line that curves over one breast and goes up to the neck. For an armhole, draw another line that goes over one shoulder. (See Figure 11-5a.)

   To create a strapless dress, draw a slightly curved line or a sweetheart neckline across the chest.

   For a dramatic ball-gown effect, draw in elbow-length gloves.

3. **For the rest of the gown's bodice, follow the sides of the model's torso to draw the side seams, and draw a waist seam across her middle.**

   Create an asymmetrical waist seam in any interesting design by going from the top of one hip to the bottom of the other. (See Figure 11-5b.)

4. **Map out where her legs are going to be.**

You won't see the legs, but you want to make sure this lovely lady looks like she's standing and balanced — she's probably wearing fancy high heels, and you don't want her to look like she's going to tip over! (See Figure 11-5c.)

a   b

Figure 11-5:
Building
the top half
of the ball
gown.

c

After you draw the ball gown's bodice, you're ready to add the skirt:

1. **Begin the skirt by drawing side seams that bell out from the bodice's waist seam. End the lines at the model's feet.**

2. **At the bottom of the skirt, draw a hem line connecting the side seams, being sure to draw wave-like shapes for the folds of the fabric. (See Figure 11-6a.)**

3. **Finish the skirt by adding a few lines going up from the hem, creating folds. (See Figure 11-6b.)**

Figure 11-6:
Finishing the
ball gown.

a

b

Putting On the Ritz for Guys

Guys may grumble when they have to suit up, but we think men are secretly pleased with the end results. A man looks elegant in a suit or tux, as long as the fit is right. What looks better than a well-cut jacket and a pair of pants that hang from a guy's hips just the right way? We show you how to draw men's formalwear in the following sections.

Sketching a suitable tux jacket

Although men's formalwear doesn't have nearly the variety of styles that women's fancy dresses do, you can still tailor the look. Tuxes can vary in the color and fabric (powder blue velvet tuxes were popular in the '70s!), the width of the lapels, the placement of the buttons, and the length of the jacket.

To draw a fitted jacket that's flattering to the male form, remember several points:

✔ Make it taper at the waist.

✔ Go for a broad-shouldered look

✔ Show the cuffs of the shirt.

Men usually wear a vest under a tux jacket. Create a vest the same way you draw the jacket — just don't draw the lapels or sleeves!

To master the look of a perfect tuxedo jacket:

1. **Draw a male torso (see Chapter 5 for details).**

2. **Add a *V* shape below the chin to mark the top of the shirt collar. For the jacket's neckline, draw a deep curved line that starts where the neck meets the shoulders. (See Figure 11-7a.)**

   The curved line forms the inner edges of the jacket's lapels.

3. **Add in lines for the shoulders and draw triangles below the chin on the *V* shape, as in Figure 11-7b.**

   The triangles form the shirt collar above the jacket.

4. **For an off-center jacket opening, draw a line coming down from the right side of the curved neckline and ending on the left side of the body for an off-center jacket opening. Add two buttons. (See Figure 11-7c.)**

   Draw buttons on the right of a buttoned dinner jacket.

5. **Angle in the sides of the torso to transform the lines from the body's outline into the jacket's side seams. This creates the sleek, fitted look. (See Figure 11-7c.)**

6. **Use angled lines along the jacket opening to draw in the one side of the tuxedo's notched collar. Add in a jacket sleeve that ends at the wrist but lets the shirt's cuff peek out. (See Figure 11-7d.)**

7. **Draw the other side of the notched collar and the other sleeve. Add in small slash lines on each side of the waist for pockets (see Figure 11-7e). Finish with a little shading.**

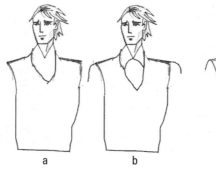   

Figure 11-7: The fitted jacket has broad shoulders and tapers at the waist.

a   b   c   d   e

Keep tuxedo shirts simple. Take a look at some photos of tuxedos from the '70s. You won't *believe* how much the ruffled shirts distracted from the lines of the jacket. Check out Chapter 9 on drawing men's shirts and imagine the fun you can have designing the next big shirt style under the tuxedo jacket.

Transforming dress pants into tuxedo pants

A perfect jacket deserves a sleek and elegant pair of pants. The secret to tuxedo pants lies in the fit; baggy or too tight pants just won't do.

Here's how to draw your figure in a perfect pair of tux pants:

1. **Map out a pair of pants around the male figure, as in Figure 11-8a.**

   Refer to Chapter 10 if you need a pants refresher. Dress pants fall in a clean line from the hip; they don't taper. The bottom of the pants hits well below the anklebone.

   Don't draw flared pants unless you want your male figure to look outdated.

2. **Draw the tuxedo stripe running down the side of the pants leg by adding a line parallel to the outside seam. (See Figure 11-8b.)**

   Tuxedo pants typically have a stripe of satin going down the side of the pant leg.

3. **Shade to show lights and darks in the sheen of the fabric and the shine of the stripe, as in Figure 11-8c.**

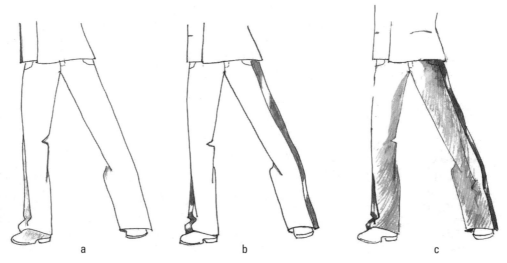

Figure 11-8: Terrific tuxedo pants.

a   b   c

Bringing on the bow tie

We know people who look pretty dopey in a bow tie (for example, one of our biology teachers from high school). But many guys can really carry off the look. Although some men choose to wear a necktie with a dinner jacket, we vote for the elegant bow tie. Why mess with a classic? (If you want instructions on drawing a necktie, see the section "Trying a tie" at the end of this chapter.)

Here's how to draw a bow tie:

1. **Sketch the head, neck, and shoulders of a man, as in Figure 11-9a.**

2. **Sketch in the pointed shirt collar using two curved triangles at the base of the neck, as in Figure 11-9b.**

   Give the triangles a bit of shape to reflect how they lie against the body and curve around the back of the neck.

3. **To make the tie's knot, draw a tiny circle in the center where the collar meets, as in Figure 11-9c.**

4. **Draw three lines coming from one side of the circle. The top one goes up at an angle, the middle one is short and straight out, and the last one angles down. Copy these lines on the other side of the circle. (See Figure 11-9d.)**

   The top and bottom lines represent the top and bottom of the bow tie. The center line shows the crease in the tie as the fabric comes out of the knot.

   Make sure the size of the bow tie you draw isn't too big; you can run into clown issues.

5. **Finish by connecting the top and bottom lines on each side of the tie to create the finished and formal bow tie. (See Figure 11-9e.)**

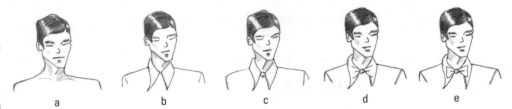

Figure 11-9:
Bow tie
magic.

a   b   c   d   e

Delighting Girls with Their Dream Dresses

Wearing a party dress makes a little girl feel like a fairy or a princess or, well, a fairy princess. You may not be able to get your girls out of party dresses — girls may even opt to wear them over a pair of jeans with high-tops! And tweens love putting on dresses that make them feel stylish and grown-up. We show you how to draw age-appropriate dresses for young girls and preteens in the following sections.

Fitting girls with a puffy party dress

Using triangles, squares, and circles can help you create the puffiest dresses on the planet. Start with the triangle bottom to give it a princess look and have some real fun creating a dream come true.

Check out this drawing exercise:

1. **Draw a square, as in Figure 11-10a.**

2. **Add a large triangle beneath the square with one of the points centered on the bottom line of the square. (See Figure 11-10b.)**

3. **Attach two circles at the top corners of the square, as in Figure 11-10c.**

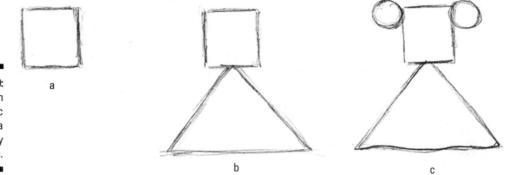

Figure 11-10:
Start with all the basic shapes for a puffy party dress.

What do you have? An instant cartoon-like dress that works surprisingly well for a young girl's party dress. By taking the cartoon-like dress from Figure 11-11 and using it as a fashion foundation tool, you can build an awesome party dress a little girl would die for!

Here's how to draw a puffy party dress:

1. **Draw a fashion figure of a little girl, as in Figure 11-11a.**

Figure 11-11:
Refine the basic shapes to finish the puffy party dress — she's such a party girl!

2. **Sketch the cartoon-like dress over her, using a square for the top, a triangle for the bottom, and circles for the puffy sleeves. (See Figure 11-11b.)**

   The bottom of the party dress hits a little above the knees.

3. **Soften the dress and sleeves with folds. Draw a curved neckline. Add some details, like a sash at the waist or some tulle peeking out from beneath the skirt. (See Figure 11-11c.)**

   When shading folds, use the side of a pencil.

Adding a touch of glitter

For a little girl, glitter is the stuff dreams are made of. You can draw party dresses that are designed with glitter appliqués for the little ones.

Here's how to draw a party dress with a glitter appliqué:

1. **Draw the top half of a girl fashion figure, as in Figure 11-12a.**

2. **Sketch in a square for the top of the dress.**

   The top of the square should fall where the arms meet the body (the under-arms). The bottom of the square falls at the waist. (See Figure 11-12b.)

3. **Draw a heart for the appliqué on the front of the dress.**

   The top half of the heart goes above the top of the square, and the other half of the heart falls within the square. This placement ensures that the appliqué isn't too high or too low on the torso. (See Figure 11-12c.)

4. **Use stippling (a bunch of random dots) for a glitter effect. (See Figure 11-12d.)**

   Check Chapter 3 for stippling techniques that create glitz and glitter.

Figure 11-12:
A glitter appliqué adds shimmer for a girly look.

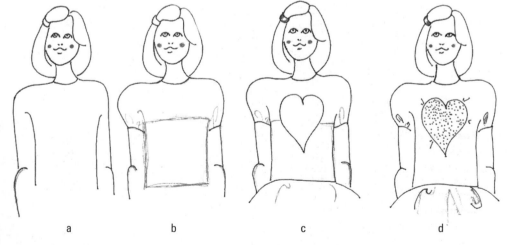

a   b   c   d

Drawing tween looks

Many of today's styles for kids look very much like teen and adult fashions, just modified for younger bodies with a lot less revealed! An older girl may want something sophisticated to wear to a party or her first boy-girl dance, whereas her parents want a dress that suits her age. You can make everyone happy. The trick to keeping tween fashion age-appropriate is to draw an adult-style dress that doesn't fit as tightly and has a higher neckline and lower hemline.

Tweens' dresses are rarely strapless, so add little straps to modify a strapless adult design. Spaghetti straps on a sheath-like dress make a girl feel grown up. For this type of sophisticated dress, go for an above-the-knee style (but not too far above the knee!).

Here's how to draw a tween in a simple party dress featuring spaghetti straps:

1. **Draw a fashion figure of a tween, as in Figure 11-13a.**

2. **Map out a rectangle for the shape of the dress. (See Figure 11-13b.)**

   A rectangle creates a streamlined look for girls who desire a simple dress (some actually do!).

3. **Add spaghetti straps — and don't forget some splashy flowers! (See Figure 11-13c.)**

   Drawing a floral pattern makes for a younger, less sophisticated look. Fabrics that shimmer also appeal to tweens.

Figure 11-13:
A simple party dress for a tween.

a   b   c

Dressing Boys in Dapper Duds

Sooner or later, a boy has to get dressed up for a holiday, a family party, or a school concert. Much to his displeasure, he has to put on a decent pair of pants and a blazer. Fortunately, you have no such problems getting your fashion-drawing boys to dress up just the way you want them to. In the following sections, we show you how to draw a boy's blazer and a necktie. If you want to outfit your young man in dress slacks, flip to Chapter 10 for the how-to on pants.

Brushing up on blazer basics

A boy's blazer is simply the mini version of a man's blazer with simple lapels, two lower pockets, and one breast pocket. By using basic shapes, we show you how to create the jacket that boys hate to wear!

Here's how to draw a boy in a blazer:

1. **Draw the top half of a boy fashion figure and add in slightly curved lines for the armhole seams, as in Figure 11-14a.**

   A boy's chest is not packed full of muscles, so draw it slim.

2. **Map out two curved rectangles for the front of the jacket, showing them a few inches apart for the jacket to be open. Draw in the sleeves. (See Figure 11-14b.)**

a

b

c

d

Figure 11-14:
A boy wears a blazer.

Draw slightly looser sleeves than you would for a man's jacket and end the sleeves at the wrist bones.

3. **Add two triangles inside the inner edge of each curved rectangle for the lapels. (See Figure 11-14c.)**

4. **Use a straight line to show pockets. Don't forget the buttons and the breast pocket! (See Figure 11-14d.)**

5. **Most blazers are of a dark hue, so shade in the jacket with the side of a soft pencil.**

Trying a tie

Getting a little guy or tween boy to put on (and keep on) a tie in real life is a challenge, but fashion drawings don't put up a fight, so deck out your young dude in a tie! Like a bow tie, a tie lies under the collar.

Here's how to draw a tie on a boy:

1. **Draw a boy's head, neck, and shoulders. (See Figure 11-15a.)**

2. **Sketch out two triangles for a shirt collar where the neck meets the torso, as in Figure 11-15b.**

3. **Draw a small square between the collars, just below where the triangles meet. (See Figure 11-15c.)**

   This square represents the tie's knot.

4. **To draw the sides of the tie, draw short angled lines out from the bottom of the square. Extend the lines down and then angle them toward each other to form a point. (See Figure 11-15d.)**

   The tip of a tie hits slightly below the waist.

a   b   c

Figure 11-15:
Try a simple drawing of the shirt collar and tie.

d

Chapter 12

Outerwear for All

*B*aby, it's cold outside — at least part of the year — so you need to know how to draw outerwear. Coats (for rain, shine, wind, and snow) as well as boots, hats, scarves, and mittens all make it into the fashion illustrator's inventory sooner or later. In this chapter, we show you how to keep your fashion models warm and cozy in every kind of weather.

Sensational Spring Jackets

Spring jackets are fun to draw because they're not as heavy and bulky as winter wear; you can actually see clothes peeking out beneath some spring jackets. Outerwear really lightens up in the spring, so we show you how to draw lightweight jackets. Spring also brings rain in many parts of the country, so we include a quick section on drawing raincoats as well. You can have a lot of fun with these jackets.

Venturing out in lightweight jackets

Casual lightweight jackets can have a fitted or a boxy look for both men and women. These types of jackets can range from sportswear suitable for an afternoon spent outdoors to more professional-looking trench coats that you can wear to the office on cool mornings. Fabrics can range from wool to nylon, depending on the look and functionality of the coat.

Casual lightweight jackets often have lots of detail. Stroll through a department store or your own closet and examine the details on your lightweight coats, checking out the zipper, pockets, and armhole ventilation. Casual jackets have pull cords, piping, and logos galore. The details make the difference when drawing lightweight jackets. Check out jackets in stores or online for inspiration or use your imagination to come up with creative details.

Draw a women's lightweight hiking jacket:

1. **Draw a front female pose with one arm bent and on the waist, as in Figure 12-1a.**

2. **Follow the sides of the trapezoids that make up her torso for the sides of the jacket. Add an oval around the neck and another above the shoulder for the hood. Include the center front line for the zipper. (See Figure 12-1b.)**

3. **Add lines on both sides of the arms for sleeves, as in Figure 12-1c.**

   For a fun design shape, draw curved lines that start below the armholes and angle up to the neckline. Add dashed lines next to those seam lines for topstitching.

4. **Finish the design with pockets at your model's waistline and a stripe down the side of each arm, as in Figure 12-1d.**

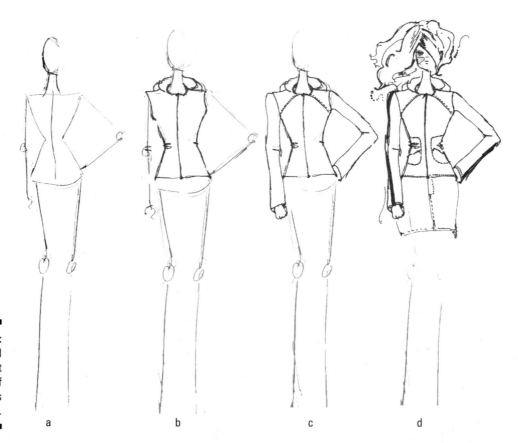

Figure 12-1:
A fitted hiking jacket shows off a model's shape.

a   b   c   d

Men's spring jackets are boxy compared to women's jackets; if you can sketch a rectangle, you're in business. Men's jackets also may feature more pockets or logos.

Try your hand at the men's jacket:

1. **Sketch a male front pose with both arms bent, as in Figure 12-2a.**

   One hand will rest in the jacket's center front pocket, and the other will be hidden behind the back.

2. **Draw the center front zipper and the collar, as in Figure 12-2b.**

   Start the zipper a few inches below the chin. For the collar, draw a *V* at the top of the zipper. Keep one side of the collar straight up and wrap a curved line around the back of the neck. Add a tiny circle beneath this collar for the drawstring hole. Draw a sideways triangle on the other side to show that that side of the collar is open.

3. **Add curved lines at the shoulder and neck to show the hood in the back, as in Figure 12-2c.**

4. **Draw side seams in a boxy shape down the sides of the torso to the hips. Add boxy sleeves with little creases at the bend in the arm. (See Figure 12-2d.)**

5. **Finish with details such as a center front pocket, two zipper pockets on the chest, a drawstring near the neck, and a seam across the chest. Don't forget to add topstitching! (See Figure 12-2e.)**

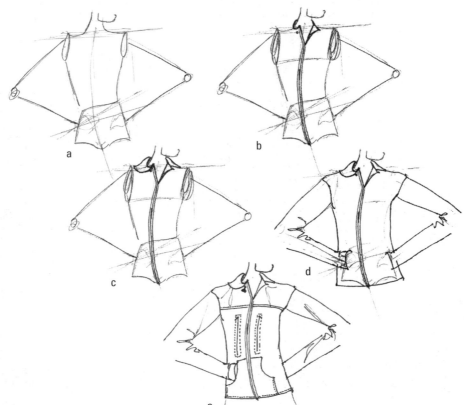

Figure 12-2:
A men's lightweight jacket features pockets, zippers, and piping.

Delighting in rainy day raincoats

Marianne lives in the Pacific Northwest, where it seems to rain every day. Hoods and waterproof gear are essential, and women love to rock their raincoats! From long, sleek pea coat styles to super-technical, boxy, mountain-climbing looks, you can have fun playing in the rain!

For raincoats made of PVC or another shiny material, leave a little white in the dark areas to indicate the shine.

To rock a girl in her raincoat:

1. **Sketch a female side pose, as in Figure 12-3a.**

2. **Draw the sleeve, as in Figure 12-3b.**

   Using the arm hanging straight down as the center of the sleeve, draw a sleeve that starts out narrow at the armholes and bells out at the wrist. Add some stripes for a fun design, leaving a little white in the stripe to indicate the shine of the waterproof material. Sketch in a hat.

3. **Follow the side profile of your model's chest above the breast, drawing a line that falls down from the point of the chest to her stomach and comes a little forward into a bell shape at her knees. Draw the back line of her coat peeking out from behind her arm. Draw a line for the hem to connect the front and back. (See Figure 12-3c.)**

Figure 12-3: A fun raincoat brightens rainy days.

a   b   c   d   e

4. **Add a seam at the waistline and draw a line down her side for the side seam. Draw a couple of short lines at the model's hip to show the side-seam pocket, as in Figure 12-3d.**

   Add boots and draw your model's hair blowing in the wind.

5. **Feel free to add a ruffle at the hem and a bold print throughout the coat (for more on patterns, see Chapter 14). Don't forget to include white areas for shine! (See Figure 12-3e.)**

Fabulous Fall Fashions

Jackets look smart in the fall. Blazers over turtlenecks convey the elegant country look, and short, snappy jackets work for the city. The fall look is about layers, because a fall day can go from chilly to warm to chilly again. A T-shirt layered over a long-sleeve shirt with a hoodie on top can make your fashion look, as can a flannel over a hooded shirt and a knit skirt over leggings and knee-high boots. The combinations are endless!

Exploring fall jacket styles

Fall jackets come in many styles. Sure, you can wear your spring jacket in fall, but who can resist all the great cuts and fabrics designed specifically for cooler temps? These fabrics include heavier cottons (such as flannel), wool, and fleece-lined nylons. Colors tend to differentiate spring from fall jackets; fall jackets tend to feature neutral and darker colors, while spring jackets sport pastels and brighter colors.

The denim or jean jacket remains an enduring classic and is a popular choice when temperatures fall and a brisk wind picks up. The true jean jacket changes very little from year to year.

Here's how to capture the jean jacket look for a guy:

1. **Sketch a male front torso, as in Figure 12-4a.**

2. **Create a boxy look by drawing side seams that come straight down from the armpit to the waist. Add a slight curve for the hem and place four buttons to the right of the center front line. (See Figure 12-4b.)**

3. **Draw the collar, neckline, and additional buttons, as in Figure 12-4c.**

   Draw a *V* under the chin to show the jacket slightly open. For the collar, add some triangles on both sides and a curve going around the neck. Add buttons on the left side of the open part of the center front line and buttonholes on the other.

4. **Add in boxy sleeves down to the wrist, as in Figure 12-4d.**

   The fit of a jean jacket requires a slightly dropped armhole seam, so be sure to draw the armhole seam a little farther down than you would for a woman.

5. **On both sides of the center front line, add in pockets and lines for fitting. Don't forget to add a seam line at the cuff of the sleeve. (See Figure 12-4e.)**

6. **Finish the drawing by adding rows of topstitching next to every seam line, as in Figure 12-4f.**

Figure 12-4:
A jean jacket can ward off the chill and create a rugged look.

Women love fall jackets, too. The younger crowd loves hoodies, especially longer versions they can rock over leggings with high boots.

Try a hoodie-based fall fashion look for a teen girl:

1. **Sketch a three-quarter pose with one arm bent, as in Figure 12-5a.**

2. **Follow the center front line for the centered zipper. Use the sides of her torso to draw the sides of the hoodie and draw a curved line at her crotch level for the hem. (See Figure 12-5b.)**

3. **Sketch in an oval at her head for the opening of the hood and add another curved line behind it for dimension. (See Figure 12-5c.)**

   Include the center seam of the hood with topstitching on both sides.

4. **Draw sleeves following both arms. Add in the ribbing at the end of the sleeves and the bottom hem of the hoodie. Just below the waistline, add in a pocket that curves down from both sides of the center front. (See Figure 12-5d.)**

5. **Finish the hoodie with two drawstrings for the hood at the neckline, as in Figure 12-5e.**

Complete the look with knee-high boots and thigh-high socks.

Figure 12-5:
A teen can look fashionable and stay warm with a hoodie.

a   b   c   d   e

Kicking up your heels in ankle boots

Who doesn't love fall, when the cold and wet weather means it's time to pull out your boots — or buy some new ones! Not only are boots functional, but they're also a classic in fashion. From wedges and heels to flats that end above the ankle, boots can be a great finishing touch to the fall look.

Here's how to illustrate some ankle-high wedge boots:

1. **Sketch a lower torso with one leg stepping forward and the other leg behind, as in Figure 12-6a.**

2. **Draw the wedge-shaped heels, as in Figure 12-6b.**

On the foot stepping forward, sketch a slightly curved triangle for the wedge. On the other foot, draw a line that goes straight back from the ball of the foot; form a 90-degree angle by adding a line that goes straight up to the heel.

3. **To create the tops of the boots, add two curved lines on each boot, with one line slightly above the toes and the other at the ankle, as in Figure 12-6c.**

   Fill in the bottom half of the legs with long cylinders that taper in at the ankle and round out at the knee. Add cylinders from the crotch to the knee for the thighs.

4. **Finish the wedge boot with laces in a zigzag pattern down the center of the shoe. (See Figure 12-6d.)**

   Add some knee socks as well by drawing ribbing just below the knees.

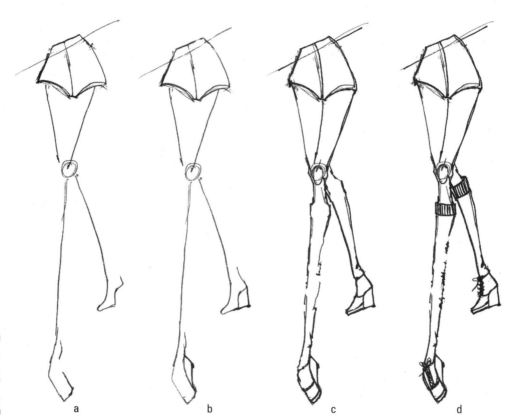

Figure 12-6:
Low boots
show off
long legs.

a   b   c   d

Layering looks

Fall is the time for layers. When dressing your model in fall fashions, you end up with outwear as the last and final layer, but many times you can see the other layers peeking out from underneath. The grunge look of long under-wear with a T-shirt over the top comes to mind for guys. Girls also have the layered look down with a tank top and a low-cut Henley shirt layered over it. Layering is a game of fashion and comfort where creativity creates trends! Watch as ladies layer leggings and socks with skirts or long shirts and men layer long sleeves under short sleeves and vests.

When drawing layers, we suggest that you draw the bottom layer over your figure first and work your way to the outer layers, erasing as you go along.

Here's how to sketch a man sporting a down vest over a cotton button-down shirt:

1. **Sketch a male upper torso with one bent arm, as in Figure 12-7a.**

2. **Draw the outline of the vest. (See Figure 12-7b.)**

   For the collar of the vest, draw a pair of curved lines that wrap around the neck; one goes right under the chin, and the other one sits at the base of the neck. Draw lines for the shoulder seams following the shoulders, curved lines for the armholes, and side seams that follow the body down to right above the crotch. Add a center front line going from the collar to the bottom of the vest. End the bottom of the vest with a pair of lines parallel to one another with vertical lines between them to show ribbing.

3. **For the cotton shirt underneath, draw loose lines on both sides of each arm and two curved lines just above each wrist for the turned-up cuffs. (See Figure 12-7c.)**

   Add topstitching lines down both sides of the vest's center front line to show the zipper seams.

4. **To finish the vest, add horizontal topstitching lines across the body. To show the vest's puffiness, add short and long curved lines that extend from the horizontal lines of topstitching. (See Figure 12-7d.)**

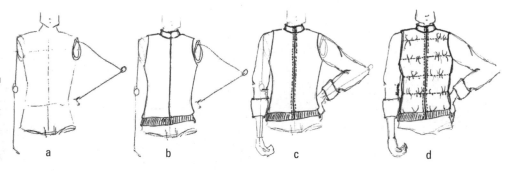

Figure 12-7: A down vest keeps a fella warm.

a   b   c   d

Women love to dress in layers. It gives them an excuse to shop and buy more clothes! Who cares if it means they have to do more laundry? At least they look stylish while they do it.

Try the layered look for women with a knee-length dress paired with a sweater coat, knee-high socks, and boots:

1. **Sketch a full length female pose in three-quarter view, as in Figure 12-8a.**

2. **The Peter Pan collar takes two steps. First draw a curved line at the neckline, and then draw two half circles below it, meeting up at the center front of the collar. For the rest of the sweater coat, follow along the sides of the body and draw the hem right over the knees. (See Figure 12-8b.)**

3. **Draw the coat buttoned at the first two buttons and open the rest of the way down. Start a center front line at the center of the collar and keep it as one line until below the breasts. Split the center front line into two lines that go down to the hem, spreading out more the farther down they go. Add two horizontal lines near the bottom of the coat's opening. (See Figure 12-8c.)**

   The lower line is the back hem of the coat. The higher line is the bottom of the model's dress. Add buttons to one side of the coat and fringe on the coat's hem.

4. **Finish the coat by drawing sleeves that end a little below the elbow. Add the model's legs, paying attention to where the thighs show in relation to the hems. (See Figure 12-8d.)**

   Use the steps from the earlier section "Kicking up your heels in ankle boots" to draw the heels of the boots as wedges. Instead of ending the boots at the ankle, end them around the middle of the calf and add knee-high socks with ribbing at the top.

Figure 12-8: Layering lets you draw a variety of clothing.

a   b   c   d

Warm and Wintry

By the time you've finished drawing a winter coat, you've just about covered up your fashion model! Floor-length coats, ski jackets, pea coats, and tailored coats paired with gloves, hats, and scarves make winter fashions fun and easy to draw — you've covered up nearly all the anatomy and don't need to worry about drawing the perfect pair of ears or hands. In the following sections, we introduce winter coats and cold-weather accessories.

Putting on a great winter coat

A coat makes a statement because during certain parts of the year (depending on where you live), it's the one garment that you can wear every day. You can be known for your look based on the coat you wear. Are you preppy and stylish? Are you bold with patterns, and do you love standing out in a crowd? Whatever your style, coats are so much fun to design!

Although many people from warmer climates use the terms *jacket* and *coat* interchangeably, coauthor Marianne is from Chicago, where the difference between a jacket and coat is that a jacket is lighter in weight. You wear a jacket when the weather is a little warmer, such as in fall and spring. A coat is heavier and warmer and is worn mostly in winter. Coats tend to be longer and made out of thicker fabrics, such as wool or down; they often include details such as fleece lining or fur collars and cuffs.

No matter where you're from, you draw winter coats in the same way you draw spring and fall jackets. Follow the lines of the torso and arms to create the main parts of a winter coat. To show that the model is wearing a winter coat, simply include wintry details that hint at the coat's function. Add design details such as collars, buttons, pockets, cuffs, hoods, extra length, and a snug fit to show the extra bulk and warmth. You can also use texture and patterns to indicate a heavier or seasonal fabric that's suitable for frigid winter days (see Chapter 14 for tips on texture and patterns).

Take a look at a series of winter coat styles:

- ✔ Double-breasted pea coat with a large fur collar and fur cuffs (Figure 12-9a)
- ✔ Long quilted puffer (Figure 12-9b)
- ✔ Short poncho style with raglan sleeves (Figure 12-9c)
- ✔ Satin bomber jacket with a ribbed hem and sleeves (Figure 12-9d)

Designing chill boots

Boots are the finishing accessory that can turn a plain look fierce — not to mention that they keep a lady's legs warm when she's dressed up. Boots come in all shapes and sizes, and they can be functional (think sledding while wearing boots with a thick tread or jumping in rain puddles in the spring) or fashionable (think thigh-high boots with a mini on New Year's Eve). And every once in a while, they're both functional and fashionable at the same time. The fun part is adding buckles, zippers, laces, studs, and whatever else you're feeling!

Figure 12-9:
Winter coat styles can be as varied as snow-flakes.

a   b   c   d

Here's how to rock some high fashion boots that have stretch in the body:

1. **Sketch two legs from the knee down with one foot sideways and the other facing forward, as in Figure 12-10a.**

2. **Draw the heel and platform of each boot, as in Figure 12-10b.**

   On the sideways foot, add two lines coming down from the heel, and on the ball of that foot, draw another line for a slight platform. On the foot facing forward, add a line around the base to show the platform from the front.

3. **Add the top of the boots, buckles, seams, and topstitching, as in Figure 12-10c.**

   Add a buckle across the ankle and a curved seam from the front of the foot around the ankle to the heel. Draw the front view of the buckle on the forward facing foot. End both boots right below the knee with two curved lines, topstitching, and a *V* shape on the side (this shows the elastic that allows the leather to stretch over the wide part of the calf).

Even kids get into the boot look. In fact, some kids love their boots so much that they want to wear them on the hottest summer days.

Boots for young girls should have a simpler design and lower heel than women's boots.

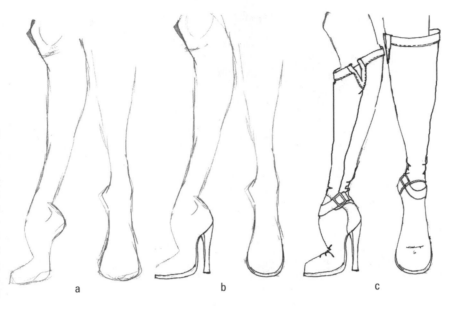

Figure 12-10: Stylish boots keep a woman's legs warm (and fashionable) when she's wearing a short skirt.

a   b   c

To draw a simple yet fun pair of boots for a girl, follow these steps:

1. **Sketch the lower torso of a little girl with one foot facing forward and the other turned in toward the other foot, as in Figure 12-11a.**

2. **Draw the outline of the boots, as in Figure 12-11b.**

   For the top of the boots, draw slightly curved lines right below the knees. Start on one side and trace along the shape of the calf down to the foot around and up the other side, connecting to the line below the knee again. Add another line at the bottom of the foot to create the tread.

3. **Add the seam details, as in Figure 12-11c.**

   On the turned boot, add a line down the side for a side seam. End the seam at the ankle, where it turns into two lines going up in a *V* over the front and around the back of the boot. On the front-facing boot, draw a curve across the ankle to represent the seam.

4. **Finish with fringe coming down from the top of the boot, as in Figure 12-11d.**

Wrapping up with scarves of all sorts

Scarves are a classic winter accessory that keeps coming back in style. Once used only for warmth, today winter scarves make appearances at all occasions, from formal events to an afternoon on the playground. Scarves come as one long strip of fabric with two ends or with the fabric connected in a large circle (these are called *infinity scarves*). They vary by weight and fabrics and of course in color and patterns.

Figure 12-11:
Fringe is a fun accessory to add to girls' boots.

a   b   c   d

Scarves aren't just for keeping you warm — they also pull together your look! You can wrap them around your neck several times, wear them in a knot (or a few knots) in the front, drape them around your neck, shoulders, and head, or come up with other creative ways to express yourself.

Here's how to create a hip, bunched scarf:

1. **Sketch a female upper torso with one arm bent on the waist, as in Figure 12-12a.**

2. **Draw a large oval around the neck and slightly above the chest, as in Figure 12-12b.**

3. **Draw a circle close to the neck, as in Figure 12-12c.**

4. **Add a bunch of short and long curved lines between the circle and oval. At the bottom of the oval, add a rectangular shape with fringe for the end of the scarf. (See Figure 12-12d.)**

Not many men wear scarves to make a fashion statement. Most men use these winter accessories for their primary purpose — warmth.

For a man rocking his down-home scarf:

1. **Sketch a male upper torso with both arms bent, as in Figure 12-13a.**

2. **For the part of the scarf that goes around the neck, draw a curved line right below the chin and another curved line just below the base of the neck, creating a curved shape that points down on one side. (See Figure 12-13b.)**

3. **For the end of the scarf, add a rectangular shape coming down from the pointed, curved shape. Angle the end of the rectangle shape and add fringe, as in Figure 12-13c.**

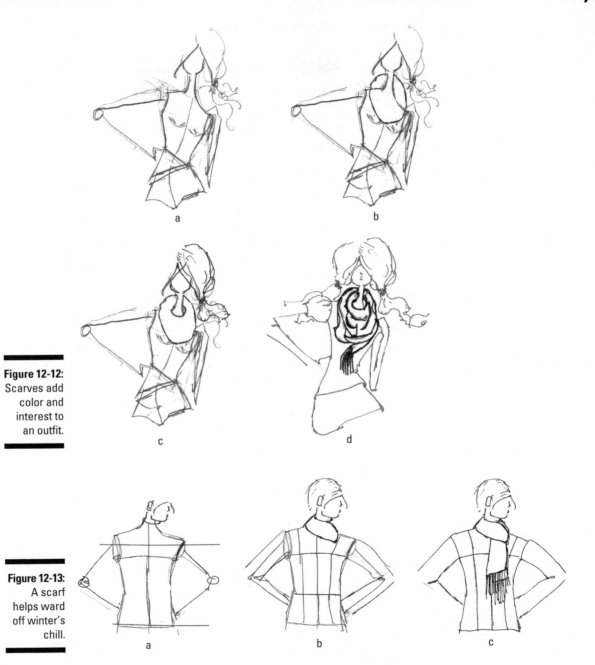

Figure 12-12: Scarves add color and interest to an outfit.

Figure 12-13: A scarf helps ward off winter's chill.

Sporting gloves and mittens

Being fashionable is one thing; being fashionable and warm is another! Mittens and gloves are so much fun because even the tamest of people can wear crazy gloves or mittens and not look silly! Gloves and mittens give everyone a chance to have fun with accessories and keep their little fingers warm. Mittens have only a thumb and a large area for all the fingers, which makes them easier to draw!

Here's how to draw a pair of elbow-length gloves:

1. **Sketch a side view of a female torso with the arm closest to the viewer hanging straight down with a few fingers showing, as in Figure 12-14a.**

2. **Add a curved line right below the elbow and trace around the forearm and hand to form the outline of the glove. (See Figure 12-14b.)**

3. **Finish the gloves with a curved-stripe pattern, as in Figure 12-14c.**

For tips on drawing stripes, turn to Chapter 14.

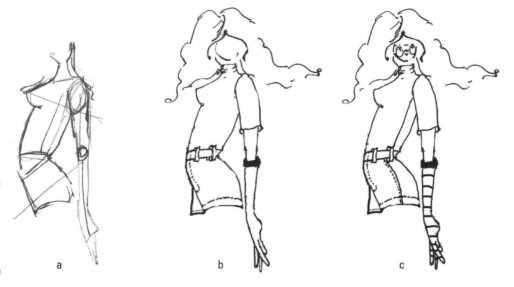

Figure 12-14: Experiment with accessories like gloves.

a   b   c

Chapter 13

Accenting the Accessories

· ·

· ·

The world of fashion illustration isn't just about clothes. Major accessories and extra bling bring a fashion look together. Accessories — hats, shoes, jewelry — can make or break an outfit; the proportions and overall statement must fit together, or your fashion illustration will look unfinished or over-done. In this chapter, we explain how to draw accessories that will have your fashion illustrations humming.

Unlike shirts and pants, accessories don't completely cover the body part they adorn, so you need to draw the hand, ankle, or foot you're featuring with the correct lines and proportions. Head to Chapter 6 if you need to practice drawing these parts.

Finding the Right Shoes

Shoes finish a fashion look. Like clothes, shoe styles change quickly, so keep up with what's new. But keep the classics on hand (or foot!) as well — they only get better with age. Many fashion artists feel intimidated when drawing shoes, but if you can draw feet, we promise that you can draw a shoe.

You need to know how to draw a foot before picking up your pencil to render shoes, so go to Chapter 6 to freshen up your skills if necessary. For more in-depth knowledge on drawing feet, check out *Figure Drawing For Dummies*, by Kensuke Okabayashi (Wiley).

Concentrating on the classics for women

Although shoe fashions come and go, most are variations on a few classics. If you can draw the classics, you can easily modify them with the latest fashion twist. Start out drawing a pair of great-looking pumps and a classic flat. From there, you can take off and draw the most fanciful shoes ever.

Women's feet are much narrower than men's. Don't draw boats at the end of a fashion woman's legs!

Hanging out in heels

Most women love the look of a pair of elegant heels. They make women feel beautiful and their legs look great, which is why heels (the higher, the better) are almost always the choice footwear on fashion runways. These shoes can cover most of the foot or barely any of the foot, depending on the season and the clothing they're paired with.

Here's how to draw a fierce looking high-heeled shoe:

1. **Draw a woman's foot featuring the Barbie arch. (See Figure 13-1a.)**

   See Chapter 6 for details on drawing this arch.

2. **Draw the sole of the shoe with a line that follows the Barbie arch along the bottom of the foot, as in Figure 13-1b.**

   Connect the sole line to the foot at both ends and shade in the area between the lines.

3. **Draw the heel of the shoe with two almost parallel but tapering lines. Shade in the bottom of the heel for the rubber tip. (See Figure 13-1c.)**

4. **Add a small reverse *S* curve just above the heel for the ankle bone.**

5. **Use curved lines to map out the shoe at the back of the heel and in the toe area of the shoe. Then connect the heel and toe with a line to show the side of the shoe. (See Figure 13-1d.)**

Figure 13-1: Draw high-heeled shoes for glam!

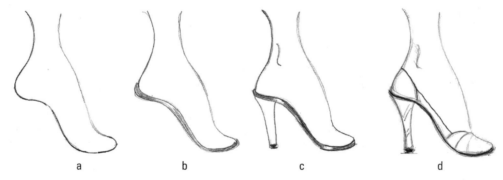

a   b   c   d

Heels don't have to be as high as the heavens to look good. You may want to show your model in a stylish yet comfortable shoe that she could actually walk in without teetering. To modify the arch of the foot, draw the line for the heel lower when following the first step for Figure 13-1. When you connect the line from the heel to the toe, the Barbie arch comes down dramatically, giving your model a shorter heel.

Staying grounded in flats

The classic flat is here to stay because it's so darn comfortable and it looks so graceful! Borrowed in design from the ballet slipper, the flat hugs the shape of your fashion figure's foot and has a teensy sole. You can dress your fashion figure up or down when you draw this style.

Here's how to draw a charming flat:

1. **Draw a shapely foot and mark the ankle bone with an *S* curve. (See Figure 13-2a.)**

   A slender ankle is a fashion artist's must when drawing flats.

2. **Follow the shape of the foot to draw in the top edge of the shoe, giving it a gentle curve. (See Figure 13-2b.)**

3. **Add a little curve for a heel under the heel of the foot and shade for highlights. (See Figure 13-2c.)**

   Even flats have heels — they're just very low.

Figure 13-2:
The classic flat never goes out of style.

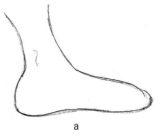 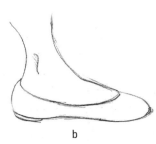 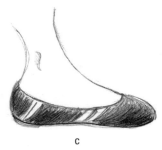

a   b   c

Fancy up the classic flat by adding bows, flowers, or buckles on the toes; stippling the shoe to make it appear sparkly; attaching ribbons that lace up the ankle; or drawing a strap across the top of the foot.

Drawing a dude's shoes

When a guy has to give up his sneakers, what does he wear? Loafers! Make sure you know how to draw a classic loafer for male fashion figures, because you can pair them with just about every style. (We've even seen men in bathing suits and loafers — but not in our fashion sketches!)

Here's how to draw a guy's shoe:

1. **Use a triangle to start your manly foot, as in Figure 13-3a.**

   Don't go too small — guys have big feet!

2. **Refine the foot by sketching in a slight arch, a rounded heel, and a slight curved dip before the toes. (See Figure 13-3b.)**

3. **Form the body of the loafer, as in Figure 13-3c.**

   Start with a line that begins at the top of the heel and goes down around the heel, along the bottom of the foot, and back up to the top of the toes. Draw the top edge of the loafer by starting at the top of the heel and drawing a line along the top edge of the foot and curving over the tops of the toes to meet the first line.

4. **Add a thin rectangular heel, as in Figure 13-3d.**

5. **Add the front piece of the top of the shoe with a gentle curve across the top of the foot. (See Figure 13-3e.)**

6. **Shade to show the grain of the leather, as in Figure 13-3f.**

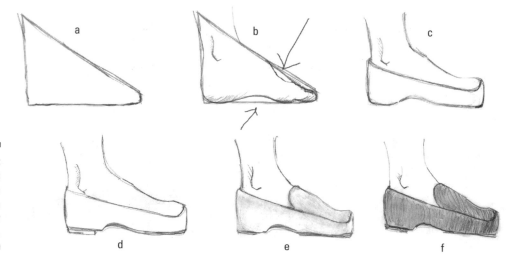

Figure 13-3: Men's loafers are suitable for many occasions.

Give loafers a different look and feel by drawing cutouts across the top (think penny loafers), adding tassels or buckles, or including heavy topstitching around the top of the shoe. You can also pencil in different textures to make the footwear look like it's made out of suede or canvas.

Booting 'em up

Boots are a go-to look for everyone these days. Women's boots can look *way* pointy, feature super-high heels, and end just below the knee, or they can be subdued granny boots that have a low heel and end at the ankle. Boots for a guy look more rugged, with an outdoorsman feel, cowboy look, or industrial, steel-toe vibe.

Boots go with all sorts of fashions, not just jeans or a sleek skirt, in all sorts of seasons. Folks even wear them in the summer! Drawing a fashion figure of a woman in a sundress and boots isn't unusual, and it's not out of the ordinary to draw a guy wearing baggy shorts and boots. The look is the epitome of youth culture, so work on drawing boots that look stylish in any season.

Here's how to draw a tall for a woman boot. (Want to draw ankle boots? We give steps for those in Chapter 12.)

1. **Draw the Barbie arch, as in Figure 13-4a.**

2. **Draw lines just beyond the foot and ankle outline to create the front, back, and bottom of the boot. Draw a curve at midcalf for the top of the boot, connecting the front and back of the boot. (See Figure 13-4b.)**

3. **Add a heel that reaches the sole of the boot and shade it in for contrast. (See Figure 13-4c.)**

4. **Add folds at the front and back of the boot for a slouchy look. (See Figure 13-4d.)**

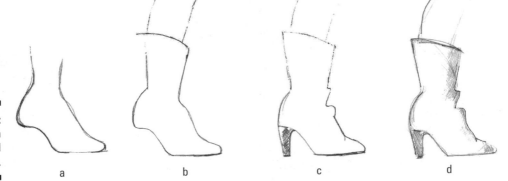

Figure 13-4: Fashion boots add elegance.

a   b   c   d

Women can slip into boots any number of ways. Some boots you can just pull on. Others zip, lace, or button, depending on how high and tight against the leg they are; these closures may be on the front, back, or side of the boot. Play around with different closures as you practice drawing boots.

Here's how to draw a hip guy's hiking boots:

1. **Start with a triangle and add a curve to the heel and a slight arch. (See Figure 13-5a.)**

   A guy's boot has a heel, too, just not a high one.

2. **Draw the general shape of a boot by loosely following the coutours of the foot, as in Figure 13-5b.**

   Draw a line just below the bottom edge of the boot to create the sole of the boot. Add a curve above the ankle for the top of the boot. Make the curve rise a little bit at the front of the leg; this will be the top of the boot's tongue.

3. **Add a cuff at the sides and back of the boot by drawing a line parallel to the top of the boot from the back to where the tongue begins. Connect the lines with a curved line to give the cuff some shape. (See Figure 13-5c.)**

4. **Draw a line parallel to the top of the foot, extending it from the top of the tongue to about two-thirds of the way down the shoe. Add in laces that cross from one side of the tongue to the other. Use a zigzagged line on the sole to add the tread. (See Figure 13-5d.)**

5. **Finish the boot by adding a line from the front to the back of the boot at the midpoint of the foot, showing where the materials change. Add shading to indicate differences in color. (See Figure 13-5e.)**

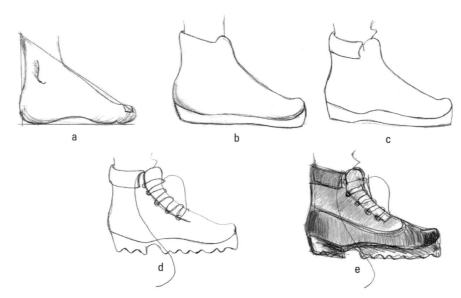

Lounging about in sandals, wedges, and flip-flops

Sandals, wedges, and flip-flops are summer classics, so drawing them (and the feet they show off) well is essential, unless you plan on majoring in winter fashions. Sandals can be nothing more than a sole and a simple strap, or you can decorate them to the max with beads, prints, and other artwork. Flip-flops, on the other hand, are all about simple lines. Wedges are a more-solid version of the high heel.

Stepping out in sandals

Everyone wears sandals these days. Women walk around in strappy sandals that wrap up to and around the ankle, men wear "Jesus" sandals, and kids run around in sandals that are easy to slip on and off. The key feature of sandals is that they're fashioned from straps of materials that crisscross the foot and show off the foot's structure.

Here's how to draw a women's sandal with style:

1. **Draw the Barbie arch, as Figure 13-6a shows.**

2. **Thicken the line along the bottom of the foot to form the sandal's sole. Sketch a high, tapered heel for a dressy summer look. (See Figure 13-6b.)**

3. **Add one curved line across the top of the toes to form the toe of the sandal, and then add two sets of parallel lines across the top of the foot for the straps. Another set of curved parallel lines forms the ankle strap. (See Figure 13-6c.)**

4. **Decorate with bling by adding small circles of different sizes to represent sparkle from glitter or beads. Vary the pencil pressure so some are darker than others. (See Figure 13-6d.)**

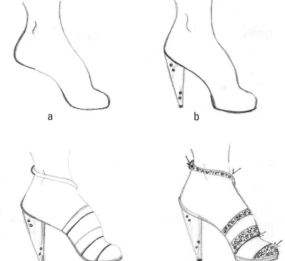

Figure 13-6: Draw sizzling summer sandals.

In addition to drawing strappy high-heeled sandals, you can modify the classic flat and the men's loafers to turn them into sandals. Draw the basic soles as described earlier in this chapter. Then, instead of drawing the solid toes or leather uppers, draw straps that cross the top of the foot and attach to the sole — use thin or thick straps for women and thick straps for men. For women, you can even continue thin straps up the calf for an ancient Roman look.

Working with wedges

The wedge is a durable classic that matches any type of summer outfit. Much more casual than a high-heeled shoe, the wedge still gives you extra height. Your fashion drawings look snappy when you draw shorts, a flirty summer sundress, or even a bathing suit accompanied by the wedge-shaped shoe.

The wedge is usually made out of cork or wood for a more casual look. You can achieve the texture of wood or cork by adding a few hatching lines and some stippling (see Chapter 14 for tips on drawing texture).

Here's how to draw a wedge:

1. **Draw the Barbie arch, as in Figure 13-7a.**

2. **Draw a straight line down from the heel to the ground and a perpendicular line that extends to the beginning of the toes. (See Figure 13-7b.)**

   Slightly angle the vertical line toward the ball of the foot for a stylish look.

3. **Add two parallel curves across the top of the foot to form sandal strap and shade it in. (See Figure 13-7c.)**

Figure 13-7:
Wedges
have a wow
factor.

a   b   c

Flipping for flip-flops

The simple flip-flop — designed for both genders, super-easy to draw, and usually made of foam rubber — follows the line of the foot and is attached by a single rubber strap.

Men are more likely to wear flip-flops than sandals, so here's how to draw flip-flops for a fella:

1. **Sketch a triangle for a male foot, as in Figure 13-8a.**

2. **Add a thin sole at the bottom of the foot by following the line of the foot. (See Figure 13-8b.)**

   Extend the line slightly beyond the toes and heel.

3. **Draw two wide parallel curves to form a thick sandal strap that wraps from the side of the foot over the top. (See Figure 13-8c.)**

   Depending on the view of the foot, you may want to make part of the strap disappear between the big toe and second toe to make the flip-flop look like a thong.

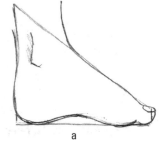
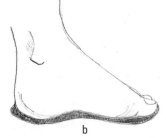
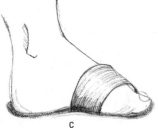

Figure 13-8:
The flip-flop
is forever.

a   b   c

Drawing Kidswear: Shoes That Play Well

Kids' shoes are all about comfort. Fashion-illustration kids often sport sneakers, but you have other footwear choices as well. Boots, flip-flops, and sandals all work for kids as well as adults (see the earlier sections for details about drawing these shoes; simply scale down the footwear for the younger crowd). In this section, we show you how to draw a kids' favorite, sneakers, and introduce you to colorful clogs.

Sneakers — always in style

How many types of sneakers can you draw on your fashion figure of a child? Too many! We could fill up pages with sneaker drawings, but we'll stick to tips on the kind kids crave. Athletic sneaks are padded, with arched and chunky-looking soles that curve up at the toes. Some have stripes and flashing lights in the heels, and others have elevated heels and soles for bounce. Sneakers are to kids as what cars are to adults: status.

Here's how to draw a stylized sneaker:

1. **Map out the shape of a child's foot, as in Figure 13-9a.**

2. **Draw a full sole following the bottom of the foot. (See Figure 13-9b.)**

   Make sure to curve the sole up under the toes.

3. **Use a curve below the ankle to enclose the shoe. (See Figure 13-9c.)**

   The front and back of the foot transform into the front and back of the sneaker because these shoes are pretty form-fitting. The curve you draw in this step connects the front and back of the shoe.

4. **Add a curve at the heel and draw a pair of curved lines around the ankle and down the front of the shoe. A simple zigzag line indicates shoelaces. Right above the laces, draw a curved line to show the tongue. Add a little loop in the back for a nice detail. (See Figure 13-9d.)**

   Kids' sneakers have all sorts of cool features these days. Add lines, lights, symbols, or other elements that appeal to youngsters' sense of style and make them stand out from their peers.

Figure 13-9: Sneakers fit for a kid on the move.

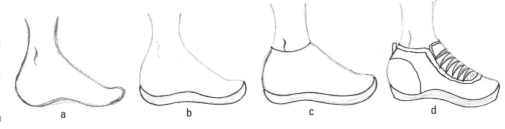

a   b   c   d

Adults wear sneakers, too. If you're drawing workout gear for grown-ups, the only modification you have to make when drawing the shoes is to keep them in scale with the rest of your fashion figure.

Clogs for kids

Fashion drawings of kids in clogs are really adorable. When a little girl is twirling about in a colorful summer dress with a matching pair of clogs or a little guy is marching around in shorts and clogs, a fashion drawing looks very in-the-moment. Clogs, which are usually made out of a foam resin, are the shoe of the moment for kids' fashion illustrations. Who cares if these shoes were originally meant for boating? This lightweight footwear is all the rage for the kid set.

Here's how to draw clogs for a child:

1. **Draw a child's foot, as in Figure 13-10a.**

2. **Draw two parallel curves around the heel for the back strap and a curve from the bottom of the heel to the top of the foot for the front of the shoe. (See Figure 13-10b.)**

   The outline of the foot transforms into the outline of the top and toe of the shoe.

3. **Draw an arched and chunky sole beneath the bottom outline of the foot. (See Figure 13-10c.)**

Figure 13-10:
Kids love
the ease of
clogs.

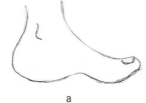
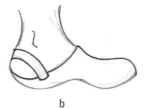
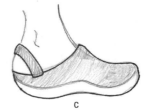

a   b   c

Jewelry and Watches: It's All About the Bling

Drawing jewelry on your fashion figures is all about using basic shapes to create necklaces, earrings, bracelets, or watches. Going back to the basics applies whether you're creating simple or elaborate jewelry.

Is bigger better? Not necessarily; be mindful of what works for your fashion drawing. You don't want the jewelry to overshadow the clothes you've drawn, nor do you want to play it too safe.

All items of jewelry must follow the curve of the neck or arm, or you'll end up with a flat look in your drawing.

Necklaces — simple to outrageous

Fashion necklaces work best when you draw them with a graceful curve and lots of little shapes. The proportion and style should match your fashion figure's outfit.

There's no fashion rule about what type of necklace looks best with a certain clothing style or how many necklaces you can wear at a time — the trendy look changes constantly! From the tight, fitted choker to the long, thin chain of fringe hanging down to the waist, anything goes when it comes to dressing up the neck. Experiment with mixing long and short together and then throwing in some bulk with pearls or large pendants.

In this exercise, you draw two styles of necklaces: one simple, one more elaborate. The elaborate piece builds on the simple necklace.

1. **Draw the head, neck, and shoulders of a woman, as in Figure 13-11a.**

   A swan-like neck is essential to show off a necklace. If you need a refresher on drawing heads, head to Chapter 7.

2. **Add a line to show the chain or metal of the necklace. Draw the line so it follows the shape of the neck; curve the edges away from the neck slightly to show how the necklace wraps around the back of the neck. (See Figure 13-11b.)**

3. **Draw a simple shape for an understated look. (See Figure 13-11c.)**

   A circle can represent a pearl or a round diamond. A diamond shape or square can represent an eye-catching bead or any cut gemstone you like. Use your imagination or browse through a jewelry catalog or website to gather ideas.

4. **Draw extra curves and lots of shapes (trinkets) for an abundant design statement. (See Figure 13-11d.)**

   Add dangles, multiple beads, or several wraps around the lady's neck to create a fancy showpiece.

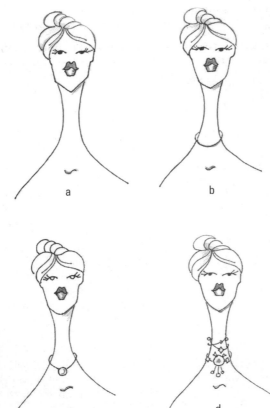

Figure 13-11:
Necklaces can be simple or elaborate.

a

b

c

d

Bangles for hands and feet

Drawing a simple curve around the wrist gets you started with the look of a basic bangle, but as a fashion artist, you want to show the thickness as well as the texture of jewelry, whether you're creating an antique heirloom or a summer hippie look with a thin chain, a piece of hemp, or a rubber bangle around the ankle.

In fashion drawings, bangles look best with short-sleeved or sleeveless blouses and dresses. In real life, women may wear bracelets with long sleeves, but when putting your fashion ideas on paper, you don't want to make your model appear cluttered. So if your model's forearms are bare and you feel like adding something, dress them up with as many bangles as suits her style.

Here's how to draw bangles:

1. **Draw a woman's wrist and hand, as in Figure 13-12a.**

   If you need to brush up on drawing hands, flip to Chapter 6.

2. **Sketch a wide curve around the wrist area for each thin bangle. Think about gravity when drawing bangles; the top of the circle should touch the wrist and the bottom should be hanging below the wrist. (See Figure 13-12b.)**

   Bangles need to be wide enough to slide over the hand onto the wrist. A thin chain bracelet often has a clasp that allows for a shorter length.

3. **For a thicker bangle, sketch two parallel curves and connect them with two short, curved lines to show the bangle's curve. (See Figure 13-12c.)**

4. **Shade for texture. (See Figure 13-12d.)**

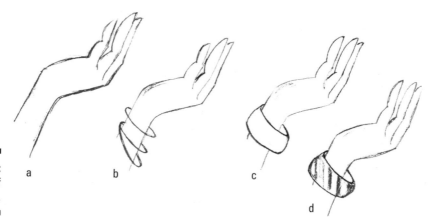

Figure 13-12: Bangles of all sorts.

a   b   c   d

Draw an anklet exactly as you would a bracelet, but curve it around a cute-looking fashion ankle rather than a wrist. (Chapter 6 tells you how to draw fashionable ankles.) Add a low sandal, and your model's ready to hit the beach.

Watching the time

The design style of watches can range from casual to opulent for men and women. Since the advent of cell phones, watches have become more of a fashion statement than a means of telling time, so don't be afraid to add outrageous design and details.

Most people wear their watch on their left wrists (although a lefty may wear her watch on her right wrist). If you need to brush up on drawing arms, wrists, and hands, check out Chapter 6.

Creating a fancy watch for a woman on the go

For a high-styled lady watch, a leather band just won't do. Heavy silver or gold links are all about luxury, and twinkling diamond edging around the face of the watch completes the image. Drawing an oval shape for the watch face adds to the elegance and makes the watch more like a jewelry piece.

Here's how to draw a women's watch that tells more than time:

1. **Draw the back of the wrist and hand of a woman. (See Figure 13-13a.)**

2. **Draw an oval for the watch face at the base of the wrist, as in Figure 13-13b.**

3. **Edge the oval with tiny circles for diamonds. (See Figure 13-13c.)**

4. **Draw little rectangles to form the links of the watch band, as in Figure 13-13d.**

   Make the links curve around the wrist.

   Add tiny markings to represent the numbers. You can put 12 of them on the face of the watch, or you can simply mark the quarter hours. Be sure to include hands on the face of the watch. Without those, your model will never be on time for anything!

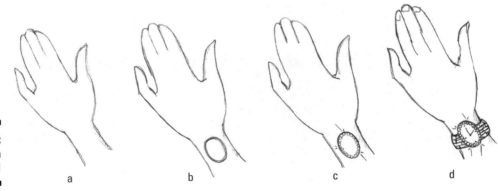

Figure 13-13: Watch in wonder!

a   b   c   d

Keeping time for the guys

If you're drawing a guy in a suit, don't forget to draw his watch peeking out from under his long-sleeve shirt, because it's a safe bet he's wearing one. Guys in suits have places to go, and they need to get there on time! Because guys don't often wear bracelets, a watch makes a nice accessory for any guy wearing a short-sleeve shirt as well.

Here's how to draw a guy's simple watch:

1. **Sketch the back of a guy's wrist and hand. (See Figure 13-14a.)**

2. **Draw a circle for the watch face on the wrist. (See Figure 13-14b.)**

3. **Add a leather strap on each side of the face of the watch by drawing two parallel lines that curve around the wrist. Join them with a curved line to show the shape of the strap and then shade in the straps. (See Figure 13-14c.)**

   Don't forget to add numbers — or marks that stand in for the numbers — and hands to the face of the watch. Or you can draw a digital face for your watch.

Figure 13-14:
A guy's watch.

a   b   c

Keeping jewelry simple for kids

A little kid should wear only little pieces of jewelry. Big, glitzy pieces scream of pageantry, and pageantry just *isn't* about fashion and style. Go easy when drawing a little girl and sketch a simple locket around her neck (yay for the heart shape!). You may draw a little guy wearing a special bead that's been threaded with twine for a miniature surfer dude look.

Here's how to draw a little lady's locket:

1. **Draw the head, neck, and shoulders of a girl, as in Figure 13-15a.**

2. **Draw a curve around her neck for the chain. (See Figure 13-15b.)**

3. **Draw a little heart shape in the middle of the curve, just below the collarbone. (See Figure 13-15c.)**

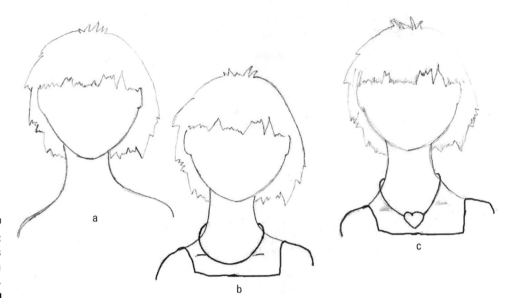

Figure 13-15:
A locket is
special for a
little girl.

Here's how to draw a surfer-dude choker:

1. **Draw the head, neck, and shoulders of a young man. (See Figure 13-16a.)**

2. **Sketch several curves around his neck to show twine, as in Figure 13-16b.**

   Keep the curves close together, because they'll all go through the bead in the next step.

3. **Draw an oval for a bead. (See Figure 13-16c.)**

   The bead should be big enough to contain all the curves you drew in Step 2. If you show the bead from the side, make sure you draw the hole that the twine passes through. You can substitute a masculine charm for the bead — think simple geometric shapes, claws or shark teeth, snakes, skulls, or dogtags.

Figure 13-16:
Twine and
a bead
make up a
guy's trendy
choker.

a   b   c

Let's Hear It for the Hat

Once upon a time, men and women wore hats just about everywhere — you just weren't dressed without a hat. Today, hats are optional, but people often opt for them when making a fashion statement. Baseball hats remain ubiquitous for guys under 30, and nothing adds elegance to an outfit like a hat straight out of the 1930s — for men or women! The Fedora is even making a comeback.

To keep you on the right fashion track, the proper fashion term for designer hats is *millinery*. Impress your friends with that!

Drawing high-fashion headgear for any occasion or season

Sun hats, brim hats, and snug-fitting hats all start with one mini golden rule: draw a shape that fits around the head before adding brims, textures, and accessories.

Here's how to draw three different hats for women:

1. **Draw the head and neck of a female fashion figure. (See Figure 13-17a.)**

2. **Map out the crown of the hat close to the head. (See Figure 13-17b.)**

3. **Embellish the hat by adding different brims, textures, or even feathers or flower shapes (not shown) to adorn the lady's hat.**

   - Sketch a wide oval that extends around the back of the head for the brim of a sunhat. (See Figure 13-17c.)

   - A small oval slightly wider than the hat works for the brim of a hip hat. (See Figure 13-17d.)

   - Extend the crown of the hat down around the ears and near the eyes for a warm cap. (See Figure 13-17e.)

Going classic with the ball cap

Some men's hats are real classics — the Fedora, the Stetson, and the Panama. And although the bandana isn't exactly a hat, *so* many guys wear bandanas around their heads that they have to be considered fashion headgear. But when opting for a hat, most guys these days wear the baseball cap whenever possible. This hat has left the dugout and shows up on every type of man, teen, or kid for every possible occasion, including black-tie events!

Figure 13-17:
Three hats
for women.

Here's how to draw the universal ball cap for all men:

1. **Draw a guy's head in profile. (See Figure 13-18a.)**

2. **Map out the shape of the crown close to the head. (See Figure 13-18b.)**

   Add some crease lines at the top of the hat to show how the fabric shapes to fit the head.

3. **Draw the bill of the cap.**

   - To draw a forward-facing cap, draw a thin half-oval for a brim above the guy's profile. (See Figure 13-18c.)

   - To draw a baseball cap worn backwards, draw the brim going down the back of the neck. To make the bill look curved, keep the top of the brim straight and curve the bottom line that connects it from the body of the hat to the front of the brim. (See Figure 13-18d.)

Topping it off with kids' hats

You can always adapt baseball caps for kids. Two other types of caps look adorable on kids but have rather odd nicknames: the Trapper Hat and the Thief Cap. These hats work for both genders. Trapper Hats and Thief Caps are often made of knitted wools or a heavy cotton with a faux fur lining.

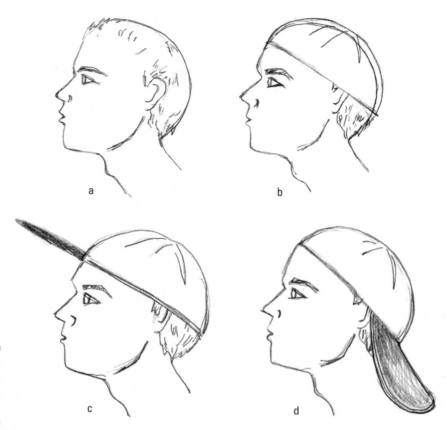

Figure 13-18:
Baseball
caps are
everywhere.

a

b

c

d

Here's how to draw a Trapper Hat without the fur:

1. **Draw the head and neck of a boy. (See Figure 13-19a.)**

2. **At the crown of the head, map out the shape of the hat rising slightly above the head. (See Figure 13-19b.)**

3. **Draw a curved line slightly above the eyebrows to cover the forehead. (See Figure 13-19c.)**

   The line connects to the sides of the hat.

4. **Add ear flaps to the sides of the head over the ears and add ties to the flaps. (See Figure 13-19d.)**

   Use one of the techniques from Chapter 14 to add texture to your hat. If you want to add fur, draw the inner line around the face jagged with a few extra lines for texture.

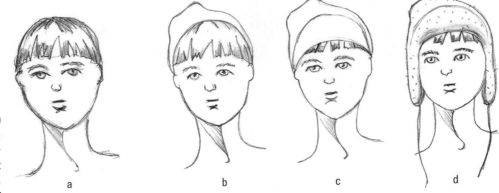

Figure 13-19:
The Trapper
Hat without
the fur.

a   b   c   d

Here's how to draw a Thief Cap, or stocking cap:

1. **Draw the head and neck of a young girl. (See Figure 13-20a.)**

2. **Map out the shape of the cap right along the head and over the ears. (See Figure 13-20b.)**

3. **Finish the cap by drawing a curve right above the eyes covering the hair and ears. Add short lines for texture. (See Figure 13-20c.)**

Figure 13-20:
The Thief
Cap looks
cute.

a   b   c

Part IV
Taking Your Fashion Drawing to the Next Level

The 5th Wave   By Rich Tennant

"I wanted them to look like real fashion models, so I drew them throwing cellphones at each other."

In this part . . .

Moving on to the next level is necessary if you want to perfect your craft. Bring your illustrations to life by mastering body movement, creating a sense of different fabrics, and conveying the way the clothing moves. We also show you how to develop your own style and, just as important, how to sell your work to the world.

Chapter 14

Fabrics: Refining Style with Draping, Texture, and Patterns

Fashion illustration is about more than drawing tall figures dressed in interesting clothing. You need to add details to your illustrations that show how the clothing fits the body and what fabric the clothing is made of.

When you show how that clothing fits and moves with the body, you focus on *draping* your model. Draping in fashion illustration is not like still-life art classes, where every fold must lie perfectly (boy, do we ever remember *those* classes!). Like the rest of fashion illustration, drawing drapery is about exaggeration — you find the few key folds in clothing and run with it. Your job is to show how both the body and cloth move and play off each other.

Other details of fashion drawing convey the feel and look of the fabric. What types of fabric are your garments made of? Denim, cotton, leather, silk? Does the fabric have a pattern, such as stripes? Including details like these in your drawings gives a more complete picture of the outfits you've designed.

In this chapter, we give you tips about draping fabric, rendering textures of fabrics, and drawing clothes with plaids, polka dots, and other patterns. Practice these skills, individually, and as you get more confident, mix and match the techniques to create innovative designs that your friends and family will be begging to wear.

Getting the Hang of Draping

When we talk about draping or drapery, we're not talking about curtains. In fashion illustration, *drapery* refers to the fluidity of clothing on your fashion models — it's how the fabric hangs on the body, creating folds. The clothing on your fashion figure can look very flat if you don't observe the way clothes fall against the fashion body and move when the model poses or struts down a runway.

Many factors influence how a garment is draped on the body:

- The obvious factor is the shape and position of the body wearing the piece. Depending on the model's body position, certain parts of the garment may become stretched or pushed together. Although gravity pulls the fabric downward, the model's motion may cause part of the garment to float away from the body.

- The weight and stiffness of the fabric determine how a piece of clothing fits and moves with the body. A pair of leather pants fits differently than denim jeans or silk trousers do, even if the cuts of the pants are similar.

- The cut of the item has an effect on draping. A skin-tight skirt lays differently on the body than a loose peasant skirt does.

Taking into account the numerous body shapes, fabrics, and cuts of clothing, you have endless ways to drape a garment. And most of the time, all three of these factors work together in your design. In the following sections, we show you how to work with various aspects of draping.

Following the folds to show how clothes move

Folds don't just fall without purpose — there are reasons why cloth pulls and moves on your fashion figure. When material moves in different directions (because you've drawn a fashion figure really working it), folds appear!

The placement and appearance of the folds partly depends on how you've drawn your fashion figure, because the folds show areas where the fabric is stretched or compressed. Include folds when you draw a shirt tucked into another garment, a super tight piece of clothing, or a gathered or draped piece of clothing.

The type of fabric also affects the draping. Lighter fabrics that fall loosely (like chiffons, light cottons, silk, and thin flannels) move more than stiffer, heavier fabrics (like leather, suitings, and wool).

As you draw a fashion figure striking a fierce pose, include some key folds. Look at fashion magazines or watch clips of runway models strutting their stuff to check out how the fabric falls against the elbows, knees, crotch, chest, and hips; you need to draw only one or two lines or curves to convey movement.

Don't draw too many fashion folds, or your drawings will look overworked and confusing. When you draw a clothed fashion figure, folds most commonly form at bended areas such as at the waist, hip, crotch, elbows, and knees.

Here's how to draw simple folds in casual clothes:

1. **Sketch a fashion figure with her right elbow and leg bent. Dress her in a simple shirt and pants, as in Figure 14-1a.**

2. **Draw a few curved lines going inside the shirt where the elbow bends, and add some curved lines outside the elbow to show the folds, as in Figure 14-1b.**

   Drawing curves is an awesome way to show the folds in fabric.

3. **Draw some curves where the knee bends the same way you drew them for the elbow. Add some curves for the breasts and crotch area. (See Figure 14-1c.)**

   Add shading around the fold lines to show depth in the fabric.

Figure 14-1:
Fashion
folds!

a   b   c

Tightening folds for body-hugging clothes

Some clothes are really tight, and why not? On the body of a fashion figure, that's often the way they look best! Draw a long, lean fashion figure and show her (or him) off in clothes that really hug that bod. No matter how tight the shirt, dress, or pants are, folds do exist — tinier ones. You need to add them to show how even the tightest of fabrics stretch.

You're your own best model for figuring out where folds should fall in your sketches. Put on a tight pair of jeans or leggings and stand in front of a mirror with one hand on your hip. Where do you see folds? You typically see them where the body bends. Notice that the tighter the area of bending, the smaller the folds are. Your body is three-dimensional and full of curves and angles, so when clothing is tight, you'll always have areas with folds.

Now try the same pose while wearing loose jeans or pants. Again, notice where the fabric folds and how large those folds are. When clothing is looser, the fabric folds in places where the body bends and where gravity pulls the fabric down.

Even the tightest articles of clothing have folds at the elbows, hips, crotch, ankles, and knees in a fashion drawing.

Here's how to draw a tight dress and even tighter leggings:

1. **Draw a female fashion figure, as in Figure 14-2a.**

2. **Map out a tight little dress and leggings on her body. (See Figure 14-2b.)**

3. **Draw a few small lines to show folds at the elbows, knees, stomach, and ankles. Add one or two diagonal folds under the breasts and use shading to add depth to the folds. (See Figure 14-2c.)**

Figure 14-2:
Tight
clothes,
tight folds!

a   b   c

Drawing folds in hanging fabric

Some fashion models are fortunate enough to wear glam dresses and gowns, where the cloth tumbles into a beautiful cascade. Many noted designers use bolts and bolts of fabric to get gorgeous hanging folds.

Don't draw little curves at the hemline of a dress and expect them to look like folds. Choose a few key folds and follow their form from where they begin down to the hemline for good fashion results. Graceful folds in soft or light fabrics originate from a focal point like a bodice, a sleeve, or the back of the dress and follow the line of your fashion figure.

Here's how to draw your fashion figure in a dream of a dress with a two-tiered floating skirt featuring loads of folds:

1. **Lightly sketch a fashion figure of a woman wearing an asymmetrical hem dress, as in Figure 14-3a.**

2. **Draw a few lines around the neckline in curved shapes crossing over and underneath each other, as in Figure 14-3b.**

3. **Draw two rows of curved lines for the hem. At the bend of each curve, draw a line going up to show the folds of the fabric. (See Figure 14-3c.)**

Give the fold lines a little bit of curve to convey the skirt's movement.

Figure 14-3:
Light fabric lends itself to long, loose folds.

a   b   c

Folding in the fabric's characteristics

Fabric characteristics such as weight and flexibility — in other words, gravity and fit of the clothing on the body — can affect the appearance of folds:

- Soft and light woven fabrics can hug the body, but they often swirl and float away from the body when a fashion model is in motion.

- Lightweight knits hang in soft folds while also fitting around the body horizontally in small, snug folds.

- Stiff, heavyweight fabrics such as denim hang with large, rigid curves.

- Stiff, lightweight fabrics such as polyester or silk taffeta can fold with sharp angles and tend to take on a shape of their own, with somewhat soft folds and other sharp folds.

Creating Depth with Texture

All fabrics work for at least one type of clothing, but as a fashion artist, you're the one who chooses the type of fabric that works for your fashion figure's clothes. Do you want to draw a cutting-edge leather coat? Do you dare to draw fierce-looking tweed pants with a high waist or to draw a long, nubby sweater? *Texture,* which in the fashion world means the feel of the fabric, suggests different fabrics and adds a sense of dimension.

Texture is significant when you zoom in on your fashion figure and showcase the details. Adding texture is a perfect way to polish your style, whether you render herringbone pants or a chunky sweater.

A mini golden rule that applies to texture is that less is more. You don't have to render every bit of fabric when drawing texture in clothes. In fact, it's quite tasteful looking when the texture fades off the clothes, leaving a blank area. However, don't leave too much blank space when drawing a textured item, or it'll look like you're taking a shortcut.

In the following sections, we show you how to draw different fabric textures. You can create fabric looks that conform to or go against common fashion rules. Pull out your bag of texture tricks and use shading, cross-hatching, and stippling to create different fabric types.

Some fashion designers choose to be *very* alternative with their fabric choices when designing; think about shoes covered in thick fur or a vinyl wedding dress with a plastic veil!

Creating a luxurious look with herringbone

The *herringbone* texture is named after a fish, because the pattern of thin, parallel lines looks just like a herring's spine. In fabric, herringbone is a texture in which the threads are woven together. Drawing the herringbone texture is about knowing how to team up your lines and point them in opposite directions to form right-side-up and upside-down *V*'s (this alternating *V* shape is called *chevron*). Fabric with a herringbone pattern is often used to make pants and men's sports jackets.

Herringbone feels raised to the touch, a sensation you need to communicate through your drawing techniques.

To draw a herringbone texture:

1. **Draw a series of angled lines in a vertical row, as in Figure 14-4a.**

2. **Repeat in a chevron pattern, switching the direction of the angle with each vertical row. (See Figure 14-4b.)**

Figure 14-4:
Herringbone
rows.

Now you're ready to draw a sporty pair of herringbone pants worn by a fashion figure who looks like an heiress in her country house. To complete the look, think tweeds, boots, scarves, and cashmere for luxurious country living.

Here's how to draw classic herringbone pants:

1. **Draw a fashion figure of a woman, as in Figure 14-5a.**

2. **Map out a wide pair of pants with a high waist. (See Figure 14-5b.)**

3. **Add your herringbone texture, leaving an unfinished area for fashion balance. (See Figure 14-5c.)**

Figure 14-5:
Classic
herringbone
makes a
comeback.

a   b   c

Conquering cross-hatching

When you add *cross-hatching* to an illustration, you draw a series of lines that parallel one another and then cross that group of lines with another group of parallel lines in the opposite direction. You can use cross-hatching to add texture to clothes or for shading. Fabrics such as tweed (a type of woven pattern for thick threads) and tulle (a stiff, stretchy, woven, lightweight fabric) generally have a cross-hatching texture.

To create the cross-hatching look, follow this example:

1. **Draw a series of horizontal straight lines, as in Figure 14-6a.**

   Keep the lines evenly spaced and not too close together.

2. **Draw vertical lines across the horizontal lines. (See Figure 14-6b.)**

   Apply the same spacing you used in Step 1.

3. **Use for texture in clothes like a tweed skirt, as in Figure 14-6c.**

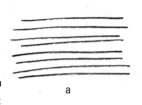

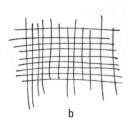

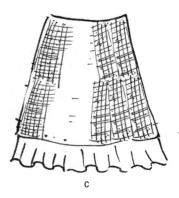

Figure 14-6:
Cross-hatch
for texture.

Cross-hatching can run in other directions beside top-to-bottom and left-to-right. The zigzag cross-hatch is another way to create texture and interest. Want to draw a sheepskin coat collar or a textured, nubby jacket on an urban guy? Start by simply drawing several zigzagging lines. They can overlap each other or curve and go from thick to thin or thin to thick — the more variety, the better.

When you draw a zigzag cross-hatch on the neckline of a tight sweater on your fashion figure, you can create fashion fluff — in a good way! Not only is zigzag cross-hatch fun to draw, but it also makes the clothing in your drawing look playful. Everyone should have at least one little number that can only be worn to a "Gay Paree" type of party.

Make sure that your zigzags overlap for an even flow. However, don't line up the zigzags in simple rows, or the excitement will go out of the look.

Here's how to draw a boa using the cross-hatch technique:

1. **Draw the top half of a female fashion figure. (See Figure 14-7a.)**

2. **Map out a tight tanktop with a curved neckline. (See Figure 14-7b.)**

3. **Draw two rows of zigzag cross-hatch around the collar line for fashion fluff. (See Figure 14-7c.)**

Figure 14-7:
Add zigzag
cross-hatch
for flair
and fun.

a   b   c

Starting with stippling

Stippling is a technique of drawing tiny little dots, and it never looks better than when you use it to add texture on a great-looking wool jacket or sensible, slimming pencil skirt. Stippling works well on fabrics with a rough texture, such as wool, crepe, and sequins. (See Chapter 3 for a review of stippling techniques and uses.) Stippling dots represent holes, nubbing, flecks in the material, or areas where the threads overlap in the weave structure.

Stippling can make the drawing of your fashion dude's jacket go from flat and dry to a richly textured look. Sound easy? Yes and no — you have to go slowly when you stipple, or you can end up with little lines instead of little dots.

Not every inch of a dude's jacket has to be stippled; let the wool breathe by leaving an unstippled area. In Figure 14-8, Marianne combined stippling with cross-hatching to give the fella's jacket a super-textured look.

Try drawing a textured jacket for a dude:

1. **Draw the top half of a fashion dude, as in Figure 14-8a.**

2. **Map out a jacket. (See Figure 14-8b.)**

3. **Stipple and cross-hatch the jacket throughout the design. (See Figure 14-8c.)**

Figure 14-8:
Stipple that jacket for texture!

a   b   c

Working with thick wool trim

Drawing a warm, shearling-trimmed coat and boots on your fashion figure is an awesome exercise in texture. The thick wool trim on the cozy, fitted coat in Figure 14-9 uses small, overlapping strokes of your pencil. Let your short lines do the talking when you're expressing texture in short, thick furs.

To show the texture of shearling, use pairs of short little lines rather than stippling. The tiny curved lines show the direction and the length of the fibers, as well as the sunken areas of the trim. Don't arrange your lines like soldiers in formation. Instead, scatter them in groups across the fabric like bowling pins after a strike.

To draw a woman wrapped in shearling:

1. **Draw a female fashion figure. (See Figure 14-9a.)**

2. **Map out a fitted coat and knee-high boots. (See Figure 14-9b.)**

3. **Draw little broken lines on the perimeter of the trim on the coat and the top of the boots. Add small curved lines on the interior to create texture and dimension. (See Figure 14-9c.)**

Figure 14-9: Staying warm in wool.

a　　　　　　　　b　　　　　　　　c

Puzzling Out Patterns and Prints

Patterns (not sewing ones) can really throw a fashion artist, but you can draw awesome fabric designs if you know a few artists' tricks. So many illustrators opt out and just shade in fashion drawings. But what happens when you want to draw a whimsical skirt sprinkled with polka dots or high rubber boots with a great-looking plaid on them? Stripes are a staple in fashion illustration; you can find them on everything from bathing suits to a winter scarf. We cover all these patterns in the following sections.

All patterns must follow the curves and folds of the fabric as it drapes on the body (see the earlier "Getting the Hang of Draping" section for more on folds). When a fabric curves up and over a curved part of the body, the pattern must curve with it. When there's a fold or an edge of a fabric, the print has to end, sometimes at an awkward part; this makes your pattern look authentic, not fake and flat like it was just pasted on.

Polka dot time

Polka dots are forever. People wear them on clothes as babies and kids, and for tweens and teens, the print is perfect for bathing suits and sundresses. And as for adults? Well, the polka dot dress resurfaces again and again on clothing such as lingerie and retro-looking tops.

When drawing polka dots, make sure that some fall into the folds, or else the look can be very flat. Not every dot has to be a complete circle — halve them as you reach hemlines and side seams. Also, remember to follow the curves and folds of the fabric on the body. At a fold or a seam, you might see only part of the dot, or you might see dots bunched up together. This also happens at the edge of a fabric, depending on where it's cut. Figure 14-10 shows how to keep your polka dots looking realistic.

Here's how to draw a tight, dotted romper:

1. **Draw a fashion figure of a woman. (See Figure 14-10a.)**

2. **Map out a short little romper for the figure. (See Figure 14-10b.)**

3. **Draw full and half polka dots that follow the folds of the fabric on the body's curves. Break dots in half and place each side of the dot on the line of the fold but a little staggered. (See Figure 14-10c.)**

   Scatter dots all over the print for a polka dot look. Polka dots can be drawn evenly spaced, almost in a grid-like fashion, but often they occur in a more random pattern.

Stripes and more stripes

Who doesn't own a striped shirt or a striped tie or a striped pair of socks? Most people choose to wear stripes that run on the vertical because they're more slimming, but when drawing a fashion figure, your stripes can go any way you choose. In fact, because the fashion figures you draw *are* so thin, drawing a woman in a bathing suit where the stripes run horizontally doesn't add 5 pounds like it does in real life.

Figure 14-10:
A
scattering of
polka dots.

a   b   c

And don't forget about diagonal stripes, which can add a fun feel to casual pieces, like a skirt. You also find diagonal stripes on men's ties. Or try just a few diagonal stripes across the front of jacket of a warm-up suit; run them from one shoulder to the opposite hip.

Stripes in a traditional striped shirt or skirt are normally evenly spaced, but you can also make them run closer together or vary the distances as a design statement.

Stripes follow the curve of the body; don't draw them in a straight line, or your figure will look flat. Look at Figure 14-11 and notice how the horizontal line of the black stripe starts on one side of the leg and curves either up or down, creating a sense of movement and perspective.

Draw a woman in a jean mini skirt and striped tights:

1. **Draw the bottom half of a fashion figure of a woman. (See Figure 14-11a.)**

2. **Map out a jean mini skirt. (See Figure 14-11b.)**

3. **Draw in stripes, making sure the lines are curving upward or downward. When coloring in the stripe, leave a little white to add dimension to the fabric. (See Figure 14-11c.)**

Draw the stripes in an upward curve on one leg and a downward curve on the other leg.

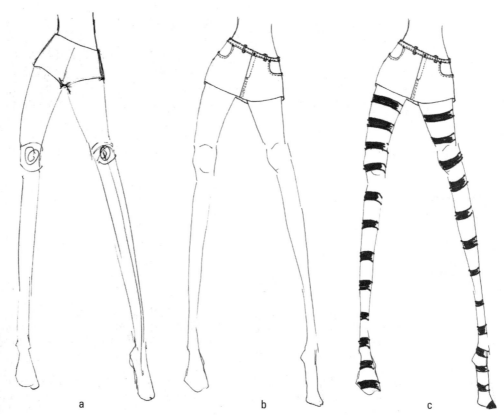

Figure 14-11:
Stripes can
add a touch
of whimsy.

a   b   c

Practical plaids

Practical plaids are just that: practical! You may use plaid on school uniform
skirts, pj pants, field hockey skirts, or flannel shirts, but chances are you'll
never draw a fashion figure wearing a plaid dress to a fancy event. Although
you never know — designers such as Vivienne Westwood might! Use your
basic cross-hatch technique with its parallel lines to create a plaid.

Plaids consists of rows and rows of threads in different colors woven
together at right angles in varying widths. That may sound complex, but
plaids can be as simple or as complicated as you want them to be. Plaid
patterns can be quite tight or much looser and larger; the colors can blend
subtly or boldly contrast.

Here's a quick step-by-step for the plaid pattern:

1. **Draw a grid of vertical and horizontal lines. (See Figure 14-12a.)**

   Leave a little more space between the lines than you do when drawing a
   cross-hatch texture.

2. **Draw tight zigzags on every other vertical line. (See Figure 14-12b.)**

3. **Draw tight zigzags on every other horizontal line. (See Figure 14-12c.)**

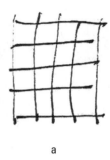

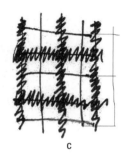

Figure 14-12:
Plaid consists of zigzag lines drawn over a grid.

a   b   c

When you're drawing plaid on an item of clothing, don't lay it out flat like a checkerboard. Make the plaid pattern follow the curves of the body and the drape of the fabric.

Draw a plaid print on an old-fashioned halter swimsuit:

1. **Draw a fashion figure of a woman. (See Figure 14-13a.)**

2. **Map out a halter swimsuit with a center front seam. (See Figure 14-13b.)**

3. **Draw a basic grid system on the swimsuit, starting with the center front line going straight down the center front of the body. Draw vertical lines that start at the neckline. The lines go straight down along her body and then radiate out at the hip area. Finish with horizontal lines that wrap around the curves of her body, such as at her breasts, hips, and waist. (See Figure 14-13c.)**

   Angling the plaid on both sides of the center front seam creates a chevron pattern. In woven fabrics, this angling is called placing the fabric on the bias. A *bias-cut* fabric has been cut at a 45-degree angle instead of along the threads, tilting any patterns (like taking a square and turning it into a diamond). This shows how the fabric stretches on your model; woven fabrics stretch slightly on the bias (the diagonal).

4. **Add the tight zigzag lines on every other horizontal and vertical line. (See Figure 14-13d.)**

Handling Unique Fabrics

Fabrics can reflect your mood. Who doesn't feel fierce wearing a leather jacket? It's hard not to strut down the street when you're wearing one! And don't forget the sublime silks when you want to look ethereal — we have those fairy-tale fashion moments, too!

Many of the clothing pieces you draw will be made of everyday fabrics — denim, different weights of cotton, and so on. But sooner or later, you'll want to draw something suitable for a special occasion or made out of higher quality materials. You can show that a fabric is more than the run-of-the-mill cotton by employing the techniques you read about in this and previous chapters. Shading, adding texture, and hinting at shine are all part of the fashion artist's technique arsenal. You can also add character to these fabrics by paying attention to details like folds and fit.

a

b

Figure 14-13:
Plaids pop
on simple
swimsuits.

c

d

In the following sections, we explain how to convey some of the more
unusual fabrics in your drawings. We use the standard garment shapes and
styles that you practice in the chapters in Part III, but we help you snazz
them up with more luxurious fabrics.

Strutting down the street in leather

Drawing leather is all about shading. Use the side of your pencil — it's a guar-
anteed tool to achieve the supple and shaded look of leather. Because leather
is a thick fabric, clothing made from it has fewer folds than clothing made
from lighter fabrics, but the folds it does have are longer and deeper than in
other fabrics. Highlight this feature by darkening the folds that are created
by the fit of the jacket around the body, and use your eraser to bring out the
areas where leather catches the light.

Try drawing a little leather jacket:

1. **Draw the top half of a female fashion figure. (See Figure 14-14a.)**

2. **Map out a short and tight little jacket. Add folds on the side where the waist might bend, on the elbow of the sleeve, and coming from the top of the sleeve. (See Figure 14-14b.)**

3. **Use the side of your pencil to block out the darkness of the leather and leave areas white for shine. Darken around the folds to show the depth of the fabric. (See Figure 14-14c.)**

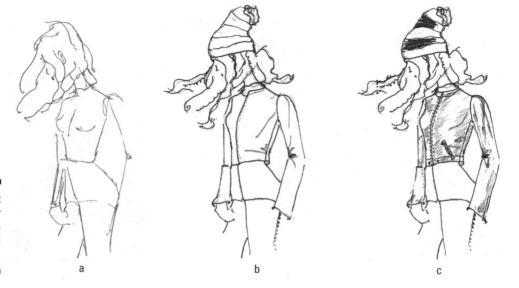

Figure 14-14:
Leather jackets are smooth and sexy.

a   b   c

Flouncing around in fluffy tulle

Tulle is the ballerina's best friend and a great addition for the crazy bouncy skirt that needs body underneath (think Carrie Bradshaw or Lady Gaga!). Layers of fine tulle create fluffy and bouncy skirts for a playful fashion look that little princess wannabes and older punkesque girls love to wear.

Use the grid system of hatching for a netted, crisp-edge look.

Try a bouncy tulle skirt:

1. **Draw a female fashion figure. (See Figure 14-15a.)**

2. **Map out a large, wide skirt with lots of gathers at the waistband. Draw the hem of the skirt with some waves to show the depth of the fabric. (See Figure 14-15b.)**

3. **Draw a grid system on the skirt, being careful to leave some areas blank. (See Figure 14-15c.)**

Add some lines that angle in toward the middle of the skirt from where the waves of the hem turn upward to indicate folds in the fabric.

Figure 14-15:
Bouncing
princess!

a   b   c

Catching the eye with sequins

Just how fun are shimmering sequins? These glinting little discs on your fashion figure's clothes make any outfit totally glam, provided you don't go overboard — which is quite tempting!

Sequins are shiny discs made of a light plastic, and they come in a vast array of colors. Gone are the days when they were sewn on by hand (except for *haute couture*). However, sequins continue to grace blouses, decorate ruffles on skirts, and add glint to shoes. They're so simple to draw, and they can give your fashion drawing a super-festive party flair or downtown chic look. You can use them as trim or create an entire fabric made from sequins.

With sequins, less is more. You don't need to fill up the entire dress with sequins. And if you're drawing a figure in a sequined top, leave the pants alone. An entire sequined suit could look, shall we say, odd?

To draw sequins on a short and strappy dress:

1. **Draw a female fashion figure. (See Figure 14-16a.)**

2. **Map out a simple cocktail dress. (See Figure 14-16b.)**

3. **Draw sequins by drawing little circles scattered across the dress. (See Figure 14-16c.)**

4. **Add sparkles along the outline of the dress to show the light reflecting off the sequins, and add random dots for some more texture. (See Figure 14-16d.)**

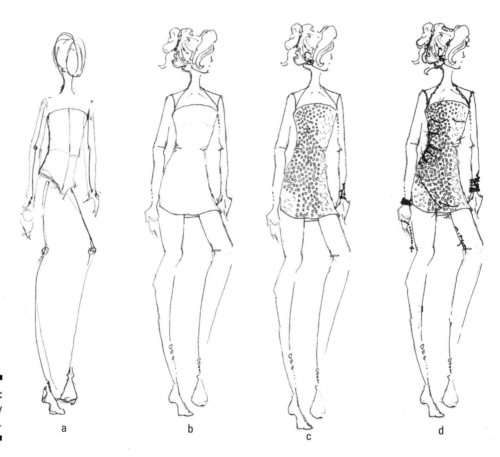

Figure 14-16:
Shimmery
sequins.

a   b   c   d

Chapter 15

Conveying Attitude and Movement through Body Language

*F*ashion illustration is as much about revealing emotions on paper as it is about drawing the fashion figure. You want to convey a drawing with an attitude, whether sassy or sweet, and that means executing a well-drawn fashion figure that tells a story. The details that you include in your fashion illustrations convey a message. Part of that message is how the clothes move with the body. In this chapter, we show you how to convey movement and introduce you to gesture drawing to help you achieve a more fluid style that suggests motion.

Producing a Fluid Torso with Gesture Drawing

In fashion illustration, a few good lines can go a long way toward creating a dynamic torso. However, consider what you can do with just one good line. Try drawing the torso with flair by using a technique called *gesture drawing,* the art of drawing quickly to capture the essence of something rather than to immortalize every detail. So you draw the torso (and eventually the fashion figure) using only one line, not ever lifting the pencil from the paper. Because gesture drawing includes only the essential elements, it gives more of a sense of motion.

Here are the advantages of gesture drawing:

✔ It forces the artist to loosen up and gives the drawing an organic look.

✔ It leads to a more fluid line, which is critical in fashion illustration.

✔ You can use it for getting an idea down on paper and refine it later.

You must draw quickly when doing gesture drawing. Don't overthink it! Otherwise, you lose the organic feel of the drawing. Getting out of the habit of erasing every little line that's out of place takes patience and practice, so stick with it.

Try this gesture drawing exercise:

1. **Start with your basic trapezoids and an oval to create a torso and head. See Figure 15-1a.**

2. **Put your pencil at any point on a trapezoid. Without lifting your pencil point from the paper, draw a line moving any direction that outlines the body and head. Check out Figure 15-1b to see what this looks like.**

   Overlapping lines is okay. The next time you do this exercise, skip Step 1 and start gesture drawing the body with a single line.

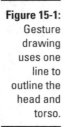

Figure 15-1: Gesture drawing uses one line to outline the head and torso.

a   b

It sounds tough, but after you try your hand at gesture drawing a few times, you'll love the results. Remember that gesture drawing isn't governed by any exact rules — just go with the flow!

Hitting the Catwalk

If models aren't posing, they're walking, and where do you most often see them walking? Down the runway, of course! The runway is where fashions come alive and are shown to the public for the first time. Designers send models down the runway to strut and play a part that sets off the look of the clothes. Illustrating movement takes some tricks, but the impression of movement adds so much life to your illustrations that mastering these techniques is worth the time and effort.

The fierce walk

There's walking, and then there's runway walking. Did you know that professionals train models to get their own signature sashshays? Browse through photos of uber-fashion models working that runway. Notice how they're never smiling or showing emotion, because the look is about being aloof; these models stride toward the viewer with cool confidence. Their hips rock from side to side, and their thin arms are, shall we say, limp. You have to nail that look with the fashion figures you draw if you want to convey high-end attitude.

Follow these steps to draw a fashion walk:

1. **Sketch a fashion figure walking with one leg forward, as in Figure 15-2a.**

   Slant those shoulders and hips for fashion attitude.

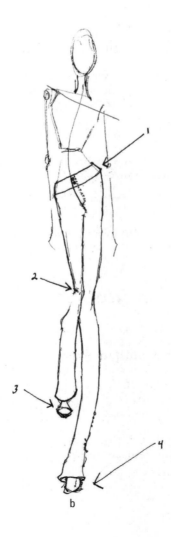

Figure 15-2:
Walk the fashion walk.

a

b

c

2. **Draw pants, as in Figure 15-2b.**

   Angle the waistband with the hips, as in Figure 15-2b, #1. Keep the knees together, as in #2. And for the back leg, draw the hem of the pant leg curving downward for perspective, as in #3. Keep the forward leg long and directly under the head, as in #4.

3. **Draw a shirt and finish the illustration with fold lines curving into the body to represent the clothing moving with the body as your model walks. (See Figure 15-2c.)**

The famous fashion turn

Drawing a fashion figure who looks like she's turning isn't impossible, although it's not as easy as a straight-on pose. There's a famous fashion expression that says a model is graceful if she can "turn on a dime." What on earth does that mean? When a model reaches the end of the runway, she pauses for a nanosecond, glares, and then quickly turns to finish walking past the fashion police in the crowd. We're not talking about a wide spin with arms a'flailing; it's a well-practiced, tight little turn that's *quite* contained.

Pay attention to your model's hands and feet when you draw a turn. When a model turns, she often puts her hands on her hips. Her feet should be close together, which allows for a quick, tight pivot away from the audience.

Here's how to draw a fashion figure who can turn on a dime:

1. **Draw a three-quarter body stance with the face looking straight ahead, as in Figure 15-3a.**

2. **Put the figure's hands on her hips during a turn. Add shoes for stepping style. (See Figure 15-3b.)**

3. **Draw a few simple lines for clothing and make them twirl to help give the illusion of spin, as in Figure 15-3c.**

The jutting hip

How far can a fashion artist kick out a hip in a fashion drawing? Pretty far if you're looking for attitude! Not only does a drawing of a fashion figure look better with a hip thrust to the side (this is true for both guys and girls), but the waist tilts and shoulders angle as well, making for fierce attitude. Do a gesture drawing of the fashion figure with hip-action galore if you want to show a striding runway model, a cocky teen, an urban dude, and more. (Bone up on hip action in Chapter 4 if you need to.)

When the hip juts out, the entire body shifts to one side. And a woman's hip kicks out farther than a dude's.

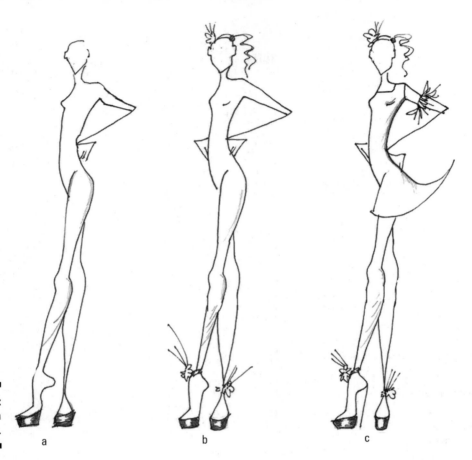

Figure 15-3:
Turning on a
dime.

a   b   c

To get that crazy hip action:

1. **Draw a torso with angled shoulders and oppositely angled hips, as in Figure 15-4a.**

   Make sure the hips are off to the side, not directly under the shoulders.

2. **Add the legs, as in Figure 15-4b.**

   Keep the higher-hip leg straight. The lower-hip leg meets with the other leg at the knee but curves away from there.

3. **Make the feet turn in and face each other for an awkward but edgy stance. Keep one arm bent and the other lying on the body along the upward hip. (See Figure 15-4c.)**

4. **Finish by filling out the lines with body shapes and clothing that follows the angles of the body. (See Figure 15-4d.)**

Figure 15-4:
Jutting hips.

a

b

c

d

The man's strut

Roosters strut, and so do male models. Your fashion drawing can show the classic strut in action when your drawing of a guy shows him pausing at the end of the runway. This pose is a fleeting one, but it can make fashion editors sigh when done right. Draw your fashion dude with the right strut potential by drawing his weight resting on one leg and having him stare straight ahead with the "I'm not really here" look. Don't forget to angle those broad shoulders and tilt that waistline in your gesture drawing.

To draw the strut:

1. **Quickly sketch a three-quarter pose of a male fashion figure with one leg to the side and one leg forward. Draw only one arm on the hip. (See Figure 15-5a.)**

2. **Indicate clothing with a few lines, as in Figure 15-5b.**

3. **Add clothing details and shadow. (See Figure 15-5c.)**

Figure 15-5:
That sexy
strut.

a   b   c

Exaggerating the Excitement

Practically every aspect of the world of fashion is all about exaggeration. Fashion design is exaggerated, the models and their attitudes are extreme, photo shoots are *crazy* and electric, and great fashion illustrations can stop people in their tracks. Once you have your fashion-drawing foundation in place, it's time to party with your pencil lines! Gesture drawings are the way to go when you want to create a bold and exaggerated style that really emphasizes movement.

Long body lines

Arms and legs must be drawn in a graceful way so they look fluid. Models spend hours learning how to stretch and leap across magazine spreads and on film screens. Although the fashion figure's legs are *wicked* long, the arms aren't exactly short. (Check out Chapter 4 if you need a review on proportion.) A great-looking exaggerated drawing shows off what you can do as a fashion artist.

Stretch out the torso and legs for a fierce fashion figure.

Shaping the legs

The fashion figure is tall, so don't forget to stretch those legs out. When you combine that with a fluid drawing, you've got yourself one long and lean fashion figure.

To show off long lines to create a fashion drawing:

1. **Do a quick drawing of a very exaggerated fashion figure with long, stretched-out legs (one bent and one straight) and the head straight up and down. (See Figure 15-6a.)**

2. **Flesh out the legs and arms, as in Figure 15-6b. Keep the arms long, reaching to about mid-thigh when straight.**

3. **Finish with clothing that follows the angles and bends of the body. (See Figure 15-6c.)**

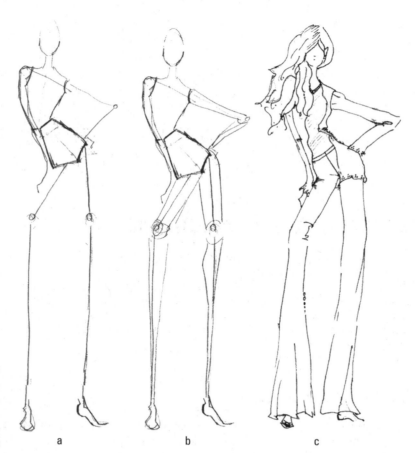

Figure 15-6:
A long, lean fashion queen.

a   b   c

Notice how models are never drawn standing straight up. Their hips and shoulders are angled, their bodies are turned away from the viewer, or their arms are held away from the body. All these techniques make for a more interesting image.

Stretching arms

Moving your arms gracefully is an art. Your fashion figure must have arms that stretch in different styles, from languid to jaunty, to show various fashion attitudes. Fluid arms moving across the waist or over the head give a soft, dancer-like quality to your pose. Angled arms with hands planted on the hips give a powerful, structured pose. Stand in front of a mirror and *S-T-R-E-T-C-H* to find some awesome poses to draw. Quick gesture drawing is still the way to achieve a liquid look for arm movement. The key is to angle the shoulders for action.

To draw arms that stretch:

1. **Sketch the head, neck, and shoulders of a woman with one arm going up and the other going down, as in Figure 15-7a.**

2. **Fill in the arms, as in Figure 15-7b.**

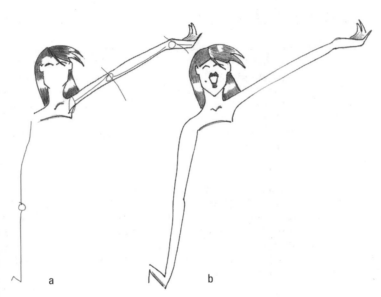

Figure 15-7:
Stretch
it out.

a   b

Side views with long arms are great for showing off accessories such as a clutch or jewelry.

To draw a sideways stretch:

1. **Draw a fashion figure in a side pose with the head in profile, one arm outstretched in front, and the other slightly forward and hanging down, as in Figure 15-8a.**

   Don't forget the *S* curve to draw a sexy back.

2. **Outline the shapes of the arms and add clothing on the body and a clutch in the higher hand. (See Figure 15-8b.)**

Figure 15-8:
Side
stretches.

a

b

Creating facial expression

Drawing the fashion face can be so exciting when you decide to go all out! Your drawing can feature penetrating eyes, have a voluptuous mouth, and look quite haunting in a most positive way. You can also draw someone with steely eyes, haughty brows, a chiseled nose, and cheekbones to die for. (Glance back at Chapter 7 if you need a refresher on drawing the fashion face.) The face of a fashion figure tells a story, and you as an artist are the visual author! Study the different styles of drawn faces from the comics to children's books to anime. Don't be afraid to take inspiration from their ideas and make them your own.

Marianne often finds students stressing over how to draw a face. She encourages them to focus on what they're good at and not try to get everything perfect. If you're good with eyes but have trouble with noses and mouths, then just draw some great eyes and add a simple curved line for the lips and ignore the nose. Sometimes it takes recognizing what you do best and working with your strengths. Remember, this is not about drawing a realistic portrait; it's about style and drama.

To draw two awesome fashion faces:

1. **Sketch the heads, hair, and necks of a male and a female fashion figure, as in Figure 15-9a.**

2. **Exaggerate the eyes in shape, size, and shading, as in Figure 15-9b.**

3. **Draw a fashion nose by using one line coming down from the inner corner of one eye, as in Figure 15-9c.**

4. **Draw the mouth — the more to the mouth, the better! (See Figure 15-9d.)**

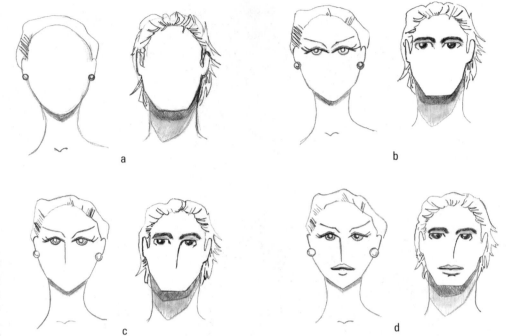

Figure 15-9:
Fashion
faces go
places.

Hair moves

Why draw a classic bob or a little flip when you can sketch towers of hair, masses of curls, or extreme short cuts? Drawing hair that has a wind-blown effect adds movement and keeps the pose from looking too stagnant. Hair can also convey attitude, with mohawks creating a powerful, rebellious look and long, flowing curls adding a soft, girlie look. A drawing of a fashion figure should be on the cutting edge (no pun intended), so use your lines and loops and shading techniques to draw hair that people *want* but don't necessarily have!

Try drawing some unforgettable hair:

1. **Draw the head, face, and long neck of a woman. (See Figure 15-10a.)**

2. **Use light pencil lines to plot out a large area that the hair is going to cover. (See Figure 15-10b.)**

3. **Add a few lines on the inside of the hair outline, as in Figure 15-10c.**

   Keep the lines loose, thick and thin, broken and moving all around the perimeter of your area with a few lines on the inside.

Figure 15-10: What woman doesn't want a flowing mane of hair?

To go even wilder with hair:

1. **Draw the face, head, and neck, as in Figure 15-11a.**

2. **Draft out the outer lines of your hairstyle, as in Figure 15-11b.**

3. **Draw long, curly loops with the tip and side of your pencil for a wild-child look, as in Figure 15-11c.**

Letting Your Figures Take Flight

Part of the fun in drawing fashion is the release of your creative spirit. Watch dancers to feel the power of creative movement. They bend, jump, leap, spin, and twist their bodies with grace and strength. And ballet dancers are about the most graceful humans going, so bring some of their moves into your fashion drawings. Fashion artists can steal ideas about movement from dancers to create beautiful, strong poses that allow creative movement in the clothing being shown on the model.

Figure 15-11:
Wild child!

Try watching yourself dance, jump, or twirl some time in a mirror — it's hilarious, especially if you're trying to move gracefully. Unless you're a trained dancer, gymnast, or athlete, chances are you look mostly silly. Here are the keys to drawing fashion figures who look good while jumping:

✔ Draw faces that are not scrunched with exertion.

✔ Draw feet pointed in a graceful way.

✔ Don't draw your figure in a folded-up flip.

✔ Draw your figure with arms and legs outstretched or bent.

Male fashion figures are rarely drawn jumping.

In the following sections, we explain how to make every part of your fashion models look graceful when they're flying through the air with the greatest of ease.

Taking a leap

First things first; think about the type of clothes you're going to draw on your fashion figure when you draw a model leaping through the air. Leggings or a flirty little dress for fun are the perfect attire for a ballerina in action.

Here's how to draw a toned-down leap:

1. **Sketch the top half of a female fashion figure with both arms and hands outstretched, as in Figure 15-12a.**

2. **Draw one leg crossing in front of the other, as in Figure 15-12b.**

3. **Draw the figure's feet, making them point downward, as in Figure 15-12c.**

   Pointing your figure's hands and feet helps your drawing to fly!

4. **Draw the hair and skirt in motion, as in Figure 15-12d.**

Figure 15-12:
A dainty
leap.

Sticking the landing

For a fashion stance that can't be topped, draw your fashion figure with one leg bending, as if she's landing from her leap. Your leg placement will make or break your illustration (but fortunately not your fashion figure's leg, no matter what you do!).

Try drawing a fashion figure who's kicking up her heel:

1. **Sketch a fashion figure with arms outstretched, as in Figure 15-13a.**

2. **Draw the front leg balancing the body while the back leg is bending. Add dancer's clothing such as a body suit and leggings. (See Figure 15-13b.)**

Draw the leg open and *away* from the pelvic region, bending the leg at the knee.

Don't draw the leg bending in front of the figure unless you want a marching effect — and trust us, you don't!

Figure 15-13:
A balanced
landing
is easy to
achieve
with a
pencil!

a

b

Jumping with one leg stretched

On a fashion figure in mid-flight, one leg bends and the other stretches out as long as possible on a diagonal angle. This look is great for a sporty outfit.

Draw a leg stretching far as a fashion figure leaps to the side:

1. **Start with the upper half of a woman's body and add outstretched arms for movement, as in Figure 15-14a.**

2. **Add the lower half of the body with the figure's left leg bending. (See Figure 15-14b.)**

3. **Give the bent leg a pointed ballet foot and add some texture to the clothing. (See Figure 15-14c.)**

   Point the feet for ballet style.

4. **Finish with the other leg facing forward but coming out of the pelvis at a slight angle for movement. (See Figure 15-14d.)**

   Make sure the leg is diagonal. If you draw the leg coming straight out to the side, it can look a tad extreme.

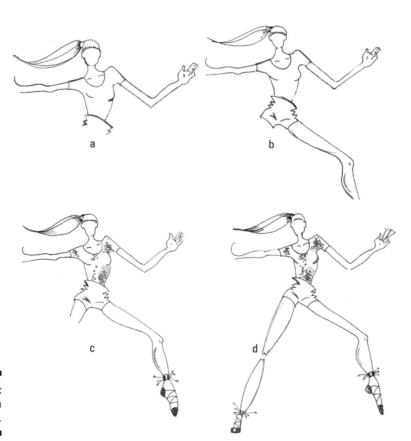

Figure 15-14:
Fashion
leaps.

Reaching up with the arms

When drawing a fashion figure jumping, not all of the action is in the legs and feet. Arms play a vital part as they reach and stretch for balance. After all, how many people jump with their arms straight down by their sides? Okay, Irish dancers do, but most fashion models don't. Try drawing a figure who has both arms reaching straight up.

Don't raise the shoulders up close to the ears; stylize them.

To draw way-up arms:

1. **Draw a female fashion figure standing on her toes with her legs crossed, as in Figure 15-15a.**

2. **Draw her arms reaching above her head with her hands bending back down, as in Figure 15-15b.**

3. **Sketch the figure's simple clothing lines, as in Figure 15-15c.**

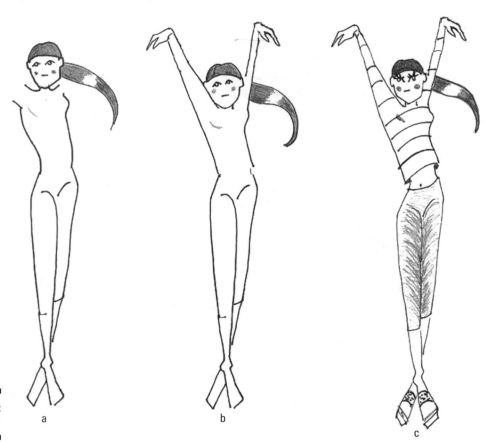

Figure 15-15:
Arms up!

a   b   c

Sinking into the Sophisticated Slouch

Slouching was never considered a fashion must until the fashion world declared it sexy. You can draw your fashion figure in a superb looking slouch, and no one will tell you to straighten up that figure! (Refer back to the fabulous *S* curve from Chapter 4 for tips on creating the perfect slouch.) The following sections tell you how to achieve model looks that are bored, laid-back, and languid.

Curving it back

Drawing your fashion figure from the side is the best way to show off a fashion pose with a curving back. The *S* curve is a great way to exaggerate a fashion stance when you want to go for a more emotional look.

Use the *S* curve as you draw a fashion figure leaning back:

1. **Draw a torso from the side, using the *S* shape to create the curve of the back. (See Figure 15-16a.)**

2. **Sketch the figure's left arm hanging straight down and her left leg straight down with her right leg stepping slightly forward. (See Figure 15-16b.)**

3. **Add a dress that drapes down the front and back to show off her fierce side view! (See Figure 15-16c.)**

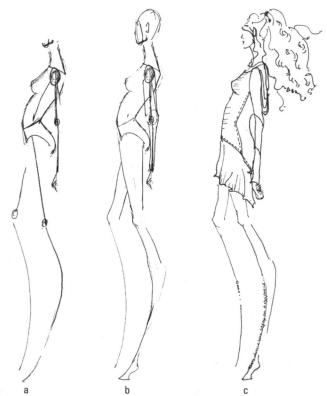

Figure 15-16:
The curve of the back is wicked sexy.

a   b   c

To draw a fashion figure in the classic teen slouch:

1. **Draw a side torso, curving the upper half forward for slouchy shoulders. Curve the bottom forward to create an *S* shape down the back. (See Figure 15-17a.)**

2. **Add in the right arm coming forward and draping down the body. The right leg curves away from the body at the calf and comes back to align with the head. (See Figure 15-17b.)**

3. **Add a top and tight pants to show off the slouch! (See Figure 15-17c.)**

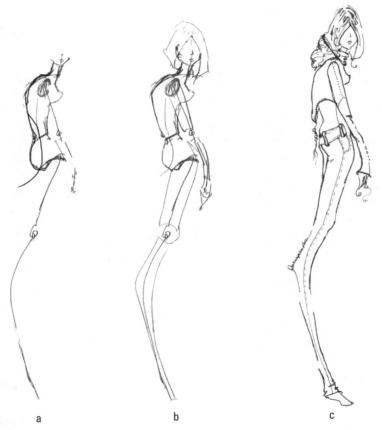

Figure 15-17: Slumped shoulders and locked knees create a terrific teen slouch.

a   b   c

Relaxing the legs

Languid legs work so well with a fashion figure with an *S* curve. Drawing relaxed limbs evokes a loose attitude if you continue your gesture drawing for easy lines. The trick is to draw the legs looking thin and without much definition.

Try drawing some long, loose legs:

1. **Quickly sketch a female fashion figure in a three-quarter view. Map out long legs that don't bend but rather curve away from the body and then back to align with head. (See Figure 15-18a.)**

   Remember to angle the torso to keep your figure looking balanced.

2. **Use long curves to draw in long, relaxed legs. (See Figure 15-18b.)**

3. **Add clothing details, keeping the legs thin! (See Figure 15-18c.)**

   Drawing a figure in low heels looks more chill.

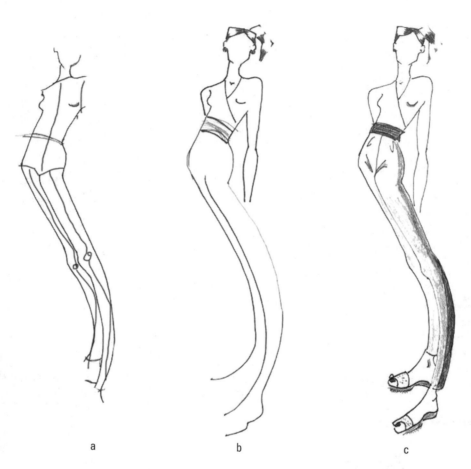

Figure 15-18:
Legs on a figure without a care in the world.

a   b   c

Languid arms

If you've drawn your fashion figure slouching, you've *got* to draw languid arms to perfect the stance. (Check Chapter 6 for a refresher on drawing fashion arms.) Practice drawing arms that look limp (in a *good* way).

To draw languid-looking arms:

1. **Draw a fashion figure's head and neck in profile, as in Figure 15-19a.**

2. **Draw a curved arm without elbows for that fluid movement, as in Figure 15-19b.**

   Arms reach mid-thigh in a fashion figure.

3. **Add the _S_ curve for the back shape of the torso and show one leg moving forward and one back, as in Figure 15-19c.**

   The forward movement emphasizes the fluid look of the arms, and the dancer-style leotard allows you to see the body.

Figure 15-19:
Relaxed
arms for a
languid look.

a   b   c

We've Got Your Back!

Drawing the fashion back with style is easy — and necessary, given all the backless numbers you see in the fashion industry. Forget rippling muscles, because drawing a fashion back is mostly about a smooth and simple style that works for your fashion figure. Drawing poses from the back conveys an attitude of confidence — both in your fashion model and in yourself. As with certain front poses, you can create striking poses with angled shoulders and hips. In the following sections, we reintroduce the inverted triangle, because it's the perfect shape to use for fashion drawing.

The sexy spine

Supple spines are graceful looking and convey just the right accent when you're using the inverted triangle for the shape of a back. A long, slightly curved line works wonders when defining the back of a fashion figure.

To draw a supple and sexy spine:

1. **Draw the back of a female fashion figure using a thin inverted triangle. (See Figure 15-20a.)**

2. **Draw a long, slight curve for the spine and fill in the fashion figure, as in Figure 15-20b.**

   Draw the hair short to show off the back.

3. **Add shading and texture, as in Figure 15-20c.**

Figure 15-20:
A sexy spine
is awesome.

a   b   c

Broad backs

Broad backs are obviously for drawing fashion figure dudes. This is the look you want when you draw an awesome guy in a bathing suit or wearing jeans only. It's show-off time, and drawing a wide inverted triangle for the back helps you do just that!

To draw a guy with a broad back:

1. **Draw the top half of a dude using a wide inverted triangle for a back shape, as in Figure 15-21a.**

   Use the base of the inverted triangle for a strong shoulder line. Draw the shoulder line at an angle.

2. **Add a strong line to show a good spine and add in the waist. (See Figure 15-21b.)**

3. **Draw masculine-shaped angel wings for muscle definition. (See Figure 15-21c.)**

Figure 15-21:
A muscled
back
with broad
shoulders.

a   b   c

Chapter 16

Going to Extremes to Develop Your Own Style

In This Chapter
▶ Using exaggeration to enhance your figures
▶ Going for a minimal look

The fashion industry is about breaking boundaries and being on the cutting edge *of* the cutting edge. As an illustrator, you want to hang out on the edge so your work stands out from the rest. After you know all the fashion illustration rules (see Chapter 4), it's time to start breaking them to create your own style. Go ahead and push the envelope to get noticed.

In this chapter, we show you how to take your drawings to two extremes. First we explain how to exaggerate everything about your fashion figure — from her height to her hair — and then we show you how to take your art in the opposite direction by drawing just enough to suggest what the viewer is seeing. Try both approaches and choose the aspects of each that you like best as you create your own style.

Letting loose is what this chapter is about! Fashion illustrations are like fashion dolls: They're not a representation of a real person, and no one expects them to be. Proportions are unrealistic to start with in fashion illustration, and sometimes the crazier the drawing looks, the edgier or more fashionable it is. Fashion illustration is about fantasy and fun; realism is neither required nor desired. Take your drawings to the limits!

Exaggerating Your Designs

Fashion illustrators have a knack for taking what's real and adding elements of fantasy. As you expand into your own style, the elements of fantasy often include lots of exaggeration. Exaggeration is effective because it involves taking what you already know about fashion illustration and simply expanding it further into the fantasy realm. Exaggeration includes taking a shape and making it twice as long or using shapes to stand in for body parts.

Standard fashion illustration preaches proportions that keep your model 11 heads tall (see Chapter 4 for details), but you can break away from that rule and exaggerate lines to create your own proportions. Putting your fashion illustrations into poses that few people could imitate is another great way to exaggerate your lines. These outrageous poses breathe high-fashion life into every illustration and grab everyone's attention. With fashion, even the weird can be beautiful!

In the following sections, we give you pointers on making everything taller, longer, or bigger. Stretch your model, give her big hair, and lengthen her arms and legs so they look like they go on forever. Creativity comes alive with exaggeration, and then your inner artist takes over. It's fun to see how the drawing looks in the end, and the journey is just as exciting!

Avoid much exaggeration in the faces — exaggerated faces take away from your clothing designs.

Extending your proportions

Although 11 heads may be the standard fashion illustration height (flip to Chapter 4 to read more), you don't have to stick to the rule. Change your drawing's proportions by adding *heads* (the height of a head as a guideline for proportion, not actual heads) to places such as the torso or the legs. You can see what we mean in Figure 16-1a, which shows a height of 19 heads instead of the traditional 11.

When creating an illustration with exaggerated proportions, you should still use your standard trapezoid shapes for the torso and cylinders for arms and legs. Add an oval for a head. You can read about using trapezoids for torsos in Chapter 5; we cover arms and legs in Chapter 6.

For some edgy front fashion poses with extended proportions, follow these steps:

1. **Create a new head template (add as many heads as you like; in Figure 16-1a, we drew 19 heads). Then draw a quick stick figure that shows the exaggerated lengths and the angles in your pose, as in Figure 16-1b.**

   Create fun poses with your stick figure. For example, put one arm on the hip for attitude.

2. **Draw two trapezoid shapes over your lines to create the torso, as in Figure 16-2a.**

3. **Following your initial lines, draw long legs using cylinder shapes. (See Figure 16-2b.)**

   Try experimenting with leg proportions by making the upper half of the leg (thigh) significantly shorter than the shin or around the same length. Try to bend the lower cylinders in unreal directions.

4. **Add cylinders for long arms, as in Figure 16-2c.**

5. **Add an oval for the head, as in Figure 16-2d.**

   If you'd like, add personal touches, such as a hand flipped up or markings for the eyes and lips of the face.

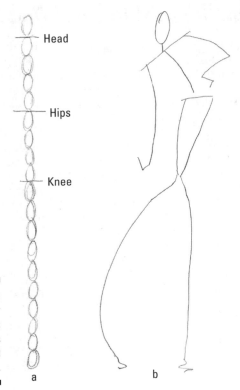

Figure 16-1:
Change your
illustration's
proportions
to add
pizzazz.

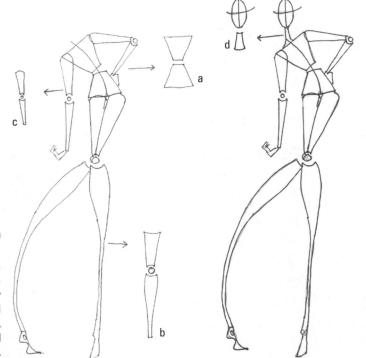

Figure 16-2:
Use shapes
to create
a newly
proportioned
torso, arms,
legs, and
head.

Keeping your arms long, thin, and flowing

Creating outrageous and unreal arm poses is always fun in fashion illustration. When you first start drawing fashion arms, you'll likely opt for typical arm placements around and behind the body. But when you're ready to move up to a more exaggerated and outrageous style, you can create long and skinny arms like snakes bending and twisting in every direction. Think long, fake, and fun to move up to the next level of fashion illustration.

Creating exaggerated fashion arms isn't simply about making the arms long; it's also about choosing the right arm placement and bending the wrist in provocative ways. Think ballerinas and flamenco dancers: Their arms are long and flowing, ending with movement of the wrist and a graceful hand gesture. Great snake arms come from poses that allow the arm to bend. Placing the arms in creative locations, such as over the head, also achieves this look.

Check out these ideas for great arms:

- ✔ Extend the length of the arm.
- ✔ Bend the arm and wrists in provocative ways, as in Figure 16-3a.
- ✔ Place one arm going up and bending back onto the head, as in Figure 16-3b.
- ✔ Make the drawing your own with whatever creative and fun ideas you come up with for arms. Instead of drawing cylinders, try vine-like or spiraling lines, as in Figure 16-3c.

Figure 16-3: The sky's the limit for fashion arms.

Looking at some leggy legends

Legs make or break 90 percent of fashion poses. Like arms, legs can go to the next level when you experiment with different shapes and creative ideas. Think outside typical cylinder shapes; use a series of hearts from wide to narrow, or try using a bunch of swirls. Don't limit your creative ideas!

A trick for keeping your pose from looking downright ridiculous is to pay attention to the placement of the head and feet. Keep the head straight up and down and have the feet end under the chin to give the pose attitude without looking silly.

Here's how to make your fashion legs legendary:

✔ **Manipulate the shape of the cylinder.** Think of how the shapes create the flow of the leg, and then add switchbacks or nudges in the middle of the shapes. Take a look at Figure 16-4a, where the lower part of the bent leg curves in an unrealistic way.

✔ **Tilt the lower half of the torso to elongate the legs and allow more creativity.** Check out Figure 16-4a to see how this tilt looks.

✔ **Draw one leg extremely long and place it directly under the body; then stylize the missing leg.** Placing one leg directly under the body keeps the figure balanced. Then you can use other shapes and designs to act as a fill-in for the missing leg, as in Figure 16-4b.

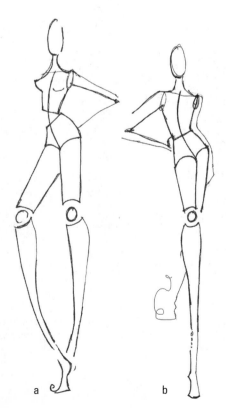

Figure 16-4:
Taking the leggy look to the limit.

a   b

Topping off your illustration with outrageous hair

Hair can add a terrific dimension to fashion illustrations. Unlike your earliest art efforts, which featured stick people with hair standing straight out from their heads, fashion hair cuts into the facial shape and uses fewer lines. Push the boundaries with big, big hair. Add hip hair accessories, and play with the face by covering one or both eyes with locks for drama.

Be free and think outside the box. No, hair isn't normally 3 feet high with ribbons hanging from it, but why can't yours be?

If you want to draw some outrageous hair on your illustrations, grab a drawing you've already created in another chapter (make sure it has a head/face and hair). Analyze your current drawing and then try adding some dramatic lines and covering part of the face with strands, as in Figure 16-5a. Add your own touches based on the kind of personality you want your figure to have — playful, sultry, gothic, or whatever. Think about what you can add to the hair to give it the feel you're going for. For example, you can add butterflies for a girlie, earthy feel, as in Figure 16-5b. You can even add words and shapes to an illustration's locks. Check out Figure 16-5c to see what we mean.

Figure 16-5: Take your hair in new directions.

a   b   c

Trying out other extreme ideas

When you're exploring your own style, experiment with every part of the body. Add extreme accessories, pose your model in impossible positions, and consider leaving some parts of your illustration to the imagination.

Feel free to exaggerate more than one part of the body at a time; with fashion illustration, you can hardly go over the top. The body you're drawing is already a fantasy; therefore, the more you allow yourself to use your imagination, the more your drawing becomes your own!

Here are some extreme ideas you can try (see Figure 16-6 for examples of these approaches):

- ✔ **Use a few lines instead of drawing an entire arm or leg.** Not every drawing has to have a completely filled in head-to-toe pose.

- ✔ **Don't be afraid to add "messy" lines all over the place.** Throughout the book, we have lots of loose lines that add character and are part of the overall process of just letting the pencil go when you sketch.

- ✔ **Have fun and incorporate objects, words, and lines or geometric shapes into your illustration.** Add out-of-the-ordinary elements by drawing a heart in place of a hand or adding a band over the eyes for drama.

Figure 16-6:
Have fun
with lines
and shapes
when you're
working on
your own
style.

Going for a Minimal Look

A fun style often seen with fashion illustration is the *minimal look*. The minimal look is a fun, unique style to adopt because it involves fewer lines and details (and it allows people who struggle to draw certain parts of the body to easily hide their weaknesses). With a minimal look, every line counts, so understanding where to put the lines and practicing to see what works are essential. You can pick up the main features of the minimal look by knowing the insider tricks in the following sections.

Staying skimpy on the lines

Sketching a fashion illustration can take hours when you pay attention to every little detail. On the other hand, drawing can take a couple of minutes if you go with the minimal look and simply focus on the garment design, giving little thought to the body, face, arms, or legs.

The main rule of the *minimal* look is to use the fewest number of lines possible. In other words, draw in such a way that those who look at your illustration have to use their imaginations to fill in the missing pieces. Not every line and body part has to be drawn and filled in to make a fashion statement. The point of fashion illustration is to show a design on a body. It's okay if the body is missing some shading or a leg or the details of a design hardly show up; as long as the main idea of the design is there, you're golden.

To practice drawing a woman in an evening gown in the minimal look, follow these steps:

1. **Start with a posed stick figure, as in Figure 16-1b. Add the trapezoids and cylinder shapes for the body, as in Figure 16-2.**

   Head to Chapters 4, 5, and 6 for information on sketching posed stick figures, trapezoid torsos, and arms and legs.

2. **Lay tracing paper over the drawing from Step 1 and use the body as your reference point for drawing your evening gown.**

3. **Draw a slightly curved line across the chest for the top of the dress. Follow along both sides of the torso, with one side ending mid calf and the other ending slightly below the mid calf.**

   You can see what we mean in Figure 16-7a. This dress is form fitting, so follow the body closely until you approach the hem.

4. **Using thick and thin lines, draw the hem of the dress with large loopy swirls to show movement, as in Figure 16-7b.**

   Extend lines up from the loops to add dimension.

5. **Add a few loose lines to suggest the placement of the arms, neck, head, and feet.**

   Add as few details as possible. See Figure 16-8 to see the finished product.

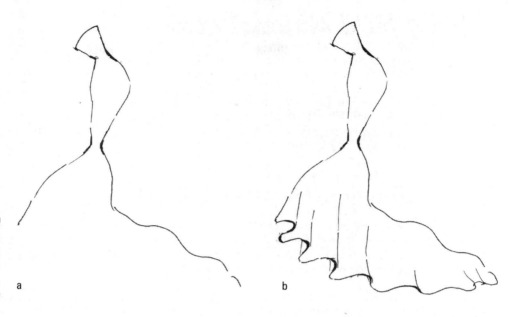

Figure 16-7:
Sketching
the outline
of the dress.

a

b

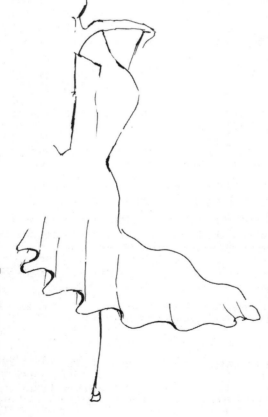

Figure 16-8:
Even
without the
details, you
still get the
gist of this
fashion
figure.

Compare the two styles of drawing of the same garment in Figures 16-9a and 16-9b. Both have the needed information for the dress and shoes, but each has an individual way of communicating that information.

Figure 16-9: Comparing detailed and minimalist drawings.

a

b

Avoiding traditional hands or feet

Hands and feet don't always have to be drawn — especially if you're going for the minimal look. Fashion illustration police aren't handing out tickets for leaving off these appendages. Veering from the typical fashion illustration can add artistic appeal and style.

Here are some ideas for dealing with hands and feet when going for the minimal look:

✔ Draw your fashion pose with arms; as you get to the hand, simply let the lines flow and disappear. Do the same for your feet; simply taper one side of the line for the leg and let it fade into nothing. See Figure 16-10a.

✔ Think of creative shapes that would work for certain markets, such as children's wear. For example, use hearts to represent hands or feet, as in Figure 16-10b.

Figure 16-10: Minimize your hands and feet.

Opting for a face without features

Faces are fun to draw because they add personality and mood to the illustration; however, they have a tendency to take over drawings because they're what viewers notice first. Other parts of the body or design get lost.

Is drawing a featureless face always a bad thing? Of course not! Often, the designer wants the attention on the clothes, not the model. Runway designers often try to play down their models by sending them all out in the same hairdo and makeup. The designer hopes you focus on the various clothes rather than the models.

When going faceless, think about the direction you want to turn the head: front, profile, or three-quarter view (refer to Chapter 4 for a rundown of the different views). No matter which direction you go, the idea is to simply create the illusion of a face.

To create your own illustration without a face, try these options:

- Simply draw the outer perimeter of the face and leave the area where the eyes, nose, and mouth would be completely blank. You can see what we mean in Figure 16-11a.

- If you have a profile or slightly turned face, as in Figures 16-11b and 16-11c, try drawing in just the chin and nose.

✔ Add just a shadow/line/mark for facial features, such as for the lips or nose, or add an eye mask for fun. Check out Figure 16-12 for an example of a mask.

Figure 16-11:
A blank or minimal face speaks volumes.

Figure 16-12:
Hide facial features with masks or other accessories.

Leaving your figures gorgeously bald (or even headless)

Drawing a fashion illustration without hair falls right in line with drawing one without a face. Leaving your figure bald is fun when you want to draw something fast or if the idea of having to get the right hairdo for your look is making you a little crazy. Believe it or not, sticking to the oval shape of a head without hair can look amazing in a fashion illustration!

Here are a few ideas to try:

- ✔ Create your fashion pose and simply add an oval shape for the head with no facial details or hair. Check out Figure 16-13a for an example.

- ✔ Try fun, creative ideas, such as adding a shape or just a squiggly line to represent the space the head would fill. See Figure 16-13b.

Figure 16-13: Bald really is beautiful.

a

b

Chapter 17

Building Your Fashion Design Portfolio

What good are fashion illustrations if no one but you ever sees them? Putting your work out there is an essential part of fashion illustration, at least if you want to make a career out of it. To keep your work organized and visually appealing across a variety of platforms, you need a portfolio that showcases your best work.

In the design industry, the portfolio is as important, if not more important, than your résumé. A *portfolio* is nothing more than a collection of your best fashion sketches. Your portfolio introduces your ideas to the world. The better you are at making your work public, the more people will see your ideas and hopefully want to buy them.

In this chapter, we tell you how to display your work in different media — and hopefully how to gain some clients in the process!

Looking at Portfolio Formats

Portfolios come in two forms: traditional, physical portfolios that you can carry around with you and digital portfolios that you can e-mail or post online for people to see from anywhere in the world.

Physical portfolios contain the hard copies of your work. Hard copies can include your original sketches or scans of your work printed out and placed in the physical portfolio. (You might want to use scans instead of your originals in your portfolio; that way, if something happens to the copies, you can go back to the original.) You slip the hard copies inside plastic sleeves that you then place inside a professional-looking portfolio, which you can take with you to interviews or networking events. You can use something as simple as a black zippered case with a handle that holds all your sketches, as in Figure 17-1.

Figure 17-1:
The brief-case type portfolio.

Digital portfolios put your work into any kind of digital presentation. A digital portfolio can include pages on a website, a folder from a portfolio-hosting website (more on those in the later section "Designing a Digital Portfolio"), a file such as a PDF with multiple pages, or a PowerPoint slideshow. After you've completed the digital file, you can e-mail it to people in another city or country or post it online for others to view. A digital file of your work may start out as a slideshow full of your sketches, as in Figure 17-2 (these sketches are by Christina Ngo, one of Marianne's students).

The best choice is to have both types of portfolios — physical and digital. That way, you can send your digital portfolio by e-mail or refer potential clients to your website before you meet in person so they can get an idea of your talents. During the meeting, you can talk through your creations as your potential client browses through your traditional portfolio.

Figure 17-2:
A few images from a digital portfolio.

In the rest of this chapter, we tell you how to pick the content for your portfolio and how to put each type of portfolio together.

Picking Material for Your Portfolio

The most common question Marianne gets from aspiring fashion illustrators is "What do I put in my portfolio?" There's no perfect answer. Although it goes without saying that you put your best work in your portfolio, choosing the exact pieces and deciding how much work to put in can be difficult when you're starting out in fashion illustration or design.

The following sections explain how many and which sketches to include, how to organize them, and how to build a portfolio that plays to the field you want to steer your career toward. Regardless of whether you're putting together a traditional or digital portfolio, the advice in these sections holds true for both formats.

Deciding on the number of pieces

When trying to decide how much artwork to include in your portfolio, Marianne's mantra is "Don't put in too much or too little." That may not sound helpful, but it covers every possible situation you may encounter in an interview.

Marianne has been to enough interviews and has spoken with enough people to know that sometimes you get 2 minutes to show someone your work, and other times a potential employer sits and talks to you about your work for 30 minutes. So you need to include a handful of knock 'em dead sketches that get your point across in 2 minutes and enough to keep a potential employer impressed for 30 minutes.

One way to figure out whether you have the right amount of material in your portfolio is to show it to people you know well, such as your friends and classmates, and people you don't know so well, such as a friend of a friend. (Don't ask your mom — you know she'll be enthralled with any little jot you've committed to paper!) Watch how much work they flip through before you start losing their attention. If they take 10 minutes or more to glance through everything, you probably have too many pieces. On the other hand, if they've flipped from cover to cover in just a few minutes, then you haven't included enough sketches to show all your skills! Marianne tells her students that ten designs are a great foundation for a budding artist's portfolio.

Choosing your best work

The pieces you include in your portfolio tell potential clients a lot about you, so make sure they say something outstanding! Portfolio pieces should show the following:

✔ What you've designed

✔ What you're capable of designing

✔ Your illustration skills

✔ Your design skills

✔ Your ability to visually communicate your design ideas

After you've decided on the amount of art to include in your portfolio, you need to winnow down your work and choose only the best pieces for your portfolio. Your best work demonstrates your ability to come up with an original idea; features your design process of ideas, notes, and sketches (see the following section for more about the design process); and showcases final versions of your original designs that illustrate your drawing ability. These are all things employers want to see!

If you're not sure what your best work is, ask other people which designs are your strongest. These people can include your teachers or professionals in any design field — it's even better if they're in fashion.

Figure 17-3 shows an example of a great sketch for a portfolio. It's a finished, clean drawing without notes on the side or other sketch lines or ideas, and it has a fun feel with a creative background. The whimsical drawing style fits with the originality of the design. The illustration also shows two views of the design: a full-length view to show how it looks on a body and a close-up view of the details from the side. The final artwork has been colored in with marker and shows texture.

Showing designs from start to finish

Although potential employers love to see final drawings, they also want some insight into your design process, from first inspiration to final garment. That's why a portfolio should contain all of the following:

✔ Rough sketches of design ideas

✔ Other work, such as collages of things that inspired your design

✔ Design processes from your notebook, which are pages that include your notes, original sketches, and inspirations you used to develop the design you were working on. These pages go with a particular design you came up with, creating a sort of diary that documents how you developed it.

✔ Your best finished illustrations

✔ Pictures of actual garments you've made from your designs

Your sketchbook, known in the industry as a *design process notebook*, contains your raw material. (See Chapter 1 for more about design process notebooks.) The design process notebook can be full of fabric swatches, magazine clippings, drawings, words, and anything and everything you use to inspire yourself when designing. It's like a glimpse into your brain working out all the details of a design. Take a look at Figure 17-4 for an example of a page from a design process notebook. Notice that it's pretty raw and not perfect, but it's what the designer used for inspiration when putting his design together.

Figure 17-3:
A great finished sketch to include.

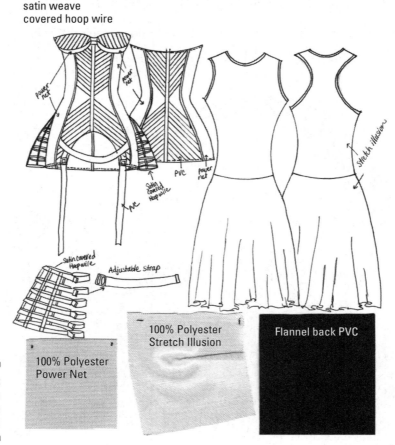

100% Polyester
satin weave
covered hoop wire

100% Polyester
Power Net

100% Polyester
Stretch Illusion

Flannel back PVC

Figure 17-4:
The design
process in
action!

Although a portfolio holds your refined work, employers often want to see
your raw ideas in your portfolio, too. For example, you may include a five-
piece collection of beautiful fashion illustrations of your original designs. A
potential employer would see your designs and wonder exactly what inspired
them, why you chose the designs you chose, and whether the designs
evolved along the way. You can show how you came to your final designs
by scanning a few pages from your design process notebook and placing
them alongside your final illustrations. These pages can include your rough
sketches, inspirations, notes, or anything else you had in your notebook. This
allows you to show the journey of your designs and the outcome.

Marianne advises her students to take their design process notebooks as well
as their portfolios to meetings or interviews. You may not need to pull out
your notebook, but if the opportunity arises, you have a great opportunity to
show how your brain works! Some potential employers will love seeing your
creativity as well as your professional portfolio.

Keeping your portfolio focused

A portfolio is a living, growing, and evolving entity because designers are always coming up with new designs. You'll probably start with a basic portfolio that will evolve into a more elaborate portfolio over time.

Even your basic portfolio should have a focus. If you're going for an interview for a bridal company, you don't need to include sketches of swimsuits and their design processes. Bring designs that meet the company's needs, like the bridal looks in Figure 17-5. Tailor your portfolio toward specific clients.

Figure 17-5:
Bridal looks for the bridal design interview.

When you're thinking about your basic portfolio's focus, consider these questions: What type of clothing do you enjoy designing the most? Is it easy for you to come up with dozens of designs for a bridal dress, or do men's jackets get you really excited? If you aren't sure, take an inventory of your sketches. Are most of your sketches women's dresses? Then that's probably the focus you want to choose.

Although you want your portfolio to have a focus, don't be afraid to include a few designs that simply feature what you would like to design. These pieces demonstrate your versatility. Besides, you'll probably do your best work on designs you enjoy the most!

Organizing your illustrations

Your portfolio tells the story of your work, so organize it like one. Use the following structure to lead your viewer through the pages with an opening page and explanations of what the work is throughout the pages:

- ✔ Create an opening page with your name or your résumé. Your résumé can also be at the back if you prefer — just make sure you have one with you!

  Alternatively, start with a beautiful drawing of something other than fashion sketches. It can grab the person's attention and entice him or her to turn the page and continue looking. This page could have your name on it or just be an illustration. The next page could then have your name followed by your work.

- ✔ Introduce your work with a lead-in page. You may not be physically present when someone thumbs through your work, so include a page with bullet points or a quick blurb telling viewers what they're looking at, including who the customer of the design is and why you created the design. For example, you may feature a section of designs inspired by water or a collection you sketched for a client's wedding party. See Figure 17-6 for a sample lead-in page explaining the designs.

- ✔ Begin with a few layouts consisting of complete design processes to final design. Start by showing the viewer the inspiration and original ideas or sketches. End the series of pages with the final illustrations of the designs.

- ✔ Next, include pages that include your original design illustrations and examples of your skills when it comes to drawing other designs (not garments you designed). Marianne includes a few extreme design ideas that are fantasy-oriented and a few that are practical, showing clothing that someone would actually wear. If you have photographs of designs you created, include a few pages showing your illustration and the picture of the garment you designed side by side.

  Some people organize their designs by season or categories, such as menswear or bridal. Marianne doesn't follow this rule, but that doesn't mean you can't or shouldn't. Your portfolio should reflect you.

- ✔ Decide whether you want to include a final page with your contact info at the end or if you want to simply end the pages on their own. This is a personal preference. Marianne has seen wonderful fun final pages and other portfolios that just end, and both looked great!

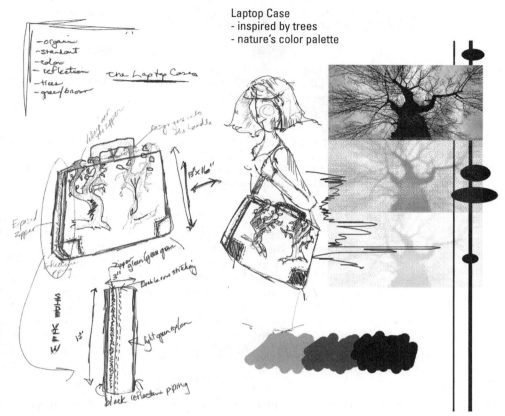

Laptop Case
- inspired by trees
- nature's color palette

Putting Together a Traditional Portfolio

Although most of life has gone digital these days, physical portfolios have their place in fashion design. You can take your portfolio to networking events, interviews, and even to Thanksgiving dinner, where you can show off your work to Aunt Jane and Uncle Fred.

In the following sections, we give you tips on purchasing a portfolio and advice on prepping your work for display.

Picking out a portfolio case

Physical portfolios are easy to find. You can buy them at almost any art or craft store that sells drawing supplies. Check large art store chains, independent art stores, college bookstores, and of course the Internet. Typing "design portfolio case" into any search engine leads to many websites selling every kind of portfolio imaginable.

Portfolios look a little like briefcases but are thinner. They usually have a handle for carrying the case and a zipper that goes around the case on three sides to keep it shut. The majority of portfolios are black and made from leather or synthetic materials. We've seen silver ones made from metal and others with wild prints on them.

Before you choose your portfolio case, you have some additional features to think about. You need to consider what size of portfolio you want (you may spend hours carrying the thing around), the type of sleeve you want to use in the portfolio, and the material the portfolio is made of.

Choosing a size

Portfolios come in different sizes, but the number to pay attention to is the size of the page *inside* the portfolio. If you want to work with gigantic page layouts, then you'll have to lug around an even larger portfolio to carry the gigantic pages! You could be flying or taking public transportation, and you'll quickly discover that a nice size is one you don't mind carrying.

The first thing we do is look at page sizes. Some good sizes include 11" x 14", 14" x 17", and 11" x 17". Choosing pages larger than 14" x 17" makes your portfolio difficult to carry, whereas sizes smaller than 11" x 14" can be difficult when you're putting together layouts that show your entire design process all the way through to the final product.

When you're shopping online, finding the dimensions of the pages can be hard. Don't be afraid to call the store or read reviews so you know exactly what you're getting.

Deciding on a design

After you decide on the size of the pages, you can choose the actual portfolio! This step is fun, so enjoy the process. Portfolio cases come in all different materials, from leather to metal to anything in between. Marianne follows two schools of thought with her portfolios:

- ✔ The safe, business train of thought says you should have a clean, slick, black professional portfolio for the interview at the type of place that would call for a serious look.
- ✔ On the other hand, you're a designer displaying your work in a design setting where creativity is encouraged. Why not go edgy with a chrome case or go wild with an animal print?

Think about the audience you're displaying your work to. If you can't choose just one style, spring for a portfolio in each style. Then you can use whichever one is appropriate for your meeting.

A handle on the portfolio case is functional and creates a nice, professional look. Portfolios may have handles at the top where you open the pages or on the binding side. Marianne likes the handle on the binding side because it allows the pages to hang nicely when she carries her portfolio.

The nicer portfolios have a closure system such as a zipper that goes around three sides of the case, keeping everything inside nice and safe. The zipper looks professional and keeps everything from falling out. Most portfolios have inside pockets where you can store papers such as your résumé or your business cards.

Your physical portfolio is an investment in your craft. Try out a few different types and see what appeals to your personal taste and needs.

Picking a sleeve type

Portfolios are made to hold plastic sleeves. The plastic sleeve is where you display your artwork.

Choosing a portfolio that has removable sleeves is a good idea. Why? Having a bunch of empty sleeves looks unprofessional when you're showing someone your work. With removable sleeves, you can decide how many pages you want to include in your portfolio and remove any empty sleeves. You can also purchase more sleeves (they usually come in sets of 10) if you need more for the amount of work you want to include. And if you have more than one portfolio case, removable sleeves allow you to move your work between cases.

You can put two pages in a sleeve, using both the front and back; therefore, 10 sleeves can hold a total of 20 pages if you count the front and back.

Sleeves come in two main types:

- ✔ Archival page protectors that are sealed on three sides, so you slide pages in from the top
- ✔ Page protectors that are open on the top and bottom

Marianne recommends using the sealed-on-three-sides archival sleeve because the work can come out only through the top; you're less likely to lose pages this way. The archival sleeve protects your drawings without exposing them to chemicals in the plastic that can damage the paper your work is printed on over time.

Prepping your work for display

After you have the portfolio and have chosen the work to put into it (see the "Picking Material for Your Portfolio" section earlier in the chapter), you're ready to fill your pages. You want to have a professional approach to the layouts and presentations.

Follow these guidelines to keep your portfolio looking professional:

- ✔ No scrapbooking! Save the cute things for the design process notebook. Stay clean and professional in your portfolio. You can include pages from your design process notebook that correspond to your final designs in your portfolio, but make sure these less professional-looking pages are scanned and then inserted into your portfolio so they have a professional feel. You don't want your notebook pages leaving glue everywhere or having fraying pieces falling off. You want your portfolio to look professional with an edge that sets you apart.

✔ If you tear out sketches to place them in the portfolio sleeve page, cut off the ragged edges with a ruler and craft knife. Mount the page in the sleeve or on another piece of paper if the sketch page is a little smaller than the size of the sleeve. This keeps your page from floating around and ending up sideways.

✔ Scan the sketches and clean them up or edit them on the computer if you'd like. Then print them out to place into the sleeve. You can find info on scanning in the next section.

If you have a nice printer at home, you can use that to print your images. If you need help or want more options, visit your local print-and-copy shop. Save your files in more than one file format, because the shop may not be able to print in every file format.

Designing a Digital Portfolio

A *digital portfolio* simply means one you can access on a computer-type device. This can be your smart phone, your laptop, or any of the other handy digital devices that are around. All fashion illustrators in today's world need to know how to use the computer to their advantage.

We're guessing that you draw most of your work by hand. In the following sections, we discuss making sure your digitized images are crisp and clean, and then we offer some options about what to do with them digitally. You can post them to a website for all the world to see, or you can create a slide-show that you can e-mail to folks who are interested in your work. Whichever method you choose is up to you, but we strongly encourage you to create some sort of digital portfolio.

Choosing work for your digital portfolio is no different from choosing images for a traditional portfolio. See the "Picking Material for Your Portfolio" section earlier in the chapter for guidance on selecting illustrations for your portfolio. A benefit of putting together a digital portfolio is that you can include more work — but not too much more — if you can't narrow your choices to 10 or 15 of your best pieces.

If you're interested in creating drawings directly on the computer, you can use graphic design software such as Adobe Illustrator. Check out *Fashion Designer's Handbook for Adobe Illustrator,* by Marianne Centner and Frances Vereker (Blackwell), for the basics on digital illustration.

Scanning your work

Scanning your work isn't quite as simple as laying a sketch on a scanner and pressing Start! Scanning is a little more complicated than that because you must pay attention to the amount of detail you want the scanner to capture. Resolution and file type are two aspects you need to know when scanning and working with digital images.

Resolution is a way of measuring the amount of information in a picture. When you scan, you have the option to choose the resolution, sometimes called the *DPI,* dots per inch. Marianne tells her students to scan their images at a 300 DPI. This setting has several advantages: It captures a lot of the detail in the image, the file size isn't too large, and you can print the picture at a fairly large size before it starts to get blurry.

You also need to pay attention to the file type the scanner creates. Most scanners scan the image as a JPEG (joint photographic experts group), TIFF (tagged image file format), or PDF (portable document format). You can control which type of file you create by checking the software settings before you hit save. For beginners, it's best to stay with the JPEG format.

Print-and-copy stores can usually help you scan images, so don't be afraid to ask for help! You can also have your work professionally scanned by someone who really knows what they're doing so you don't have to figure out how to use complicated design programs. Talk to the employees at print stores or graphic design firms for professional help.

Fixing your images

Digital sketches don't always have the same look as the physical sketch. Scanning in sketches may not capture the beauty of the drawing; you may need to edit the scan to adjust the colors or erase dust spots. For this, you may need to master an image-editing program such as Adobe Photoshop.

Photoshop is the most common editing program in the fashion industry. After you scan your image, Photoshop allows you to play with the colors, draw new lines, add text, and crop and collage images together. It's a powerful tool that allows endless amounts of creativity. Marianne used it throughout this book for almost every drawing!

Because we're not technology experts and because Photoshop has so many wonderful features for editing your work, we don't include any how-to details here. Consider browsing through *Photoshop 7 For Dummies,* by Deke McClelland and Barbara Obermeier (Wiley), or check with your local community college or other local programs to find available classes. We're just going to urge you to make the most of the technology and make sure that your scanned images are the best they can be before you add them to your digital portfolio.

Posting to a website

Using a website to host your work is great if you have the smarts about website building or are lucky enough to have an awesome friend who can do it for you! A website costs some money for hosting it (and possibly building it), but think of the website as an investment. It's great for getting your work out there, and it makes viewing your work easy for potential clients. What's easier than introducing your work to a potential employer simply by giving them your website address?

If creating a website sounds overwhelming, don't fret. Many free portfolio-hosting websites are available. Search the Internet, and you find many sites where you can sign up and post your files in a portfolio-type setting. These sites give you your own link to send to people so they can go right to your portfolio. Some free portfolio-hosting websites that are user-friendly include the following:

- ✔ Carbonmade.com
- ✔ Coroflot.com
- ✔ Styleportfolios.com

Posting to these sites is as easy as scanning your sketches, saving them as JPEG files (see the earlier "Scanning your work" section for more on file types), and uploading them on the site. Usually the websites have little tutorials to walk you through how to post your files. In 10 minutes, you can have your files online!

If you have a fashion blog, link to your portfolio from your blog instead of posting your portfolio on your blog.

If you post your digital portfolio online, be sure to put the web address on your business card.

Creating a slideshow

You can also create a digital portfolio that consists of a slideshow file, which you can e-mail to potential clients. The two most common types of slideshow files are the PDF file and the PPT (PowerPoint) file. Most computers have the programs to run these open-and-read file formats. Save your portfolio in both formats in case the person you're sending the file to doesn't have one of the programs to open the file. Marketing yourself includes making things as easy as possible for your clients!

To create a portfolio in either program, use the picture files you created when scanning your images. Place the picture files in the order you want them to be seen in either program.

Both file formats allow you to place files on multiple pages. The viewer can simply click a button to flip through the pages of your portfolio. The order of your pages, the amount of work, and the type of work you include should follow the same guidelines as those for the physical portfolio. Only the presentation format differs.

If you want to add slides with supplemental information to your slideshow, you can, but stay away from animation or sounds because they can come across as unprofessional.

Part V
The Part of Tens

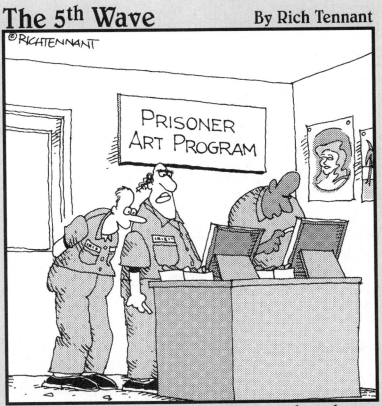

The 5th Wave — By Rich Tennant

PRISONER ART PROGRAM

"Nice fashion art, Randal. I love the whole innocent look your models project as they're being frisked by the police."

In this part . . .

The fashion world is always changing — that's what makes it so exciting! So how do you keep up? We give you ten tips for staying current in Chapter 18. And while you're trying to stay on the cutting edge, you may be trying to get your foot in the door as a new fashion artist. To help you along, we give you ten suggestions for getting noticed in Chapter 19.

Chapter 18

Ten Ways to Stay Current

Not only is staying current on fashion trends fun, but it's also essential in today's fashion world. Your fashion drawings must be timely or even cutting-edge if you want anyone to take a look at them. Read about, watch, and study all that's current in the fashion world, which is constantly changing. Here are ten ways to stay in the loop.

Peruse Fashion Publications

Although digital is cutting-edge in a lot of areas, in the fashion world, nothing is better than reading or paging through fashion magazines and catalogs. You have a variety of periodicals to choose from, targeted at different ages, styles, and looks, from luxury to rough-and-tough and more. As you page through magazines and catalogs, you can tear out photos to save for inspiration or to use when you want to practice drawing a new piece of clothing. The pages are wonderful to trace over, too.

Here are some of Marianne's favorite fashion publications:

- ✔ *Elle* magazine
- ✔ *Nylon* magazine
- ✔ *Seventeen* magazine
- ✔ *Urban Outfitters* catalog
- ✔ *Vogue* magazine
- ✔ *W* magazine

You may prefer one or two magazines or catalogs over others, but we encourage you to at least flip through other publications. You never can tell when something offbeat or not typically your style will catch your eye and inspire you to draw something fabulous. You need to keep up with all the trends if you want to do fashion illustration.

Check Out Celebrity Styles

Pick up a copy of *People, Us Weekly,* or even a weekly tabloid and see what the stars are wearing. You can check out the women's dresses and the men's suits, note what sorts of accessories they're sporting, or study what kind of 'do they had done for the latest awards show or movie premiere. The outfits they wear off the red carpet may inspire you to design something a little less fancy but just as eye-catching.

Celebrities are always on the cutting-edge of fashion. When you see the same style of clothing worn by several A-list celebs, take note; the look is here to stay for a while.

Keep Up with New Music

Fashion and music have been best friends at least since the 1920s, when people poured into speakeasys and danced to the rebellious sounds of jazz! Just the word *speakeasy* brings to mind the flapper girl. Music stars in every genre all over the globe promote and publicize fashion. Music connects people around the world and allows them to see what's fashionable in other countries just by studying the stars of the music world.

The minute kids leave elementary school behind, their walls become covered with their favorite singers and bands. And kids and teens want to dress like the musicians they hear. Think about trends and styles of dress such as punk, hip-hop, grunge, and emo. Where did they come from? Music, of course! Those genres of music were associated with a certain look and style of dress. When a rock star spikes his hair or wears buttons on his hat, waves of people adopt the look just because they like the star's music.

Great magazines to check out about the newest bands — and the fashion they may be inspiring — include the following:

- *Alternative Press*
- *Ray Gun*
- *Rolling Stone*
- *SPIN*
- *Vibe*
- *The Wire*

Don't forget music videos! MTV may not play them anymore, but YouTube is crawling with homemade and professional videos of up-and-coming bands. When you read about a new artist or hear a group's song on the radio, check out the video. The visual part of music videos is all about style and image.

Log onto Fashion Websites and Blogs

Just about any designer, fashion illustrator, or student has some sort of online presence. You can visit the fashion giants' incredible websites, check out what they're tweeting about, or see a student's work on Facebook or Deviant Art. Blogs can introduce you to other illustrators' work, connect you with the art and fashion communities, and inspire you to experiment with your own drawings.

Some designers even write about the process they go through when they're designing a new line of clothing or the challenges they face when creating a new look. When you understand how other fashion artists go about their work, you can adopt some of their habits as your own.

 If you have a favorite designer, fashion illustrator, or any other person in the fashion world who interests you, follow them on Twitter. You'll definitely stay current with the fashion world when you read their up-to-the-minute Tweets.

When you're ready to launch your own site or blog, you can look at other sites to gather ideas you'd like to incorporate in yours. Here are a few fashion websites and blogs to check out:

- ✔ Bleachblack.com
- ✔ Fashionpaparazzis.com
- ✔ Fashiontribes.typepad.com
- ✔ Thesartorialist.com

People-Watch in the City

There's no better place to people-watch and see the latest in fashion than a big city. Lisa lived in a large city for much of her life, and now that she no longer does, she still makes it a point to visit often. Big cities have a different energy, and the people who live there tend to have more interest in making a fashion statement to stand out in a place that's home to all types of people.

City people play with their clothes in a special way. Experimenting is a way of saying who they are in a sometimes-anonymous place. Seeing all types of people together in one area also results in a cultural mix that blends different fashion styles in a new way. Looks start to flow between areas of the city, and before you know it, a new trend emerges.

When you go places in the city, study everyone's clothes! These are the styles and looks you might not find in magazines. Emerging subcultures develop right in front of you when you watch a group of teenage girls hopping on the subway and then study the way they dress. Go to outdoor events, hang out at the park any time of the day, and catch the fitness crowd in the mornings and the teenagers after school. Concerts of all kinds are a must! Immerse yourself in life happening around you. Wherever people gather is where you want to be.

When you visit a big city and sit down to check out what people are wearing, make sure you bring your sketchbook or fashion journal and record what you see. Don't be afraid to pull out your phone and discreetly take pictures!

Drop into an Art Museum

Museum hop! Take a look at paintings, from historic to contemporary time periods, and pay attention to colors, shapes, textures, and poses. You never know where you'll find inspiration for your next design.

There's more to many art museums than magnificent paintings and sculptures. Some museums dedicate special wings for the sole purpose of showing fashion exhibitions. In addition to looking at gorgeous and outrageous clothing, you can view the designer's sketches, swatches, and notes about the garments. Sometimes the stories behind the pieces are just as fascinating as the clothing itself. After the death of designer Alexander McQueen, the New York Metropolitan Museum of Art put on an exhibit of his work. It was one of the museum's most popular exhibits. Imagine all the trends that could come from a look at his masterpieces!

Don't forget to sneak glances at the people attending the exhibit, too. You can be pretty sure that anyone who is taking in a fashion exhibit is probably as into fashion as you are.

Don't think that the famous museums have it all — there are some little jewels of museums as well as galleries that have fabulous fashion exhibitions. And check out fun places such as the Rock and Roll Hall of Fame in Cleveland, Ohio, and anthropological exhibits at sites such as the Field Museum in Chicago.

Browse Boutiques and Department Stores

When the seasons change, we make it a point to explore clothing lines in all types of stores, from discount stores to department stores to the tiniest of privately owned boutiques. You'll be quite surprised what you can discover in an unknown store off the beaten path. Visiting stores is inspiring and fun, and it doesn't have to cost a lot of money — as long as you look and don't buy!

You can get tons of hands-on info when you see and touch a garment. Check out how an item is constructed, feel the fabric, and look at seams. Notice how the garment is draped (or not), and you'll see the why certain designers are stars.

Pay attention to everything about the store. Notice the music and the artwork or pictures of models wearing the clothes. How are the styles shown on the models? Who is the store trying to attract and dress? What are the colors of the store and displays? What are the customers wearing? All of these details can be fodder for your next design.

Hit the Vintage Stores and Thrift Shops

Stop off at vintage and thrift shops when you're prowling around for fashion ideas. These shops can be a hit-or-miss experience, but if you find a few favorite shops, frequent them often. You never know what you may find. Be on the lookout for beaded sweaters, shimmering gowns, funky handbags, and more.

If the price is right, grab inspiring items at a vintage or thrift shop fast, because these treasures won't be around the next day! It's always easier to draw a garment when it's right in front of you, and thrift shops provide some out-of-the-ordinary design ideas for very little money. You'll find vintage and modern pieces, as well as items whose original price may have been $10 or $500.

Not only can you find terrific items to draw and incorporate into your designs or illustrations, but after you're finished sketching the piece, a quick trip to the dry cleaners can make your find wearable and as good as new for a fraction of the price of a new garment.

Catch Fashion Shows on TV

Reality TV shows about fashion draw super-high ratings. Lisa absolutely loves them. You're exposed to some creative and quirky talent, you find out a ton about style, and you get an idea of just how hard fashion designers work.

Watch how the designers create their fashions. Notice that they often sketch out their ideas before doing anything else.

You can also check out cable shows that show endless loops of designers' work on models working the runway. Hypnotic and inspiring, the fashion shows let you see how clothing falls on the models' bodies as they strut up and down the catwalk. Watch this stuff late at night when you can't sleep, and your insomnia may pay off in some new ideas that will keep you awake with a purpose and working through the night.

Watch Old Movies for New Ideas

If you want to look at fabulous clothes from the twenties through the sixties or beyond, stream a bunch of old movies and settle in with a good blanket and bowl of popcorn. Knowing a little fashion history is great, and what better place to learn about it than from a movie? If you watch movies from several different periods, you'll also see that certain fashion looks circle around and show up again 20 or 30 years later! Fall in love with flapper dresses, swoon over bejeweled gowns, laugh at go-go boots, and marvel over capes and other dramatic clothing that made a fashion statement.

You can also be inspired by modern directors' takes on period pieces. One of Marianne's favorites is Sofia Coppola's film *Marie Antoinette,* for which designer Milena Canonero won the 2006 Academy Award for Best Costume Design. Look at the cuts of the clothing, the colors, the way the skirts move as they're supported by the gigantic panniers. What can you take from a movie's costumes to inspire you when designing?

A great to place to start is with films that were nominated for Oscars, Golden Globes, or Costume Designers Guild Awards. Check out the various costume categories for ideas; think period pieces, fantasy, and contemporary.

And don't stop at movies! Check out Broadway shows (either in NYC or when they come to a major city near you) and study the lists of productions that have won for costuming. Marianne was lucky enough to hang out in the Gershwin Theatre where *Wicked* is performed and got to see the 2004 Tony Award-winning costumes up close. She even had the opportunity to try some on, and the inspirations just started bubbling up in her head!

Practice gesture drawing as you watch a movie and get inspired by certain fashion looks. Keep your sketchbook by your side. We cover gesture drawing in Chapter 15.

Chapter 19

Ten Steps to Kick-Start Your Career

In This Chapter

▶ Putting together a portfolio

▶ Promoting yourself online

▶ Getting out and about

*1*f you want to have a career in fashion illustration, you need to do more than create a portfolio and wait. Be proactive! Putting your portfolio together is the first step toward marketing your work, but it's far from the last. Making a name for yourself also involves putting yourself out there in the fashion world, using every possible medium to promote yourself, and never passing up a chance to network. These ten tips get you started on making a name for yourself in fashion.

Build a Portfolio

A digital portfolio of your illustrations works for marketing in many cases, and a hands-on portfolio is great for client meetings and networking. We recommend that you build both types of portfolio (see Chapter 17 for details).

Be your own critic when putting together a portfolio. You probably have quite a number of drawings at this point, so choose your best fashion drawings and pull together an excellent body of work. Pick only choice pieces that you feel best reflect your style. We strongly advise you to whittle down your fashion work to about 10 to 15 pieces. You don't want to lug around a cumbersome portfolio, and art directors, designers, art schools, and any other prospective clients don't have the time to skim through dozens of art pieces.

Start and end your portfolio with your strongest pieces in order to impress and be remembered.

Don't walk around with original pieces of artwork in your portfolio. Make copies of your work and put them in your portfolio in case of damage or loss.

Create an Online Presence

The world is definitely going digital, and so should you in showing your work. An online portfolio lets you show your work to clients, friends, galleries, and others all over the world. See Chapter 17 for information on creating a digital portfolio.

Set up a website or blog to show your work and to keep people up to date on what you're doing. Many websites and blogs that are free for artists provide a variety of templates, so anyone can create a great-looking site to display his or her work.

If you're more computer savvy, try making your own website — you have complete freedom on everything from the placement of your art to the font, colors, and page design. If money is an issue, you can find plenty of free portfolio websites to check out. Type "portfolio websites" into a search engine and browse through the choices.

Make sure your web address is listed on your business card so people can find you. See the later section "Hand Out Business Cards" for info on these handy handouts.

Tweet Your Own Horn on Social Media

Connect to people through social media. Twitter provides moment-by-moment descriptions that anyone can put out to describe details of their lives, so feel free to tweet about yourself on your own site. You may find that you have a group of fashion fans following your every move in the art world before too long! Don't worry about not being famous *yet;* marketing is all about getting your name out there. Some fun topics to tweet about could be new designers and their work, your favorite fashions, sketches you made, and anything you find inspirational for design.

If you aren't up to tweeting your every fashion thought, consider promoting your work on Facebook. Everybody seems to be on Facebook these days, and they're not all gossiping about last night's party. Facebook is a great place to upload your artwork and create a photo album for friends and potential clients to view.

You can create folders to group your drawings by type. You can also post updates on which gallery or coffee shop is showing your drawings. Facebook is great for networking with other illustrators and designers and lets you see what forecasters and designers are predicting as the next big thing. Facebook has fashion-related fan pages for brands, stores, and designers. Be sure to visit these pages and like them on Facebook to receive updates, event listings, and invitations.

Any work you put online can be seen and copied, no matter what type of security feature you put on the image. One way to prevent someone from claiming your work as his own is to put a watermark on the image. A *watermark* is a faint, semitransparent marking digitally placed over an image to prevent anyone who virtually copies your work from passing it off as his own. For example, you can use design software such as Photoshop to write your name across the drawing in a fairly see-through watermark (look for Photoshop's Watermarking feature in the Output Settings panel). That way, someone can't just cut out your name from a corner and pretend your artwork is his!

Show Off Your Technique on YouTube

If you've ever watched YouTube, you already know that people make videos about anything, and we mean anything! Why not make a little fashion video about fashion drawing, showcasing examples of your work and videos of you drawing or talking about your designs? You can film yourself drawing and time-lapse the video to quickly show how you go from a blank piece of paper to a finished sketch. Or simply walk around town filming what inspires your drawings. You could be the next YouTube sensation and grab some new clients. Don't forget that if you have a website, you can post these videos there as well!

Network

Never skip going to a party when someone who has fashion connections will be there, whether he's a superstar or not. A boutique owner may need some fashion sketches, or a young designer may need some promotional help. And let's not forget someone who knows somebody who knows somebody. Pass your business cards around (see the next section), and don't forget to get business cards from the contacts you make as well. Go to parties, openings, charity functions, and school events with an eagle eye for potential contacts or clients. You never know who you'll meet.

Follow up with people you meet by sending a nice e-mail telling them it was fun chatting. Don't forget to drop a valuable thank-you card to anyone who introduces you to a client or brags endlessly about you (your mom being the one exception!).

Hand Out Business Cards

Business cards are a must-have. Don't limit yourself to one type; make different types for different purposes. Cards can be large or small and can stress different aspects of your talent. You can make them on the computer or have them printed professionally. Always include your website info as well as your name, phone number, and e-mail address.

If you're working on a budget (and who isn't?), color photocopies on cardstock paper or computer printouts can save you money. Websites offer free business card templates, so be sure to check them out!

Always, always, always carry several business cards with you to hand out — you never know when you're going to meet people who might be interested in your work! They can look up your work on the web if you've handed them your business card.

Exhibit Your Work

Just because you're a fashion illustrator doesn't mean there's no place for you to exhibit. You don't have to be a painter to show your work, and fashion art is a wonderful form of commercial art that many people enjoy. Do a little research in your area and see whether any galleries have an interest. If you're a student, enter all school art shows, and don't forget to visit the owners of small clothing stores to show your portfolio. Lisa got her first fashion illustration job drawing large fashion posters for a local trendy boutique. She had total freedom to draw anything fashion-y — an awesome opportunity! Marianne got her first fashion illustration job from a stranger who walked into her office and saw some of her drawings hanging up!

Be creative when hunting for places to exhibit your fashion drawings. Don't pass up the little shops — they may provide you with your first professional breakthrough!

Create Your Own Promo Pieces

You may need to create promo pieces to advertise shows or to reach a large number of contacts from time to time. Paper is thin, so use paper for the promo pieces you mail rather than hand out to people. If you want something to pass around in person, use heavier cardstock.

You can save a lot of money by printing professionally in bulk, but that means you have to get a lot of promo pieces printed. Lisa usually does this when she's sending out an invitation to an art show or a promo piece to many clients. Check with several local printers to compare price rates.

You can also send out an e-mail blast. Upload a piece of your work, write the necessary information, and e-mail it to everyone you can think of who needs to see your drawings. If you choose this route, remember to post the same information on Facebook, Twitter, and your website. You can never have too much self-promotion when you're trying to break into the business!

Dress the Part

If you're a fashion illustrator, you gotta walk the walk and play the fashion part. You can't make a fashion statement sauntering into a showroom or a magazine office in your comfy sweats and casual shoes. You don't have to spend a ton of money to look terrific, but any in-the-moment accessories like a fabulous long scarf or a pair of terrific shoes can spice up a long winter coat and jeans. Add a fun and furry hat, and you're set to make an impression the minute you walk in the door.

Don't overdo your look unless you're going to a cutting-edge scene where fashion is all about looking extreme and bold. Do some fashion research about the company or designer before making an appointment. Most jobs involving fashion encourage their employees to have a definite fashion look; it's like a form of advertising. You won't find an employee of Ralph Lauren strutting around in tight black leather, for example. Dress for the job!

If you live in a big city, strut your fashion stuff for the nightlife; you never know who's people-watching and who you might end up meeting. Everyone dresses up to club, so make sure you get noticed with your signature style.

Alert the Press! It's All About You!

Put any modesty or shyness behind you and find out how to write up a press release when something good happens to you and your work. If you're showing your fashion drawings in a gallery, you're about to graduate from a fashion school, or you've designed something that's awesome, do some homework and find out where to send this important info.

Fashion magazines look for editorial stories or write-ups about an interesting fashion journey. Local newspapers love stories about local artists and often print exhibition announcements. Find out which editor handles fashion news in the publication so you don't send fashion news about your career to the wrong department, where it may never find its way to the right hands.

Index

• G •